MOSAIC SOURCEBOOK

Published in the UK in 2003 by
Apple Press
Sheridan House
112-116A Western Road
Hove
East Sussex BN3 1DD

ISBN 1-84092-421-7

Cover Image:
Top left: Bobbie Bush Photography,
    www.bobbiebush.com
Top center: Alan Labb
Top right: Bobbie Bush Photography,
    www.bobbiebush.com
Bottom: Expert Imaging

For work previously published in the following listed books, grateful acknowledgment is given to Doreen Mastandrea and Livia McRee for their work from *Mosaics Inside and Out* on pages 6–49, 81–131, and 136–149; to JoAnn Locktov and Leslie Plummer Clagett for their work from *The Art of Mosaics* on pages 150–283; to Georgia Sargeant, Celie Fago, and Livia McRee for their work from *Polymer Clay* on pages 50–53; to Mary Ann Hall for her work from *The Crafter's Project Book* on pages 54–58 and 134–135; and to Anna Kasabian for her work from *Decorating Interiors with Tile* on pages 59–80.

Printed in China

10 9 8 7 6 5 4 3 2 1

MOSAIC
SOURCEBOOK

ASFC LEARNING CENTRE

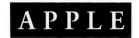

CONTENTS

Essential Tools and Materials   6
Basic Mosaic Designs   11
How to Cut Tiles   14
How to Lay Out a Pattern   16
Making Mosaics on Wood   18
Making Mosaics on Cement   18
Making Mosaics on Metal   20
Making Mosaics on Glass   20
Using Color Effectively   22
Choosing Grout Colors   24

Mosaics Inside   27
     Playroom Floor   29
     Ceramic Relief Mirror   34
     Framed Kitchen Mosaic   37
     Classical Entryway   41
     Wall Hook Rack   45
     Mosaic Plaque   50
     Terra-cotta Mosaic Frame   54
     Mosaic Candy Dish   57
     Eggshell Mosaic Frame   58

Interior Mosaics and Murals   59

Mosaics Outside   81
     Wrought Iron Patio Table   83
     Glass Patio Lights   89
     Three-Season Window Planter   93
     Sunshine Stepping Stones   97
     Seascape Mirror   102
     Mixed-Tile Birdbath   105
     Ornamental Garden Rocks   109
     Garden Animals   113
     Trout Rain Catcher   117
     House-Number Plaque   124
     Tool Mailbox   126
     China Birdhouse   128
     Mosaic Address Plaque   133
     Mosaic Chime   134

Artist's Gallery   137

Artist Directory   284
Resources   286
About the Authors   287

Essential Tools & Materials

TOOLS

1 HAMMER
Use a hammer for breaking large ceramic pieces into smaller ones. First, wrap the pieces to be smashed in a towel to prevent shards from flying, and always wear safety goggles.

2 GLASS CUTTER
Use a simple glass cutter like this one to create straight edges on stained glass, vitreous glass, and mirror tiles. Use a ruler and a grease pencil to measure and mark the glass for cutting. Then, use firm, even pressure to score the glass with the cutter along the mark. Next, lightly tap the glass along the scoring with the ball end of the cutter, then gently snap the glass into two pieces.

3 CRAFT KNIFE
A craft knife is the best tool for scraping off dried adhesive that has accidentally spilled onto the tops of tiles. A craft knife is also useful for cleaning away any extra adhesive that is clogging up the crevices between tiles before grouting a project.

4 PAINT SCRAPER
A paint scraper is just one of many tools that can be used as an adhesive spreader. A palette knife or craft stick also works well. Always clean the scraper with water immediately after using it, because it is difficult to remove adhesive after it has dried.

5 UTILITY KNIFE
If a larger area needs to be scraped clean of dried adhesive, use a standard utility knife rather than the smaller blade of a craft knife.

6 HEAVY-DUTY UTILITY KNIFE
A heavy-duty utility knife is the best tool for cutting cement board, which is used to make the entryway on page 46 and the sign on page 45. First, deeply score both sides of the board with the knife, then snap the excess off. To do this, simply align the score mark with the edge of a table, then apply pressure to the pieces that extend past the table's edge.

7 SMALL NIPPER
This smaller-bladed nipper gives more control, which is essential when cutting irregularly shaped tiles.

8 SCORER AND PLIER
This combination scorer and plier has a wheel attached to the front that is used to score the piece to be cut. Grasp the tile with the tool and align the scoring with the guide mark. Press firmly, and the tile will break along the scoring. Use this tool for cutting pieces when straight lines are called for.

9 NIPPER
A tile nipper is the basic tool used for cutting ceramic, marble, and glass pieces into basic shapes. A nipper is perfect for cutting straight-edged tiles, such as triangles, or for halving or quartering square tiles. Nippers are also used to custom-cut tiles for hard-to-fit areas.

10 CHIPPER NIPPER
This chipper nipper acts as a mosaic scissors. Use it to refine the shape of tiles and to make curved pieces such as circles or semicircles.

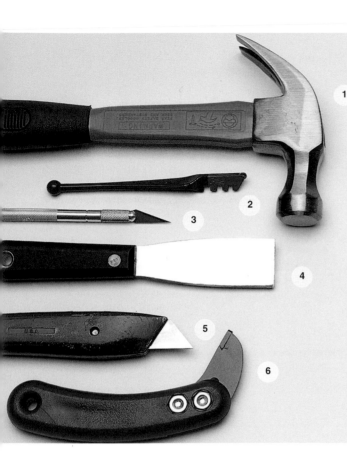

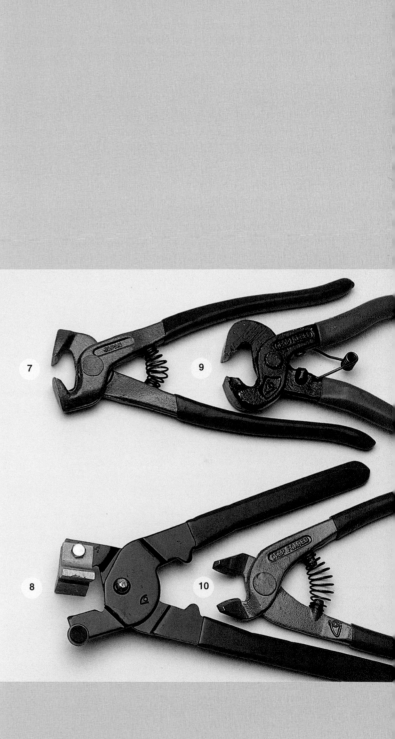

1 BUCKET
Buckets of various sizes are perfect for mixing and transporting cement or grout. Set aside several for mosaic use only.

2 SPONGE
Large sponges are crucial for wiping away grout effectively, which prevents filmy build-up. Wipe away grout continually as you work to prevent it from drying on tile surfaces.

3 SCRUBBING PADS
Ordinary kitchen scrubbing pads can be used to sand grout to a perfect finish. Use the pads dry so as not to soften or smear the grout, and always wear a filter mask when sanding.

4 SAFETY GOGGLES
Safety goggles are important to wear when cutting glass or ceramics to protect the eyes from the inevitable shards.

5 FILTER MASK
Filter masks are a necessary precaution because of the fine particles generated during mosaic work, especially when sanding grout.

6 TOWEL
A lint-free cloth is the best thing to use for buffing glass tiles after grouting. Buffing rids the surface of any residual grout film.

7 LATEX GLOVES
Latex gloves help prevent cuts and scrapes when working with sharp and jagged materials like glass and ceramic shards. They allow more control than kitchen gloves, which is helpful when applying grout by hand rather than with a tool.

8 DUSTPAN AND BROOM
A small dustpan and broom are essential for keeping a workplace tidy and for whisking away broken bits of tile. If an area is particularly dusty, use a damp sponge to clean up rather than sweeping.

9 RUBBER GLOVES
Durable kitchen gloves protect hands when mixing or applying grout and cement. Also wear them when using a large sponge and water to wipe off excess grout from the tops of tiles.

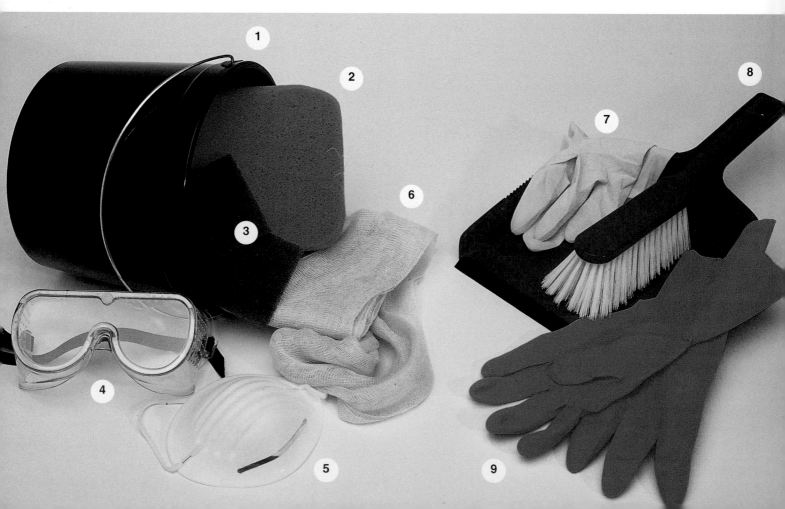

ADHESIVES

Mosaic suppliers carry an array of specialty glues for the various types of tesserae and surfaces involved in creating a mosaic work. When selecting an adhesive, make sure it is suitable for both the tesserae and the base of the mosaic. For indoor projects, tile mastic is a great choice because it is available in a premixed paste and is very strong. It may not hold up in a harsh winter climate, however. For outdoor projects, cement is the best choice because of its durability and strength. It needs to be mixed from powder and specially prepared to make it weatherproof (see Mixing Cement & Grout, below). Finally, when bonding glass tiles to a glass surface, a clear-drying adhesive specially formulated for the purpose is necessary to preserve translucency.

CEMENT & GROUT

Cement is often used as an adhesive in mosaic work because it is durable, reliable, and inexpensive. Use it for both indoor and especially outdoor projects. Grout, used to fill the spaces between tiles, adds to the strength and durability of a piece and is available in many colors and types. It can be purchased premixed, but the powdered form is very easy to use and is less expensive. Always follow the manufacturer's directions for mixing and using cement, grout, and additives and for applying grout sealant.

Many of the projects in this book call for sanded grout, which lends itself to mosaic work because it simulates textured grouting often found in traditional mosaics. It also complements the inherently dimensional surface of mosaic work, adding to its tactile beauty. Unsanded grout, such as the kind used for tiled bathroom floors, provides a smooth, caulk-like finish.

MIXING CEMENT & GROUT

Mix powdered cement and grout in small batches as needed, and always wear rubber gloves. Both cement and grout mixtures should be loose, spreadable pastes, but not too runny. Add the powder slowly to a small amount of water, mixing thoroughly, and continue to add powder until you achieve a fudge-like consistency. Once cement or grout is mixed, it should be used quickly before it becomes too dry.

For outdoor projects, use cement and grout formulated for outdoor use – they contain an acrylic additive, which provides extra strength. To guarantee lasting durability, mix the powder with a weatherproofing acrylic admixture, instead of water. The plastic nature of this additive prevents grout and cement from cracking when the mosaic is subjected to winter's freeze-thaw cycle. To be safe, cover outdoor pieces with plastic or bring them in during harsh or snowy weather.

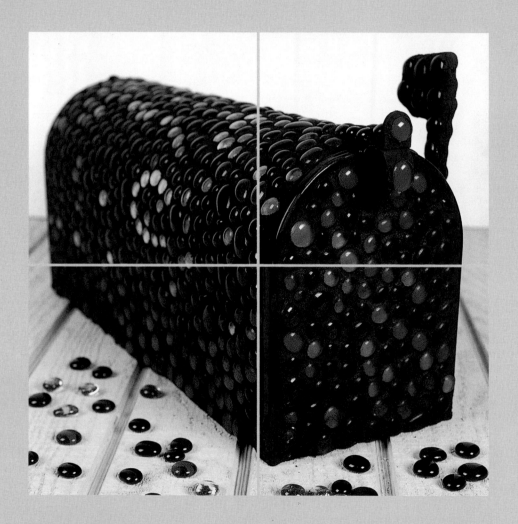

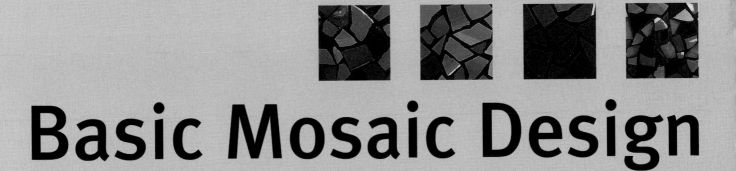

Basic Mosaic Design

CREATING A DESIGN

Mosaic designs usually start with a personal theme or a particularly inspiring material, such as a gorgeous, but broken, china teapot. Perhaps there is a favorite chipped mug lingering in the cupboard that can be restored to usefulness as a coaster, or a damaged ceramic casserole cover with a vegetable motif that can be reused as a focal point in a framed piece for the kitchen.

CHOOSING A BASE

Another good way to come up with a design is to begin with a surface or a base for the mosaic. Is there a table, a birdbath, or an old flowerpot that is in need of refurbishing? These are all great items to begin with. After selecting a base, choose a color scheme according to where the piece will go. A flowerpot in shades of yellow and blue will brighten a dreary window; earth tones would look delicious covering a window box planted with kitchen herbs. Then, create a simple design for the mosaic inspired by the chosen base and colors.

FUNCTION AS INSPIRATION

The function of an item will often inspire a design as well. Picture water bubbling over the trout in the rain catcher on page 92, and it's obvious that the design works on many levels. Use it at a seaside cottage, and it's found the perfect home! Similarly, the stepping stones on page 97 are inspired by the bright, bold flowers of high summer. The simple, stylized design captures the multiple-petal beauty of many flowers, without replicating them exactly. This is the secret to a successful design! Don't be afraid to be too simplistic. Mosaics are inherently detailed and textured, and a simple design will enhance the beauty of the tiles and the workmanship.

TURNING A SKETCH INTO A PATTERN

First, begin with a hand-drawn sketch or a photocopy of a picture. For small works, the pattern can be easily drawn at actual size. For large pieces, such as a floor, the design needs to be scaled to the size of the mosaic surface. Sketching the design on graph paper or a grid will help set guidelines. For very large pieces, use a photocopier to enlarge the pattern in sections to the necessary size.

CREATING COLOR GUIDES

A sketch can also be simplified by outlining it on tracing paper, making it easier to transfer and read. Photocopy the outline on white paper and experiment with different color combinations, using pencils or markers. Having a colored pattern to refer to while working is extremely helpful, especially with very large pieces that have many colors and images. Then, cut out and trace the pattern on the mosaic base using a permanent marker or pencil. It is also helpful to sketch in colors or a numbering system directly on the base, to more easily distinguish which tiles go where.

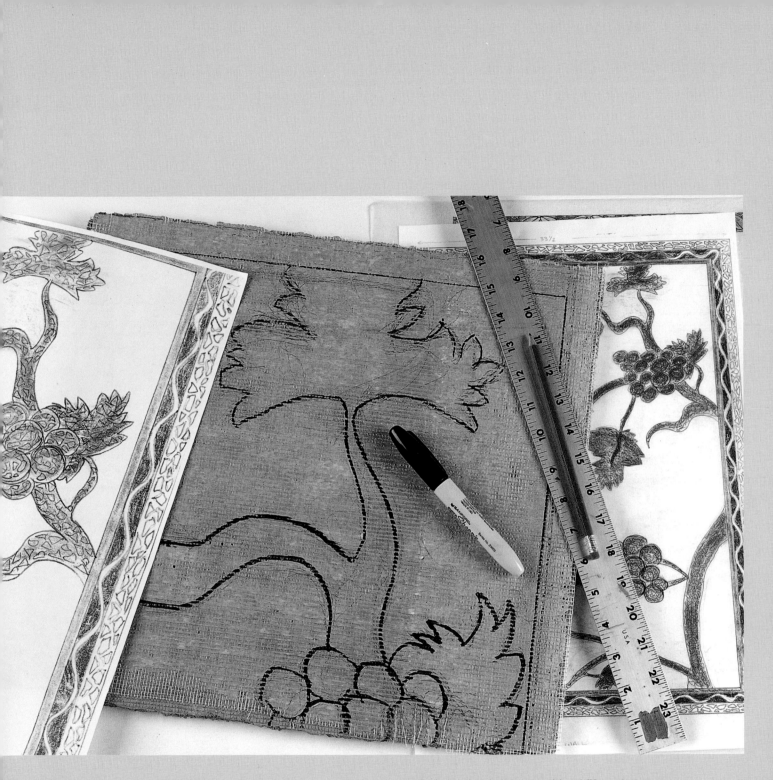

This design, inspired by a traditional fifteenth-century mosaic, was updated for the classical entryway project on page 40. Since it will eventually be covered up, don't be afraid to draw the pattern directly on the surface to make applying tiles easier.

How to Cut Tiles

BREAKING CHINA & CERAMIC TILE

Many of the projects in this book make use of shards rather than perfectly trimmed tiles, which is a great way to recycle beautiful ceramics. To break whole dishes, cups, or large tiles, use a hammer. First, wrap the pieces to be smashed in a towel to prevent shards from being scattered, and always wear safety goggles. Then, use tile nippers to refine the shape of the pieces as necessary to fit them into a mosaic. To keep an image on patterned ceramic pieces intact, try to break them into a few very large pieces, then trim around the design with tile nippers and/or chipper nippers.

MAKING STRAIGHT CUTS

Use a combination scorer and plier to make straight cuts. It is important to apply firm, even pressure while scoring. Use a metal ruler to prevent the scorer from slipping and to keep the line perfectly straight. Then, grasp the tile with the tool and align the scoring with the guide mark, or the center of the tool's mouth. Press the handles together slowly and firmly, and the tile will snap off along the score mark.

SHAPING TILES

Once tiles have been broken or cut to the approximate size needed, additional shaping may be necessary to fit pieces into a mosaic. Use chipper nippers, which act as mosaic scissors, to cut away tiny bits of tile. Don't try to cut too much at once; rather, chip away at the tile, going over the same area a few times. Use this technique to make rounded or curved tiles, too. With a bit of practice, a variety of unusual and interesting shapes are possible. Try making ovals, hearts, or leaf-shaped tiles.

1 MAKING SHARDS
Use a hammer to break china and ceramic ware into use-able shards and then refine the pieces with a tile nipper.

2 MAKING STRAIGHT CUTS
Any kind of tile can be cut into several pieces with a scorer and plier and used for mosaic work.

3 SHAPING TILES
Both glass and ceramic tiles can be further refined and shaped by using chipper nippers. Even teardrops and circles are possible!

4 CUTTING GLASS
Glass can be cut just as easily as ceramics using the same techniques.

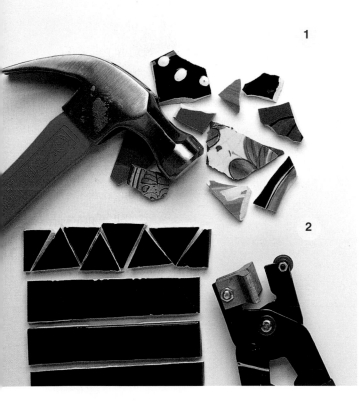

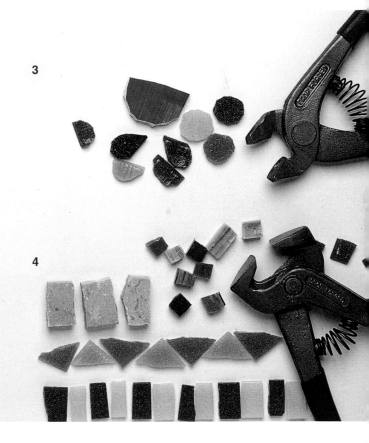

How to Lay Out a Pattern

The first thing to remember about assembling a mosaic is that the more closely tiles are placed together, the more solid the design will look; if the tiles are spaced more widely apart, the design will appear fractured. An intricate design, such as one that illustrates a scene, should have closely spaced tiles; but a geometric floor mosaic would look stunning with wider grout lines.

DIRECT TILE APPLICATION

There are two ways to apply tiles to a surface. The *direct method* involves placing tiles one by one, face up, on the base. This method can be used to apply tesserae to both rounded and flat surfaces and is good for any small project. Beginners should be sure to choose a rigid surface to work on, because any flexibility could cause the grout to crack or the tiles to pop off.

INDIRECT TILE APPLICATION

The *indirect method* involves placing tesserae face down on a temporary base, such as adhesive vinyl, then laying the tiles all at once onto a base covered with adhesive. This method is helpful when trying to achieve a flat surface, such as a floor, tabletop, or wall, or when working with flat, even tiles. Always make sure the surface is strong enough to support the weight of the tiles, grout, and adhesive, which can become extremely heavy.

For intricate or tricky areas of a design, use a chipper nipper to cut the tiles. Any oddly shaped or curved tesserae will need to be shaped carefully to ensure that they fit smoothly into the mosaic. Chipper nippers are specially designed for more precise cutting than tile nippers. Chip carefully and slowly away, checking the tiles against the pattern often and making adjustments as needed. If necessary, mark the tiles with a grease-pencil guideline.

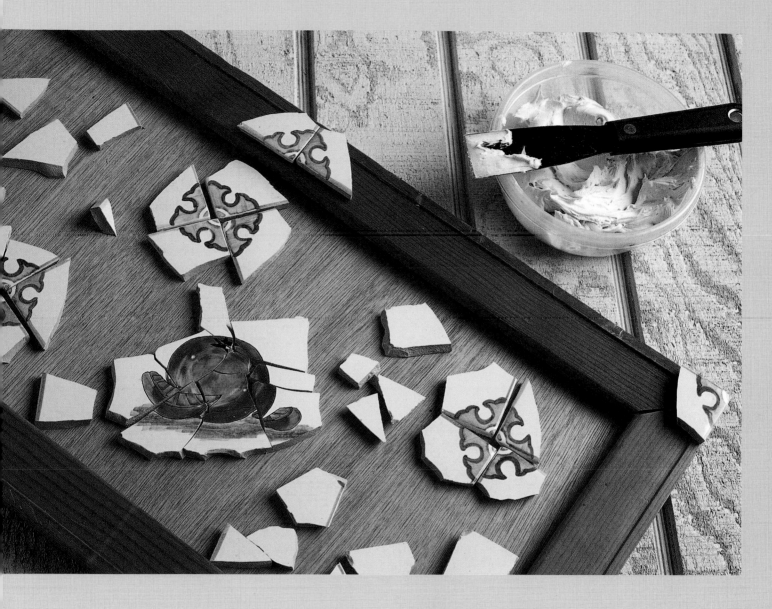

The tiles used for the framed kitchen mosaic on page 36 had corner decorations that were reassembled to make the blue floral accents throughout the piece. When working with patterned ceramic shards, play with the pieces to discover interesting ways to rearrange the images. Tiles that extend past the edge of the mosaic, like the accent at the top of this frame, make a composition more dynamic.

Making Mosaics on Wood

Wood is the perfect choice for a custom-made mosaic base, such as the house-number plaque on page 124. Particle board and plywood are inexpensive, easy-to-use materials that can be cut to any shape with a jigsaw. Lumberyards and home-improvement centers will cut wood to the desired shape and size as well.

Any wooden item can be used, but if it has been varnished or painted, use coarse sandpaper to remove as much of the finish as possible. A sealer and primer may also be necessary to make sure that the mosaic adhesive bonds properly with the wood. A solution of white craft glue or carpenter's wood glue and water works well. Used furniture, frames, and unfinished items are all great choices for a mosaic base.

Wood is one of the most versatile materials for mosaic bases because it is comparatively lightweight, is available in a variety of thicknesses, has a porous surface, is easily customizable, and is generally easy to work with. However, wood will warp over time if left outdoors. Bring wood-based mosaics inside during harsh weather, and don't use wood for patio tabletops.

Making Mosaics on Cement

Cement bases work well for outdoor projects because they are inherently durable and weather resistant. Use cement prepared for outdoor use as the adhesive for any cement-based project that needs to be weather resistant (see page 9 for guidance). Check the local garden or home center for paving stones, flower-bed edgers, garden sculpture, and other cement items for inspiration. Pavers are available in many shapes, such as octagons and circles. Cement board, which is available at home-improvement centers, provides a flat, strong, durable surface for tabletops, floors, or wall panels.

When working with a cement base, be sure to clean it thoroughly first with soap and water. Then, let it dry completely before beginning the mosaic. Dust and grime can interfere with the adhesive bond.

Cement floors are also a suitable base for mosaic application, but it's best to have them professionally cleaned and prepared, especially if they are old or abused. Any paint will need to be removed, and all cracks should be filled.

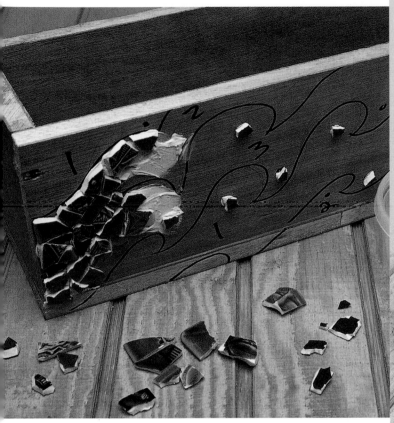

This ordinary window box is just one of the many wooden items that provide a suitable surface for mosaic. The easy-to-draw-on surface makes transferring patterns a breeze. See page 92 for project instructions.

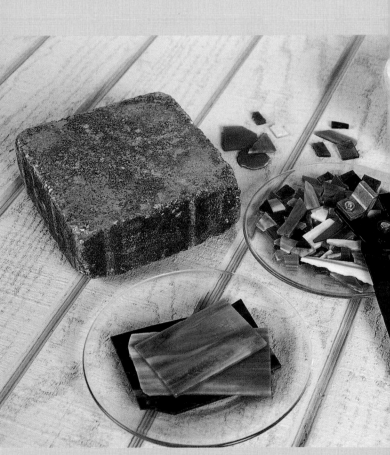

This old stone is soon to be transformed with an elegant stained-glass sun mosaic. The flat, small surface makes this project a perfect introduction to mosaics. See page 96 for instructions.

Making Mosaics on Metal

Any metal object can be used in mosaic work. Try refurbishing rusty garden furniture or transforming yard-sale finds. Mailboxes, doorknockers, shelf brackets, and wastebaskets would all make interesting and unusual surfaces for mosaic work. Try turning a coffee can into a decorative container, or turning a simple steel mixing bowl into a birdbath.

To prepare a metal surface for mosaic, first remove any rust with steel wool. The smooth surface of new metal items needs to be roughed up in order to take the adhesive properly, so give the entire piece a rubdown with steel wool until it feels coarse. Otherwise, the tiles may slip and slide, especially on curved surfaces.

This standard metal mailbox was decorated with flat-backed glass jewels, which are used whole rather than cut to fit. Cement is a good adhesive to use with metal bases, especially on outdoor projects. See page 126 for project instructions.

Making Mosaics on Glass

The variety of glass objects suitable for mosaics is staggering, and when paired with glass tiles, a luminous result is inevitable. Take advantage of the translucency of glass by decorating candle shades, votives, electric lampshades, or suncatchers. Old window panes, still in their frames, and vases are also good choices for mosaic work.

Always use glass cleaner and a lint-free cloth to prepare the surface. Fingerprints or oil from hands will interfere with the adhesive bond. Equally important is to use clear-drying adhesive specially formulated for glass. This will ensure that the translucency of the glass is uninhibited and that the adhesive is not visible from behind the tiles.

Since glass is translucent, keep in mind how the back of the project will be viewed. Be sure grout doesn't settle behind the tiles, as this will be visible from the front and the back. A good way to avoid this is to use enough adhesive to bond the entire surface area of each tile, but not so much that it oozes up into the grout lines. Practice on a scrap of glass first, to determine how much adhesive is necessary.

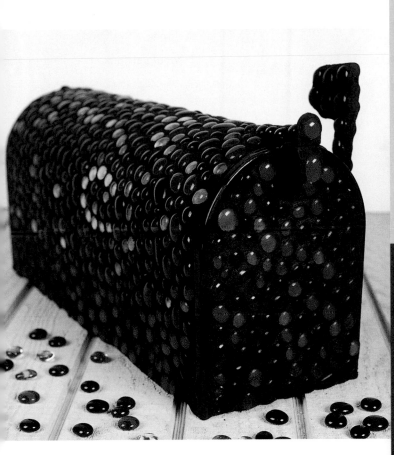

An ordinary mailbox can be the perfect storage container for garden tools. Covered with multicolor glass beads, this box will sparkle in the sunlight.

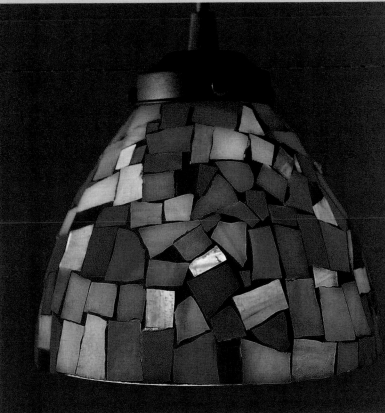

Electric patio lights can be turned into elegant stained-glass shades, which filter light beautifully. A string of lights enhances the effect by filling a whole space with colored light; it's well worth the effort. See page 88 for instructions.

USING COLOR EFFECTIVELY

The use of color in a mosaic has a profound effect on the overall mood and feeling of the piece. Consider not only the colors of the tiles, but the color of the grout as well. If colors are too contrasting, the design may become choppy and lose focus; if the colors are too similar, detail can be lost.

When selecting colors, many things should be taken into consideration to successfully render a mosaic design. Ask the following questions to determine what factors or results are most important:

Should the piece convey a relaxing or energetic feeling?
Will the mosaic be placed indoors or outdoors?
What sort of light will the mosaic be viewed in?
Are the mosaic images intended to be realistic or whimsical?
Is the mosaic inspired by a certain time period or artistic style?
Last, but certainly not least, what colors appeal to you personally?

COLOR SCHEMES

1 BRIGHT COLORS
Bright colors confer energy and vitality to their surroundings. Use them for bold, dynamic designs or to draw attention to a specific area of a mosaic.

2 EARTH TONES
Earth tones are comforting colors, ranging from brown to blue, red to green. Drawn from nature, they can't help but be harmonious when used together. Use them to seamlessly integrate a mosaic into the garden.

3 BLACK AND WHITE
Use black and white together for a classic, dramatic look. Since they are neutral, they can be used to easily accent other colors and are great for borders.

4 MONOCHROMATIC COLORS
A monochromatic palette can be intriguing and sophisticated when the boundaries of color are tested. A pattern of light-to dark-blue tiles is more interesting with a few teal tiles and gives the arrangement shading and depth.

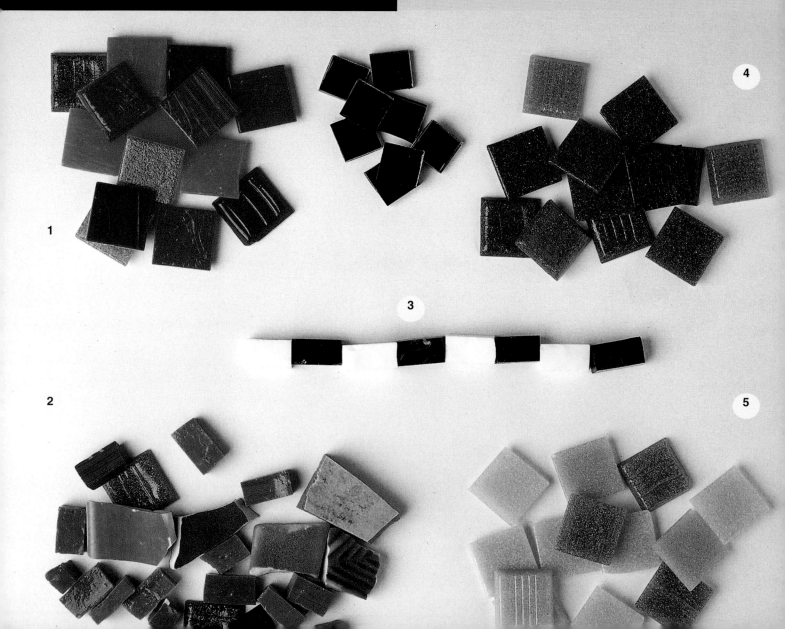

5 SOFT COLORS
Pastels are soft colors that can be worked into virtually any design, because they enhance brighter colors without detracting from them. Use them for a subdued, calming effect.

6 CONTRASTING COLORS
The central blue tile in each of these arrangements shows how different a color can look depending on the hues surrounding it. True blue, paired with an orange of equal intensity, makes for a high-contrast color scheme. When surrounded by greens of equal intensity, the blue almost disappears.

7 ENHANCING MONOCHROMATIC COLORS
Use several shades of the same color to add depth to a monotone arrangement. This technique can be used to create an interesting background pattern that enhances the focal point of a design without detracting from it.

8 OUTLINING DESIGNS
To make patterns, and especially letters, stand out, try outlining them with a darker or lighter color. The outline has to be sufficiently contrasting to be effective, as in the blue-and-white example here.

9 COMPLEMENTARY COLORS
Complementary colors, such as green and red, appear to vibrate or flicker when placed together. Yellow-purple and blue-orange combinations also share this characteristic. Use a lighter shade of either color to minimize the vibrating effect, which can be distracting. Use shades of the same color for minimal contrast.

10 DEFINING DESIGNS
The same design can be highly defined or subdued, depending on the colors involved. Play with highly contrasting and minimally contrasting designs to see what works best.

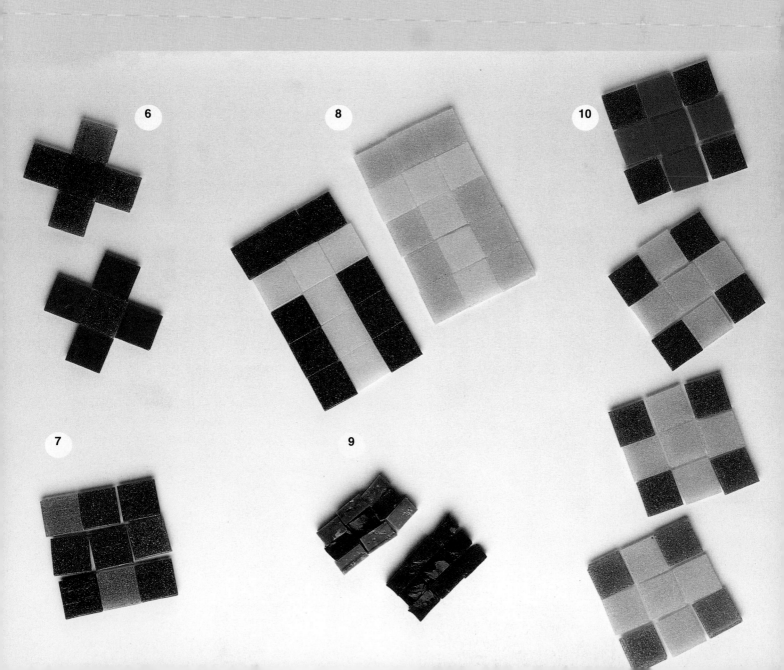

CHOOSING GROUT COLORS

In a mosaic, the color of the grout is just as important as the color of the tiles. Grout lines can pull a range of colors together, highlight or minimize the fragmented feel of a piece, or be barely visible. The color of grout that should be used in a piece depends entirely on the desired effect. Make a few thumbnail mosaics using the same kinds of tiles in the original, then experiment with different grout colors.

In general, the more the grout color contrasts with the overall color scheme of the mosaic, the more visible and fragmented the piece will look. The more closely the grout matches the overall color scheme, the more unified the piece will look. Try combining different grout colors in the same piece to highlight or subdue certain areas.

These palettes, which range from warm-to cool-colored tiles, also show various grouting styles. Use them as a handy reference for the moods and effects possible by combining different grout and tile colors.

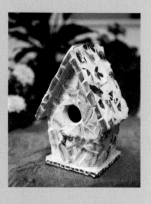

Delicate china patterns pair well with the simplicity and purity of white grout. See page 128 for instructions.

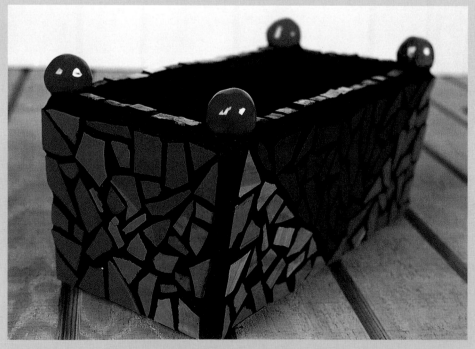

To make bright colors pop, outline them with black grout. See page 68 for instructions.

1 NO GROUT

The farther apart the spaces between the tiles in an ungrouted mosaic are, the more unfinished and broken the piece will look. If tiles are placed very close together, the design will read well. Smalti are traditionally left ungrouted because the pitted and uneven surface traps grout, causing the handmade glass to become dulled. Instead, the tiles are pushed into a bed of adhesive such as cement, which partially fills the spaces between them.

2 BLACK GROUT

Black grout accentuates the brighter colors in this palette and gives the whole panel a leaded, stained-glass feel. The shapes of the yellow shards are clearly defined, while the darker purple and blue tiles meld together.

3 WHITE GROUT

White grout is useful for pieces with light or pale color schemes. With bright, dark, and medium-toned colors, white grout highlights the shape of each tile, giving the piece a fragmented feeling.

4 GRAY GROUT

Gray grout was used on this palette. The rainbow of color is pulled together into a harmonious whole by the neutral, soft gray grout lines, which are obvious but not overpowering. This grout also looks like cement, which works well for outdoor projects like birdbaths. For the most harmonious look when a mosaic incorporates a wide range of colors, use a grout that is neither too dark nor too light, or for less harmony, use different colors of grout in each area.

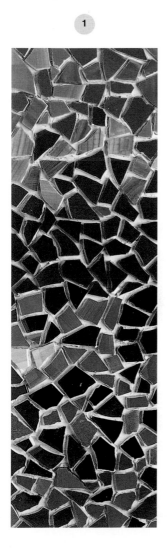
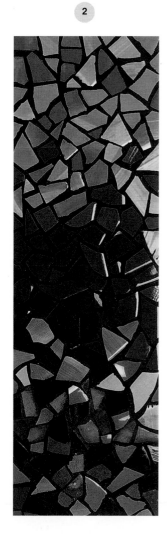
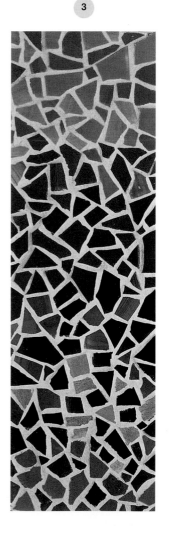
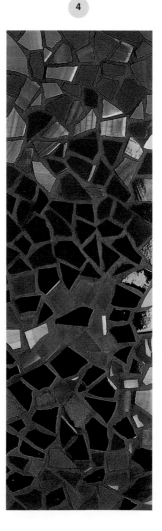

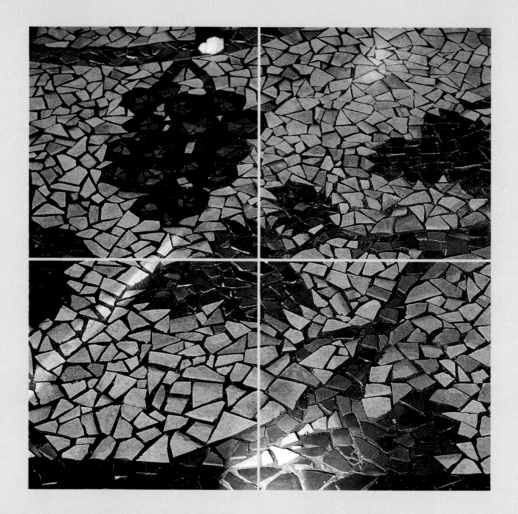

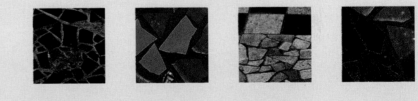

Mosaics Inside

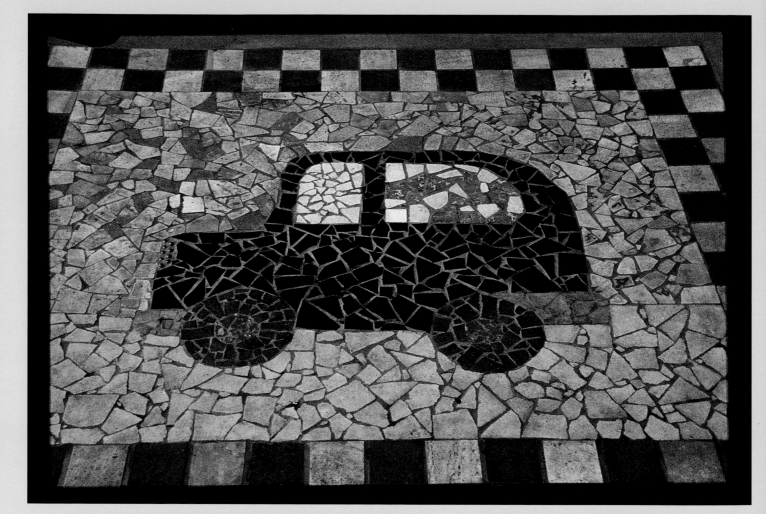

Artist: Twyla Arthur
Photo by Twyla Arthur

cement board

stone or porcelain ceramic tiles, all the same thickness

black and white tiles for the border

palette knife

heavy-duty utility knife

hammer

tile nippers

cement

sanded gray grout

large sponge

safety goggles

latex gloves

filter mask

mixing bowls for cement and grout

Playroom Floor

This truck features marble headlights, which are sure to delight children

and adults alike. Simple, fun touches like these marbles make a mosaic

engaging, and that is certainly a welcome quality in a child's playroom.

Choose simple, easy-to-recognize designs, such as a rainbow or an animal,

or just bright geometric shapes. Encourage the kids to help by choosing the

pattern or placing some of the tiles themselves!

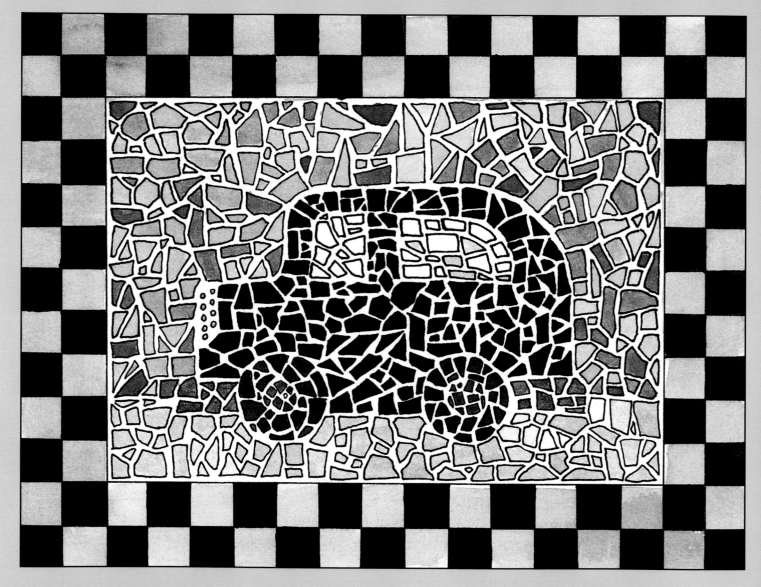

Illustrator: Mary Newell DePalma

STARTING OUT

A section of the original floor will need to be removed in order to place the mosaic. Consult with a contractor about the best way to do this. Prepare a pattern by sizing the illustration to your selected tabletop. You can enlarge the pattern in sections using a copier, or sketch or photocopy the illustration onto graph paper to determine scale.

STEP 1

Wearing safety goggles and protective gloves, break the ceramics to be used into large shards using a hammer (see page 14 for guidance). Then, cut the cement board to the desired size by deeply scoring it using a ruler and heavy-duty utility knife. Snap the excess off by simply aligning the scorings with the edge of a table and applying pressure to the pieces that extend past the table's edge. Next, cut each design element out of paper and trace around it with a permanent marker to transfer the pattern directly onto the cement board. Use 4-inch (10-cm) by 4-inch (10-cm) or 6-inch (15-cm) by 6-inch (15-cm) whole tiles for the border.

Tip: The stone used here measures 3/4 inch (2 cm) thick. For beginners, high-fire or porcelain tiles of the same thickness are easier to work with. They come in a variety of colors and are strong enough to withstand the wear and tear of children playing.

STEP 2

Prepare the cement for indoor use (see page 9 for guidance). Using a flexible palette knife, spread the perimeter of the board with a 1/8-inch (3-mm) layer of cement and begin applying the black and white border tiles. Leave out four tiles for screw holes so that the floor can be easily installed. Fill in the rest of the design according to the pattern, spreading cement over a 6-inch (15-cm) to 8-inch (20-cm) -square area at a time. Finally, apply the marble headlights, using extra cement for a secure bond. Let it dry for twenty-four hours.

Prepare gray sanded grout for indoor use (see page 9), then begin spreading it over an 8-inch (20-cm) to 10-inch (25-cm) area of the floor with glove-protected hands. Work the grout completely into the crevices between the shards using a circular motion. Continue until all the spaces between the shards are filled. Keep wiping excess grout off the surface of the shards. When the grout has dried enough to become powdery, no more than fifteen to twenty minutes, use a large damp sponge to clean the tiles. Rinse the sponge frequently, and wipe the tiles until all the grout film is gone. Buff with a dry cloth when the grout is completely dry. Let the floor dry for a week before installation.

To install the floor, use flat-headed screws in the empty spaces and make sure they are flush with the surface of the board. Next, apply tiles to cover the spaces. Let it dry twenty-four hours, then grout.

VARIATION

The timeless appeal of a rainbow motif is perfect for a playroom floor. The simple pattern seen here is a great starting point for beginning mosaicists, because it can be easily drawn and laid out. Follow the directions for the main project to ensure the floor's durability.

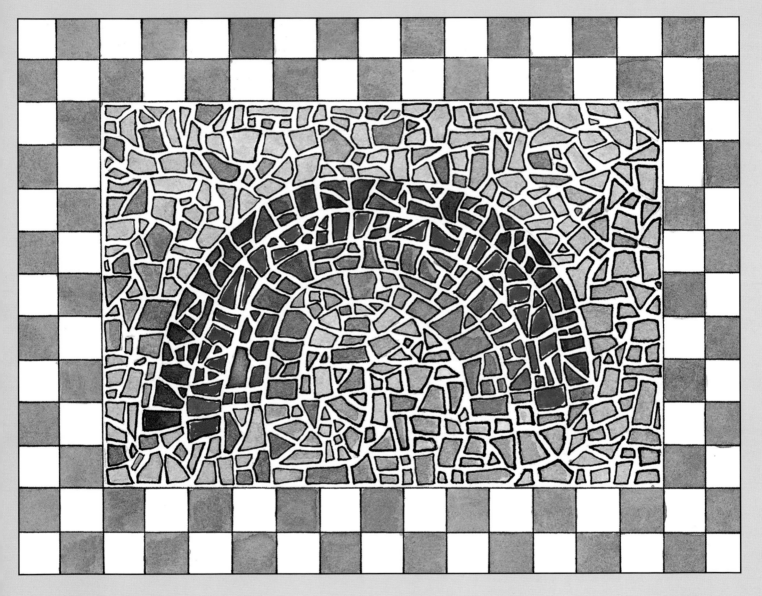

Illustrator: Mary Newell DePalma

Materials

framed mirror

broken ceramic dishes

palette knife

hammer

screws

tile nippers

tile mastic

white sanded grout

kitchen scrubbing pad

cloth towel

safety goggles

latex gloves

filter mask

mixing bowls for cement
and grout

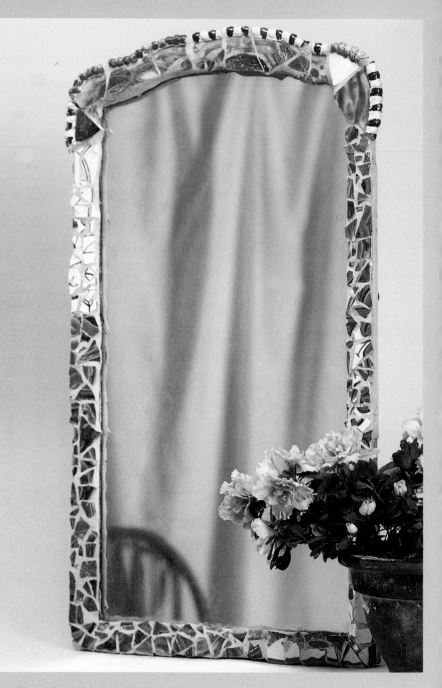

Artist: Doreen Mastandrea

Ceramic Relief Mirror

A framed mirror of any size can be used for this project. Choose one that has an interest-

ing shape, then select ceramic pieces that will accentuate it. Beautiful, handmade plates

with a dimensional rope pattern were used here to outline the scalloped border at the top

of the frame. Take advantage of curved plate edges to create striking rounded borders.

STARTING OUT

Experiment with different ways of arranging the shards by laying them out on a piece of paper next to the frame. There is no need to plan out the entire frame, but it is helpful to work out the focal points beforehand.

STEP 1

Wearing safety goggles and protective gloves, break the ceramics to be used into shards using a hammer (see page 14 for guidance). Try to keep interesting designs intact by using tile nippers to extract them safely from large, broken pieces.

Tip: Having a variety of shapes and sizes of ceramic pieces on hand will make it faster and easier to fill the space on the frame and will add interest to the design.

STEP 2

With a palette knife, spread a 1/8-inch (3-mm) -thick layer of mastic on approximately 6 inches (15 cm) of the frame. Start applying shards side by side until you cover the area. Spread on more mastic and continue applying shards all the way around the frame. If you decide to cover the edges of the frame, be careful because this is a delicate area and shards may chip off over time. You can grout or paint the edges instead after the mosaic is completed. Let it dry for twenty-four hours.

Tip: Be careful not to apply too much mastic, because the excess will be displaced into the spaces between the tiles, leaving little room for grout.

STEP 3

Prepare grout for indoor use (see page 9), then apply a small amount on the frame with glove-protected hands. Work the grout completely into the crevices between the shards using a circular motion. Fill all the spaces between the shards. Continue wiping excess grout off the surface of the shards, because it will be difficult to sand off once dry. When the grout has dried enough to become powdery, no more than fifteen to twenty minutes, use a dry kitchen scrubbing pad to sand excess grout off the surface of the shards. Wear a filter mask while sanding. If the scrubbing pad scratches the glaze, wipe off excess grout while it is wet with a damp sponge, let it dry, then buff with a lint-free rag.

Tip: If the grout has not dried enough before sanding, the scrubbing pad will get saturated with moist grout. If this happens, wait a little longer before trying again with a dry pad.

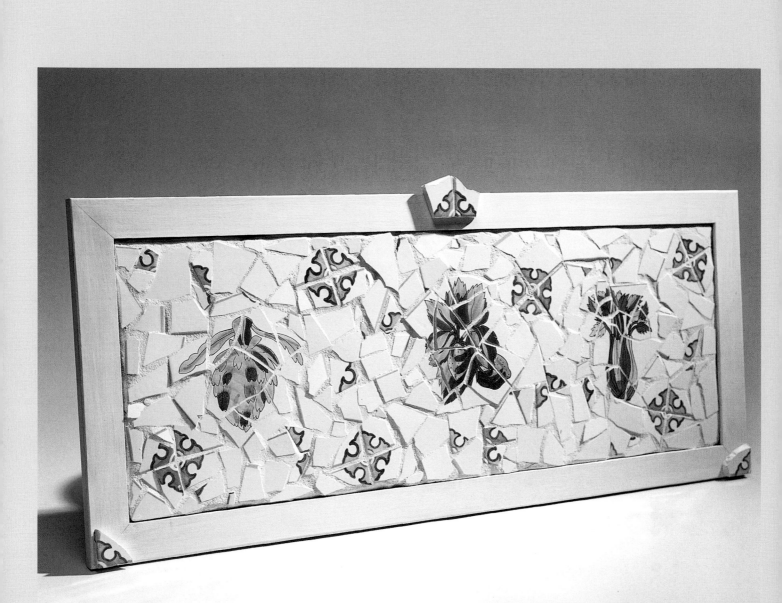

Artist: Aimee Southworth

Materials   wood-backed frame

decorative kitchen tiles

palette knife

hammer

tile nippers

tile mastic

white sanded grout

kitchen scrubbing pad

safety goggles

latex gloves

filter mask

mixing bowls for cement and grout

Framed Kitchen Mosaic

This framed project is an easy way to incorporate mosaic art into any

space — just customize the size, shape, and theme to match a particular

decor. With the variety of decorated tiles available, almost any pattern is

possible! When breaking tiles, keep special designs whole, or try combining

shards in new ways to make innovative patterns. The blue flowers in this

design were made using four corner pieces from the tiles used here.

Retrofit any store-bought frame for this project by nailing a thin piece of wood to the back. Then, paint the frame if desired and let it dry completely before beginning the mosaic.

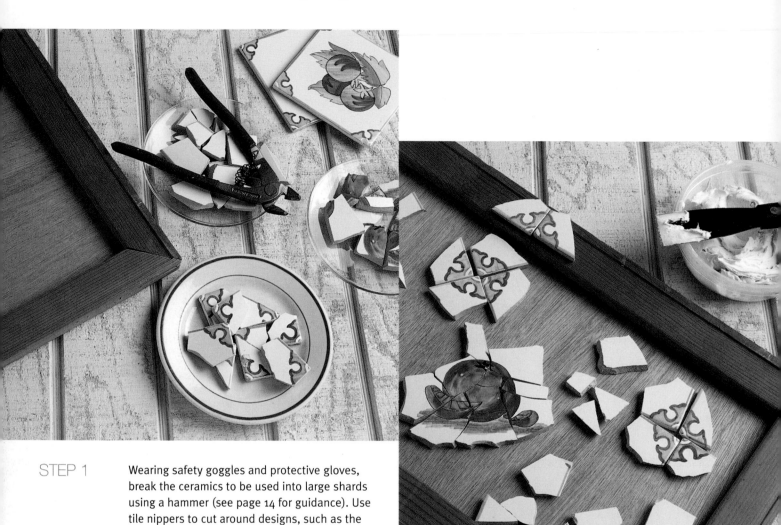

STEP 1

Wearing safety goggles and protective gloves, break the ceramics to be used into large shards using a hammer (see page 14 for guidance). Use tile nippers to cut around designs, such as the vegetables here, and keep them together.

STEP 2

With a palette knife, spread the backs of shards with a 1/8-inch (3-mm) -thick layer of mastic. Begin applying shards that need to be placed in specific areas first, then fill in the rest of the space using solidly colored, plain remnants from the decorative tiles. Here, the three vegetable motifs were applied first and spaced evenly apart. Let it dry for twenty-four hours.

Tip: Use a piece of paper cut to the same size as the frame to plan the placement of the tiles before applying them.

Tip: When using mastic, try not to move tiles that have already been applied; any movement before drying will weaken the bond.

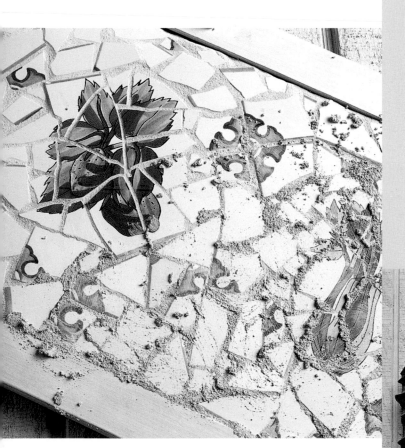

Use cement board, available at hardware stores, and a lettering stencil to make a weatherproof sign like the one seen here. First, cut the board to the desired size by deeply scoring it using a ruler and heavy-duty utility knife, then snap the excess off. To do this, simply align the scored edges with the edge of a table, then apply pressure to the pieces that extend past the table's edge. Next, trace the lettering using a permanent marker directly on the cement board. Try making a custom alphabet for tracing with a computer and printer.

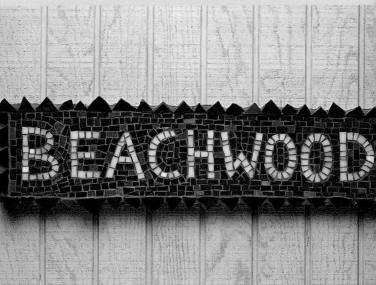

Artist: Doreen Mastandrea

STEP 3

Prepare white sanded grout for indoor use (see page 9 for guidance), then apply a small amount on the mosaic with glove-protected hands. Work the grout completely into the crevices between the shards using a circular motion, or use a rubber spatula if the shards are flat and of the same thickness. Fill all the spaces between the shards. Continue wiping excess grout off the surface of the shards. When the grout has dried enough to become powdery, no more than fifteen to twenty minutes, use a dry kitchen scrubbing pad to sand excess grout off the surface of the shards. Wear a filter mask while sanding. If the scrubbing pad scratches the glaze, wipe off excess grout while it is wet with a damp sponge, let it dry, then buff with a lint-free rag.

Apply the lettering tiles first, then complete the border, and finally fill the remaining background areas. The vitreous glass tiles on this sign were applied using cement mixed for outdoor use. Be sure to also use grout mixed for outdoor use (see page 9 for guidance). Finally, apply grout sealant according to the manufacturer's directions.

Tip: If there are any large, hard-to-remove spots of grout that have dried on the tiles, use a craft knife to scrape them off.

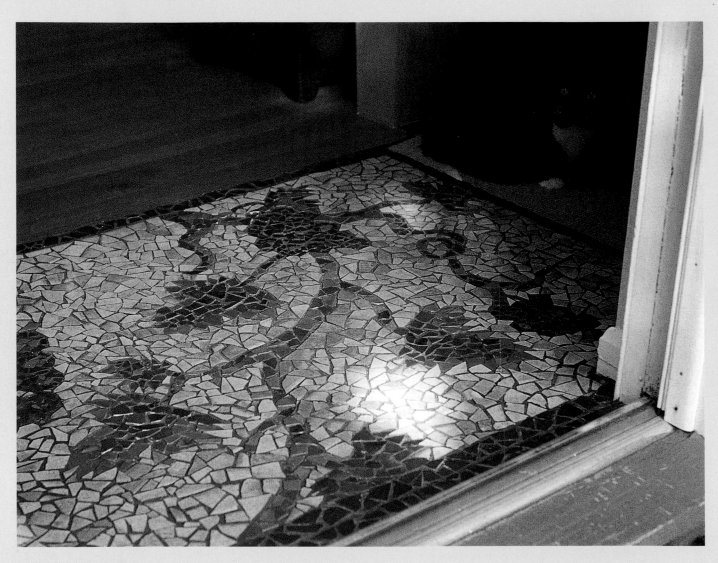

Artist: Doreen Mastandrea
Photo by: Regina Grenier

Materials

cement board

ceramic tiles or shards

palette knife

heavy-duty utility knife

hammer

tile nippers

cement

grout

acrylic admixture

kitchen scrubbing pad

safety goggles

Classical Entryway

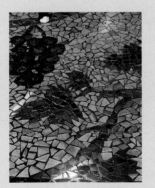

This entryway was inspired by traditional mosaic designs but is made with broken ceramic tiles instead of handmade glass smalti for a modern appeal. When planning a design, take into consideration the colors and the lighting of the room where the floor will be installed. Vary the colors of images within the pattern to create added detail and depth. The grapes here incorporate several shades of red and maroon, and the foliage is made with several shades of green. Many copy shops will enlarge a pattern to scale, which makes it easier to transfer the design. This mosaic measures 3 feet (91 cm) by 4 feet (122 cm).

STARTING OUT Cement board, available at hardware stores, is used to make a durable base for this entryway. Make sure that the subfloor is sufficiently stable; consult with a contractor if you are unsure. If the subfloor has any flex to it, the tiles will also flex and eventually pop out. To use the board, first cut it to the desired size by deeply scoring it using a ruler and heavy-duty utility knife. Then, snap the excess off by simply aligning the scorings with the edge of a table and applying pressure to the pieces that extend past the table's edge.

STEP 1

Wearing safety goggles and protective gloves, break the ceramics to be used into large shards using a hammer (see page 14 for guidance). Use tile nippers to cut the shards into smaller pieces for the images and the vines. Use the larger pieces for the background. Next, cut each design element out of paper and trace around it with a permanent marker to transfer the pattern directly on the cement board. Alternatively, try using graphite paper, usually found in art and craft supply stores, to transfer the design. Slip a sheet under the pattern, then trace over the lines of the photocopy. Because graphite paper only comes in 8 1/2-inch by 11-inch sheets, it will not be large enough to transfer a design 3 feet by 4 feet. So, you will need to transfer the design bit by bit by moving the graphite paper around to each area.

STEP 2

Prepare the cement for outdoor use (see page 9 for guidance). Using a flexible palette knife, spread a small area of the board with a 1/8-inch (3-mm) layer of cement, then begin applying the shards. Start with shards that need to be placed in specific areas, such as the vines, leaves, and grapes seen here, then fill in the rest of the background. Leave several empty spaces for screw holes so that the floor can be easily and securely installed. Finally, complete the border. Let it dry for twenty-four hours.

Tip: When selecting tiles for this project, be sure to test the durability of the glaze with a kitchen scrubbing pad. If it gets scratched easily, consider using other ceramics.

Tip: A large mosaic such as this one requires many tiles. When using ceramic shards, double-check that there are enough of each color and pattern to complete the project before beginning it.

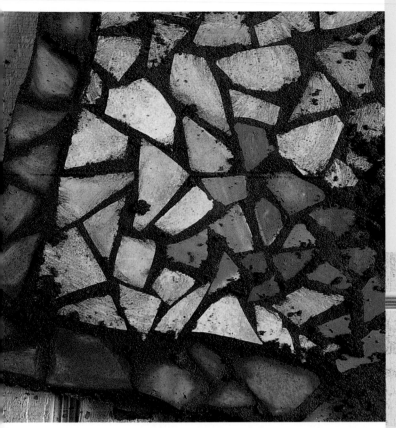

Try making a special frame for a mosaic picture
by experimenting with different motifs and
colors borrowed from the main design. This
border uses purple and green from the entryway to create a repeating, stylized grape-leaf
pattern. To help define the pattern further, two
colors of grout are used – midnight blue around
the leaves, and terra cotta within them.

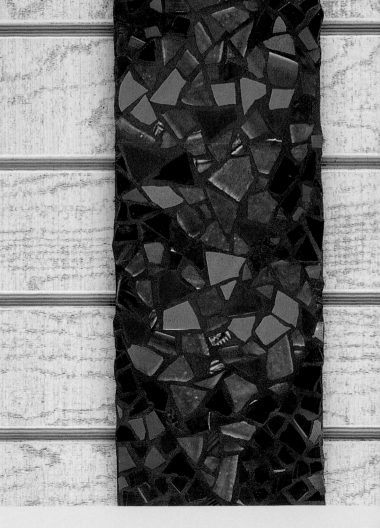

STEP 3

Prepare grout for outdoor use (see page 9),
then begin spreading it over one-third of the floor
with glove-protected hands. Work the grout
completely into the crevices between the shards
using a circular motion. Continue until all the
spaces between the shards are filled. Keep wiping excess grout off the surface of the shards.
When the grout has dried enough to become
powdery, no more than fifteen to twenty minutes,
use a large damp sponge to clean the tiles. Rinse
the sponge frequently, and wipe the tiles until all
the grout film is gone. When the grout is completely dry, buff with a dry cloth. Then, complete
another third of the floor in the same way and,
finally, the last third. Let the floor mosaic dry for
a week before installation.

To install the entryway, use flat-headed screws in
the empty spaces and make sure they are flush
with the surface of the board. Next, apply tiles
to cover the heads of the screws. Let it dry for
twenty-four hours, then grout.

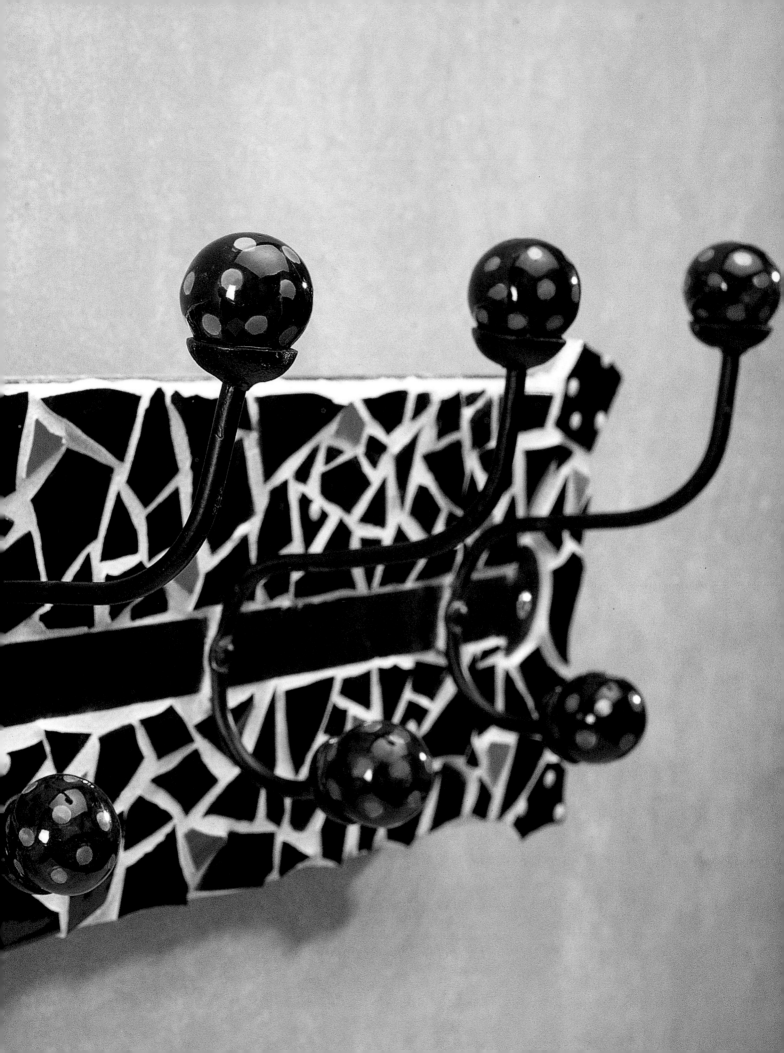

Materials   hooks

plywood board

yellow ceramic shards

polka-dot pieces

solid blue tiles

palette knife

hammer

screwdriver

screws

tile nippers

tile mastic

white sanded grout

kitchen scrubbing pad

safety goggles

latex gloves

filter mask

mixing bowls for cement and grout

Wall Hook Rack

Patterned ceramics provide an inspiring array of decorative elements

that can be used to great effect in mosaic work. Images can be broken

Artist: Doreen Mastandrea   apart at random and rearranged or carefully broken out and kept whole.

In the rack seen here, solid blue, dotted blue, and yellow ceramic tiles

were used to match these decorative ball hooks perfectly. Alternatively,

try selecting ceramic pieces with interesting designs, then find hooks

that complement them.

Plan the arrangement of the patterned shards on the rack before applying them, especially if there is a limited supply. They should be spaced out somewhat evenly, so that one area of the rack does not seem·to have more than another.

STEP 1

Wearing safety goggles and protective gloves, break the ceramics to be used into shards using a hammer (see page 14 for guidance). Use tile nippers to refine the size and shape of the shards as necessary. To make the rack, cut a piece of plywood to the desired size, then attach the hooks to the board with screws.

STEP 2

Spread the back of four polka-dot shards with a 1/8-inch (3-mm) -thick layer of mastic, and apply them so they are partly running off the four corners of the board. This is a visually play-ful way of breaking up the rectangular shape of the rack. Next, randomly apply the yellow shards and some polka-dot shards on all parts of the rack, spaced somewhat evenly apart. Then, spread mastic on a small area of the rack and apply solid blue shards. Continue until the rack is covered. The tile nippers can be used to shape pieces for hard-to-reach areas around the hooks. Let it dry for twenty-four hours.

**Artists: Deb Mandile,
Dawn Dimadona, and
Doreen Mastandrea**

VARIATION

Make your own customized rack using antique hooks and plywood. Begin by cutting a piece of plywood to the desired size, then attach hooks to the board with screws. Next, select patterned ceramic pieces that match the shape, color, or decoration of the hooks. A broken ceramic lamp base with a swirl pattern was used here to complement these curved antique hooks. Follow the steps from the main project for applying the shards and grouting. The neutral gray grout used here is a perfect match for the black-and-white color scheme of the shards.

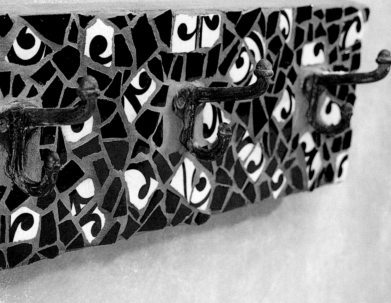

STEP 3   Prepare grout for indoor use (see page 9), then apply a small amount on the rack with glove-protected hands. If the shards are of a uniform thickness, try using a flexible rubber spatula to apply the grout. Work the grout completely into the crevices between the shards using a circular motion. Fill all the spaces between the shards. Continue wiping excess grout off the surface of the shards, because it will be difficult to sand off once dry. When the grout has dried enough to become powdery, no more than fifteen to twenty minutes, use a dry kitchen scrubbing pad to sand excess grout off the surface of the ceramic shards. Wear a filter mask while sanding. If the scrubbing pad scratches the glaze, wipe off excess grout while it is wet with a damp sponge, let it dry, then buff with a lint-free rag. Attach hardware to the back of the rack for hanging, if necessary.

Tip: Mount each hook on a small piece of ply-wood before attaching it to the board. This will raise the hooks up enough to accommodate the thickness of the shards that will cover the rack.

BITS & PIECES: WORKING WITH GLASS

Glass was used to create many of the classic mosaics that adorn ancient buildings and cathedrals throughout Europe. The highly reflective, translucent, shimmering qualities of glass tiles can make a two-dimensional image spring to life, especially when viewed in a sunbathed spot. The vibrant color and tonal variation inherent in this material make it easy to create images with shading effects, giving pieces an illustrated look. Try using mirror or freeform sea glass with traditional tiles for an eclectic design.

1 VITREOUS GLASS TILES

Vitreous glass tiles come in a variety of colors, are easy to cut, and have a corrugated back to aid adhesion. All of these qualities make them a great option for beginners, as well as more experienced mosaicists. They are generally 3/4 inch by 3/4 inch by 3/16 inch (20 mm by 20 mm by 4 mm) and are sold by the pound or on sheets of paper. Their beveled edges also work well with three-dimensional and curved designs, and the flat upper surface makes them perfect for decorating tabletops and floors. Since they are weather resistant, they are also a good choice for outdoor mosaics.

2 GLASS BEADS

These flat-backed glass jewels come in many colors and sizes. They are generally transparent and bright and can be found at stained-glass supply stores as well as home centers. The natural shape of these beads makes it easy to incorporate round elements into a design, rather than trying to cut circular tiles.

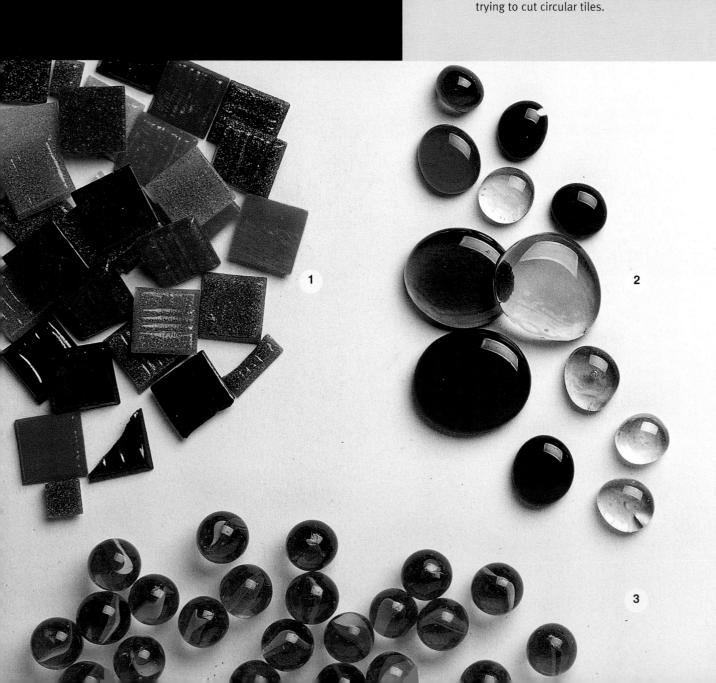

3 MARBLES

Marbles of all kinds can be used in a mosaic. Because they are completely round, pay special attention when applying them. Use extra adhesive, and place them last, if possible, to minimize the possibility of knocking them loose.

4 STAINED GLASS

Stained-glass pieces are spectacular on mosaics that will be viewed in a sunny spot. Cut custom tiles from sheets of glass, or ask a stained-glass artist about their scraps. They will usually have an abundance of shards in a variety of textures, shapes, and colors.

5 METALLIC VITREOUS GLASS

Vitreous glass tiles are also available with metallic finishes or inclusions, which add a luxurious feeling to any design. These are dappled with flecks of gold.

6 SMALTI TILES

These Italian tiles are made of opaque glass and are the classic material used for mosaics. Sold in approximately 1/8-inch by 1/2-inch by 1/4-inch (10-mm by 15-mm by 7-mm) rectangles, they have an irregular and highly reflective surface that catches light beautifully. Because of their uneven surface, smalti mosaics are usually left ungrouted, so that the pits and recesses do not become filled with grout. Traditionally, smalti are pressed into a bed of mortar. The mortar is consequently pushed into the crevices between the tiles, creating a grouted look. Smalti are ideal for walls and decorative pieces rather than projects requiring a flat, finished surface like floors.

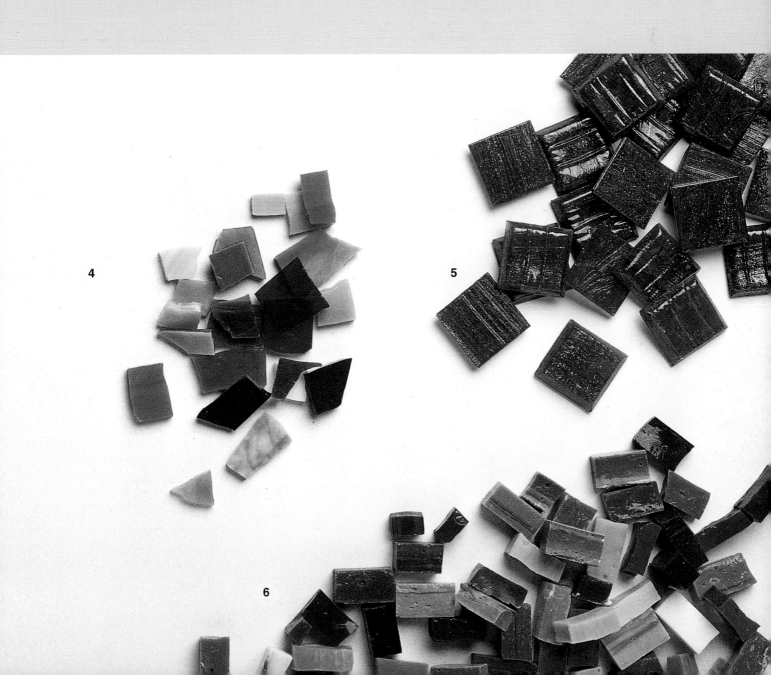

Mosaic Plaque

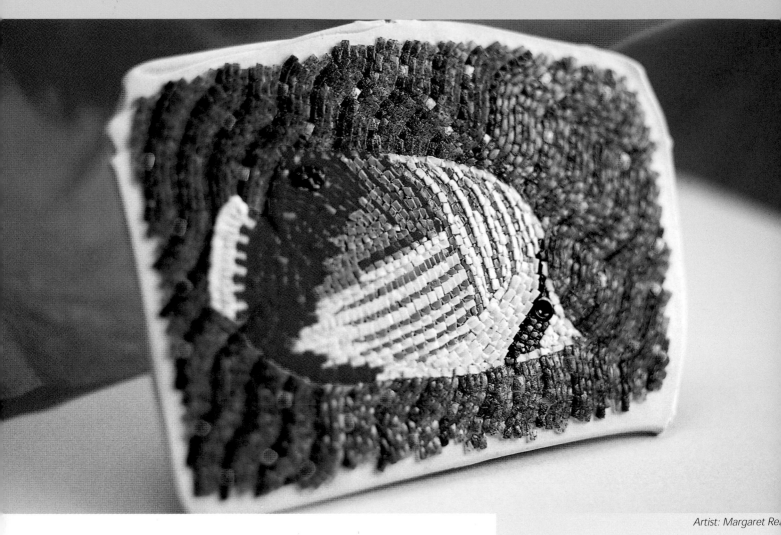

Artist: Margaret Re.

Creating a polymer clay mosaic can be thrilling, because there's no limit to the colors that can be used, as there is with other mosaic materials. The "water" in this mosaic was created by blending blue and translucent clay with embossing powder in various amounts to create an array of shades. The final result is a beautiful water scene with shimmery depth and sophistication. This ungrouted mosaic was created by placing uncured "tiles" on an uncured background, eliminating the need for adhesive. The resulting classic look is reminiscent of the intricate, expressive works created by the ancient Romans.

Materials

- basic polymer clay equipment and supplies
- picture for reference and tracing
- 1 block of white clay, Fimo or Premo
- 1 block of translucent clay, Fimo or Premo
- dark blue embossing powder
- 1 block of blue clay, Fimo or Premo
- 1 block of black clay, Fimo or Premo
- 1 block of yellow clay, Fimo or Premo
- imitation gold leaf
- tracing paper
- matte varnish, Fimo or Sculpey
- pasta machine
- tapestry needle
- penny or penny-size circular cutter
- paint brush

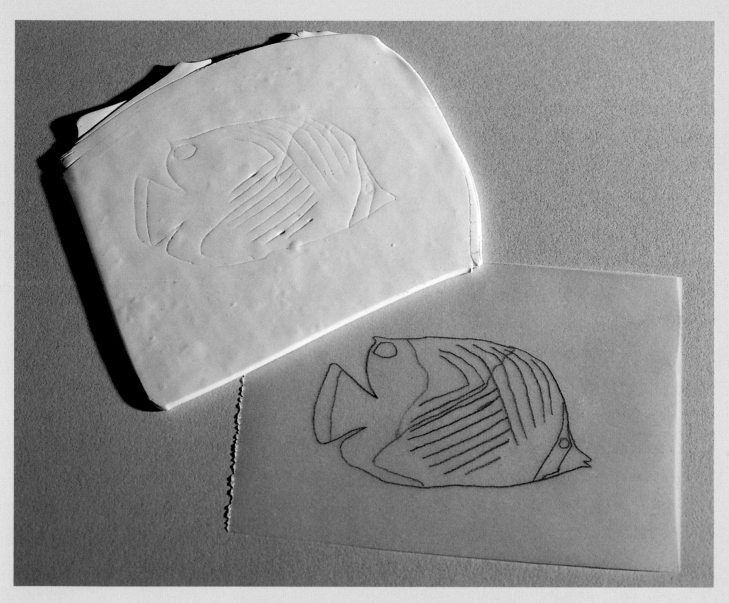

Getting Started

Be sure to include the most important details when tracing an image for a mosaic, such as the eye, fins, and gills of this fish.

1 Transfer the mosaic pattern to the clay.

First, trace the selected image in pencil. Next, use a pasta machine to roll out a piece of clay about 3½" x 2¾" (9 cm x 7 cm) on setting #1. Make the rectangle as even as possible, but don't trim the edges. Place the clay on a bakeable work surface.

Then lay the tracing face up on the rectangle of clay, and smooth it out. Run a tapestry needle over the lines of the pattern to create slight but visible indentations in the clay. Remove the paper after tracing all the lines.

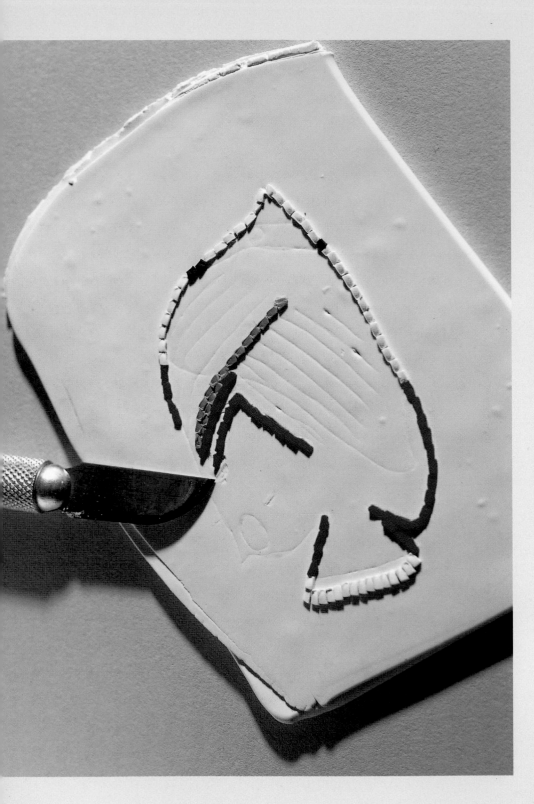

2 Fill in the traced pattern with tiles.

Roll out the clay to be used for the tiles on setting #5, and place the slabs on baking parchment or waxed paper. From these slabs, cut several short strips ⅛" to ³⁄₁₆" (3 mm to 4 mm) wide. Using a craft knife with a curved or angled blade, cut small squares from the strips, and begin placing the tiles along the image outline.

To create the shades of blue for the water, first roll out a sheet of translucent clay using a pasta machine on setting #1 (the thickest setting). Then, cut out a 1½" x 1½" (4 cm x 4 cm) from this sheet. Mix in about ¼ to ½ teaspoon of embossing powder, a little bit at a time, until the clay is denim blue. Cut the clay into four equal pieces. Set one aside to be used as is. Then cut out six penny-size pieces of clay from the remainder of the translucent sheet, using a craft knife and a penny or a circle cutter as a guide. Mix one piece of translucent clay with one denim blue piece; two pieces of translucent clay with another denim blue piece; and the re-maining three translucent pieces with the last denim blue piece. Finally, create a blue-gray color by mixing 2 parts white, ½ part blue, ½ part black clay. For the gold accent tiles, roll translucent clay through the pasta machine on setting #6 (very thin). Then, carefully lay the metal leaf on top and smooth it out.

TIP

To make an eye like the one seen here, press a small ball of clay into place with a ball stylus tool or ball-headed pin.

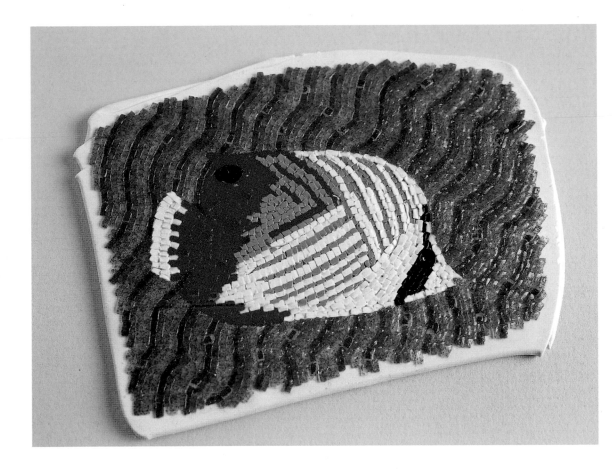

TIP

To enable you to hang the plaque, adhere a looped string to the back using permanent glue, or drill two holes at the top for a knotted cord. A smaller piece would make a striking brooch or pendant.

3 Fill in the remaining parts of the image.

For guidance and inspiration, refer to the image used to create the traced pattern. Fill in the major features, such as the fish's stripes and spots, then continue with the background. Place the tiles in rows to keep the mosaic neat. Pay attention to the flow of the lines that the rows create. The tiles in the body of the fish here have been laid in diagonal rows, but the tail is made up of horizontal rows; this helps to define the image

and creates movement in the piece. To create the illusion of water, alternate between shades of blue, and lay the tiles in wavy lines as seen here.

Once the mosaic is complete, put a piece of blank tracing paper over the tiles and use a smooth roller, such as a brayer or jar, to gently embed them into the slab of clay. Then remove the tracing paper, and bake according to the manufacturer's directions. Once the piece is cool, finish with two coats of matte varnish.

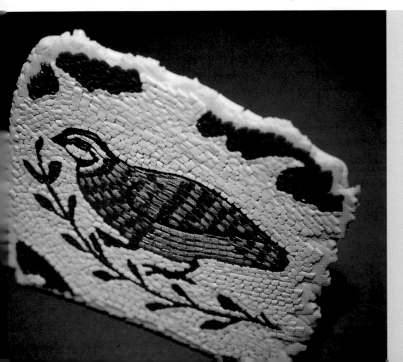

Variations

Like all surface techniques, this one could be used to ornament many different objects. Glue your plaque to a plain journal cover, clock case, or vase. Want to wear it as a brooch? Add a pinback (first clean the metal with alcohol, roughen it with a nail file, then glue it to the plaque with cyanoacrylate glue). Make a mosaic disk to fit commercial bezels for a pendant, earrings, ring, or brooch.

I work wet-on-wet, but that isn't the only way to make polymer clay mosaics. Some artists place prebaked "tiles" ranging from tiny threads to substantial pieces on top of unbaked clay. And some artists make canes that look like mosaics.

Recycle your broken pots into lively and beautiful frames and bring a patio garden feel indoors. Make a plaster frame as a base for the mosaic to enhance the irregular, casual look of terracotta, or revitalize an old frame with this simple technique. This is a wonderful frame to highlight images of flowers, landscapes, or other natural images, and it will enhance many decorating schemes, from European country to American Southwestern.

terracotta
mosaic frame

Makes one frame

MATERIALS
- craft plaster
- picture frame mold
- broken terracotta pot
- tile nippers
- silicone sealant or tile adhesive
- sanded tile grout
- grout float
- photo corners
- general craft supplies

1 Follow manufacturer's instructions to mix craft plaster and pour into mold. Allow to harden; remove from mold. Cure plaster according to manufacturer's recommendations.

2 Use tile nippers to even edges of terracotta pieces if desired. Adhere terracotta to the front of the frame with tile adhesive or silicone sealant. Let dry completely.

3 According to manufacturer's directions, mix sanded grout with water in a disposable container until it has a fudge-like consistency. Wearing rubber gloves, spread grout into spaces between pieces with a grout float or wet sponge, making sure to press grout firmly into cracks. Follow with another clean, wet sponge to wipe off excess grout. Allow to dry.

4 Sand rough edges with sandpaper. Clean frame with a damp cloth.

5 Adhere photo corners to the back of the frame to hold a picture or photograph.

VARIATION
Substitute glass pebbles, broken china or tiles, shells, coins, stained glass, or pebbles for the terracotta pieces.

TIPS
To break terracotta, wrap a pot in several layers of newspaper, enclose in a plastic bag, and tap pot gently with a hammer until it is broken into pieces of the desired size. Moisten the surface of the terracotta before applying grout so less grout adheres to mosaic pieces. Spread grout at an angle to the terracotta edges to fill in spaces without forming air pockets. When grout is partially dry, wipe with a damp sponge to even grout lines and smooth rough edges.

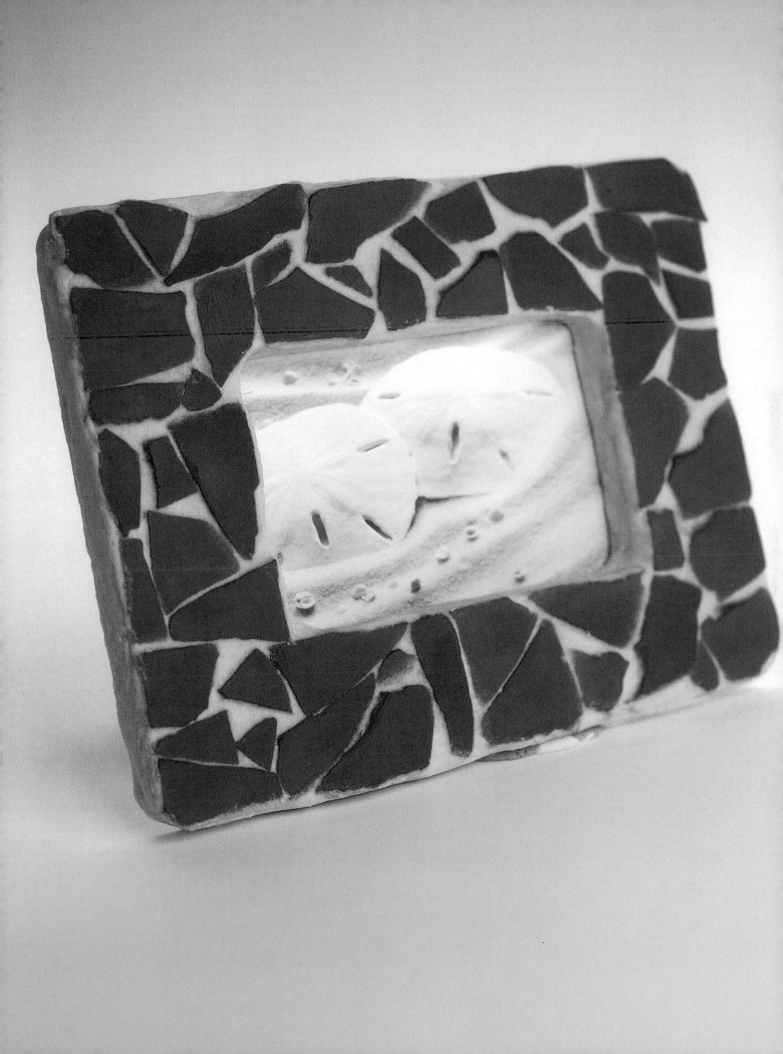

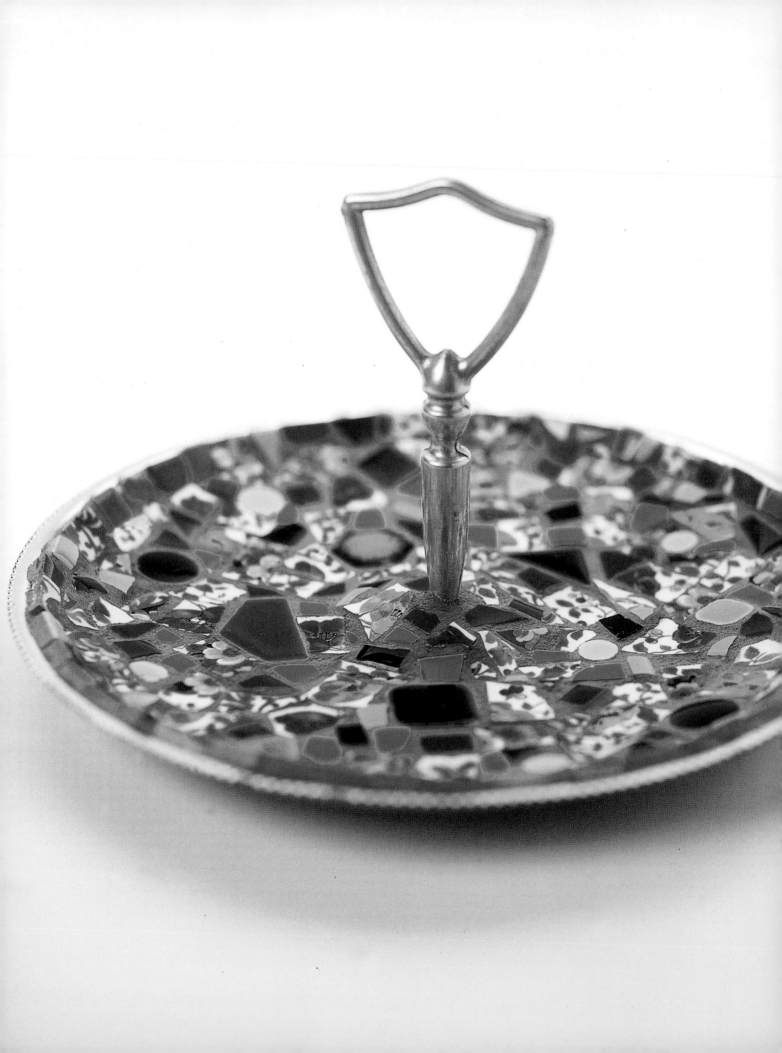

Revitalize thrift-shop and yard-sale finds by adding fun mosaic accents. The eclectic mix of recycled broken china and tile is unified by sanded grout, which is available in many colors or can be tinted at home (see Tips). When looking for china pieces, notice the colors and patterns that will give your piece its identity, then choose plain tile pieces to complement them. Because this project is meant for inside use, you can use thick, tacky craft glue to adhere the mosaic, a less expensive option than tile adhesive.

mosaic candy dish

Makes one dish

1 Clean and dry dish. Make a paper template of the area to be covered. Snip tile and china pieces into irregular shapes with tile nipper, and arrange on template until area is filled.

2 Apply a layer of tacky craft glue to the tray and transfer the cut shapes onto the glue. Let dry.

3 Following the manufacturer's directions, mix sanded grout with water in a disposable container until it has a fudgelike consistency. Wearing rubber gloves, spread grout into spaces between tiles with a grout float. Let set for 10–15 minutes, then brush away excess grout with a stiff brush or an old toothbrush. Allow to dry for another 10 minutes. Wipe away remaining loose grout with a damp soft cloth or sponge, then polish tiles with a dry cloth to remove any leftover haze.

4 Apply 2–3 coats of grout sealer according to manufacturer's recommendations.

VARIATION
Accent ashtrays, cake plates, flat faced frames, or trivets with mosaic patterns.

MATERIALS
- metal tray or dish
- tile and china pieces
- tile nippers
- tacky craft glue
- sanded grout
- grout float or flat-blade spreader tool
- grout sealer
- general craft supplies

TIPS
Wear safety glasses and gloves when cutting tile with nippers. If the tray's finish is chipped, spray on two coats of metallic spray enamel or touch up finish with metallic leafing pens. Always use sanded grout rather than premixed latex grout for mosaic projects with spaces larger than 1/8" (.3 cm) between pieces. Sanded grout is available in many colors, but to save money, purchase off-white grout and add a small amount of acrylic paint, paste food color, cold-water dye, or strong tea or coffee to tint the dry grout before adding water.

ARTIST: CONNIE SHEERIN

Delicate eggshells create striking mosaics when tinted with liquid watercolors, offering a unique and inexpensive way to update a flat frame. Pieces of dyed eggshell are carefully placed on the finished frame and are cracked even smaller by hand into a mosaic. Collage glue will dry clear, letting the painted frame "grout" show through and minimizing color bleed from the tinted eggs.

eggshell mosaic frame

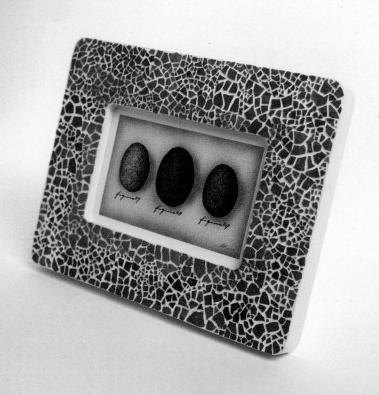

ARTIST: LIVIA MCREE

Makes one frame

1 Crack the eggs in half and reserve the insides for later use. Rinse shells and let dry completely. Paint eggshells with liquid watercolor paint, and spatter with accent colors if desired. When dry, spray the eggs with the fixative and let dry.

2 Paint the frame with white acrylic paint; let dry. Brush a layer of collage glue on the front surface of the frame. Break off a 1" (3 cm) square piece of colored eggshell and press it flat to the frame with your thumb until it cracks into smaller pieces. Separate the pieces apart slightly with craft knife to create mosaic. Continue in this manner until the entire frame is covered with the eggshell mosaic. If pieces of the eggshell extend past the frame edge, turn the frame over on a cutting mat and trim off excess shell with a craft knife.

3 Cover the entire frame with a coat of acrylic fixative and let dry completely.

VARIATIONS
Experiment with other pigments and decorative painting techniques when coloring the shells—try gold metallic paint or fabric dyes, and sponging or crackle finishes. Or, use naturally colored brown or speckled eggs for a simple, pure tone.

MATERIALS
- one frame
- one dozen eggs
- liquid watercolor paints
- white acrylic paint
- spray acrylic watercolor fixative
- collage glue
- general craft supplies

TIPS
To spatter another color on top of the base color of the eggs, let the base coat dry completely. Using a dry toothbrush lightly dipped in a contrasting watercolor, gently rub your thumb along the toothbrush to release color in a light spray of pigment. We left the membrane on the eggshell to help prevent the watercolor pigment from bleeding, but if you use other paints to color the shells remove the membrane from the eggshells after breaking.

Interior Mosaics and Murals

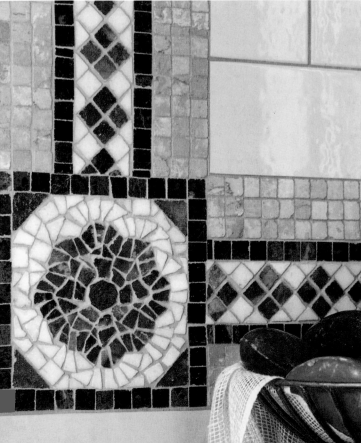

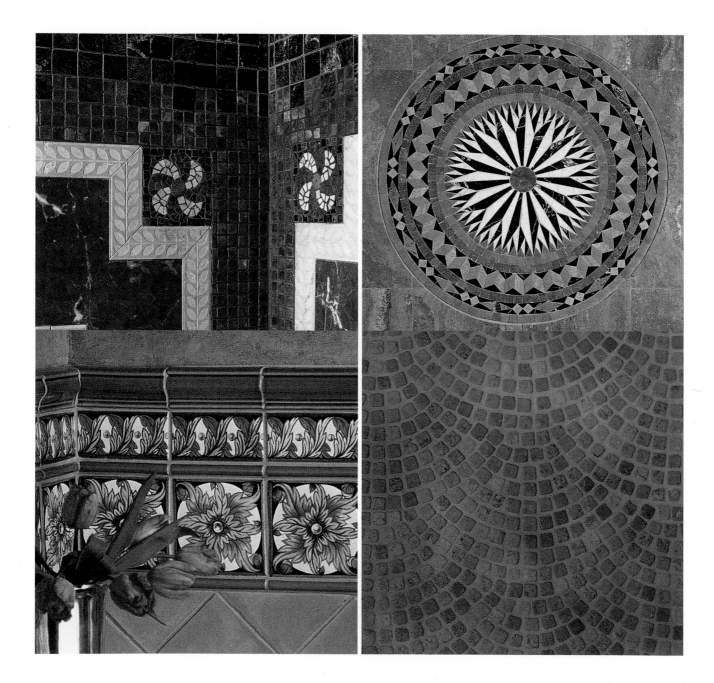

Exotic and colorful, mosaics are among the most ancient forms of decoration. Clay mosaics ornamented the walls of Sumerian temples in Mesopotamia five thousand years ago. The great civilizations of the ancient world produced magnificent mosaics, still visible in Egyptian tombs, Roman pavements, and Byzantine churches.

Today, mosaics and murals are experiencing a renewal of popularity as designers rediscover the creative possibilities of the medium. In interiors, mosaics are applied lavishly to decorate entire walls and floors, or used sparingly to enrich monochromatic tiled surfaces with the addition of color accents and elegant borders.

Mosaic designs are made by setting small squares or pieces (tesserae) of tile, stone, glass, or other materials into a background of cement or grout. Mosaics are small, multicolored stones cut into various shapes that, when viewed from a distance, can coalesce into photographic-style portraits or patterns.

Viewed up close, each small tessera is just one square or spot of color and texture. Assembled and blended, they can form shapes, patterns, images, pictures, and words. The repetitive patterning of the tiny mosaic tesserae is hypnotically pleasing to the eye.

The designer working with mosaics uses tesserae with slight differences and variations in color and shape to achieve soft outlines and a uniquely handmade feel. Arranging mosaic tiles according to subtle gradations of color can produce a full tonal range and the illusion of three dimensions.

Creating elaborate mosaic designs is a laborious and meticulous art, but the advent of the computer has made it possible to produce intricate patterns in a fraction of the time it takes to assemble tesserae by hand. Of course, mosaics set by machine cannot duplicate the subtle variations and slight imperfections that make handmade mosaics distinctive and highly prized. They are best used for repetitive designs, such as borders and trims, where precision is desirable. Intricate or simple, geometric or figural, mosaics and murals add color, texture, and dimension to your rooms.

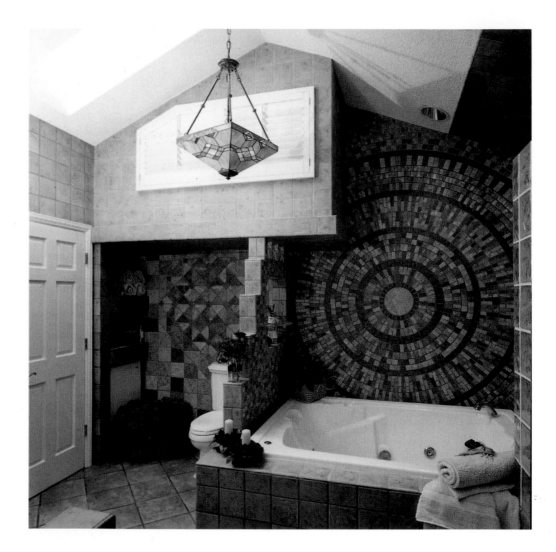

If you have a special vision for your bath, consider plotting out your own tile design. This bathroom, a mix of 4,186 hand-cut tiles and thirteen colors, is just what the owners in Cedar Falls, Iowa, ordered. Tile: Sunny Days Flooring; Design: Robert Cisar.

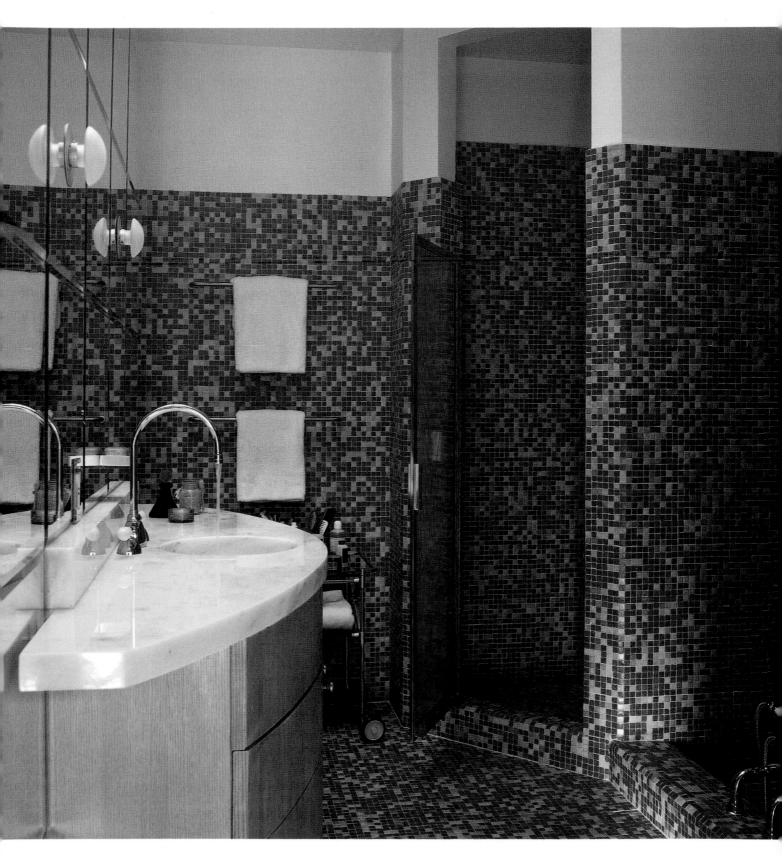

Convey an elegant look with earth-toned mosaic tiles. In this bathroom, the neutral colors meld into a complex, interesting texture off which light is free to play. Interior Design: Scott Johnson; Photo: Tim Street-Porter.

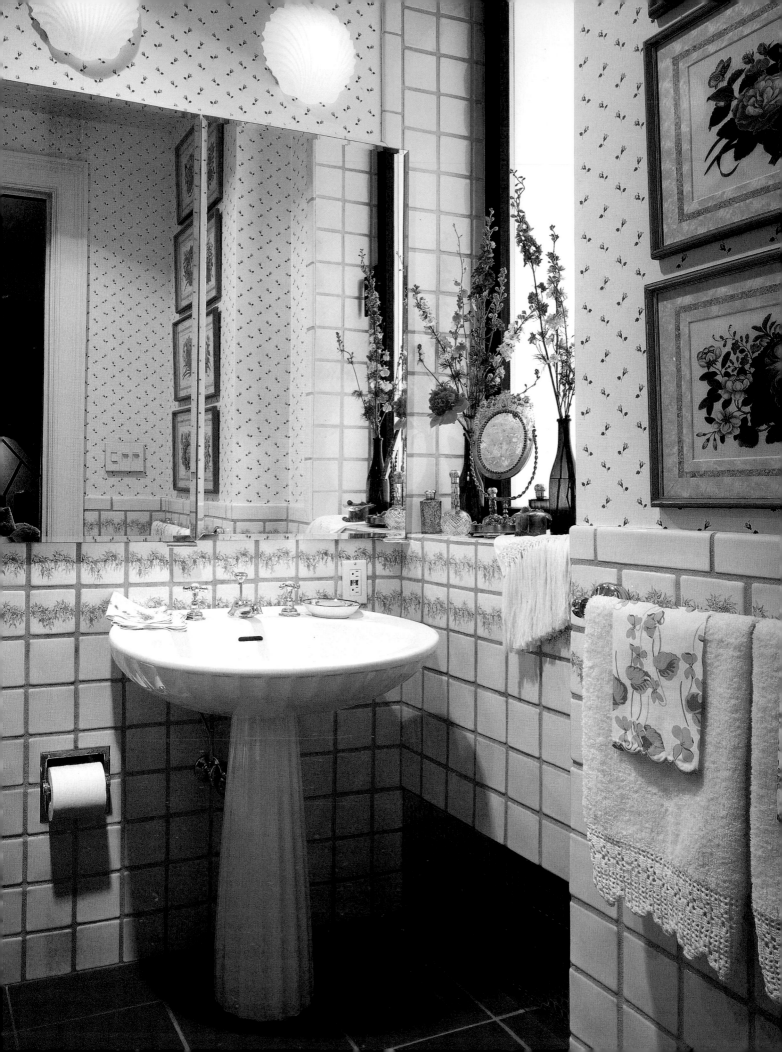

Enhance both color and a visual theme by adding a repeated mural pattern to tilework. In this bright bath, the flower theme is catalyzed by the purple wisteria that works its way around the room. Interior Design: Sam Botero; Photo: Philip H. Ennis Photography.

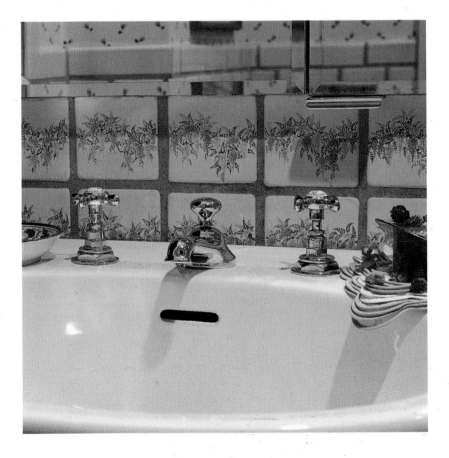

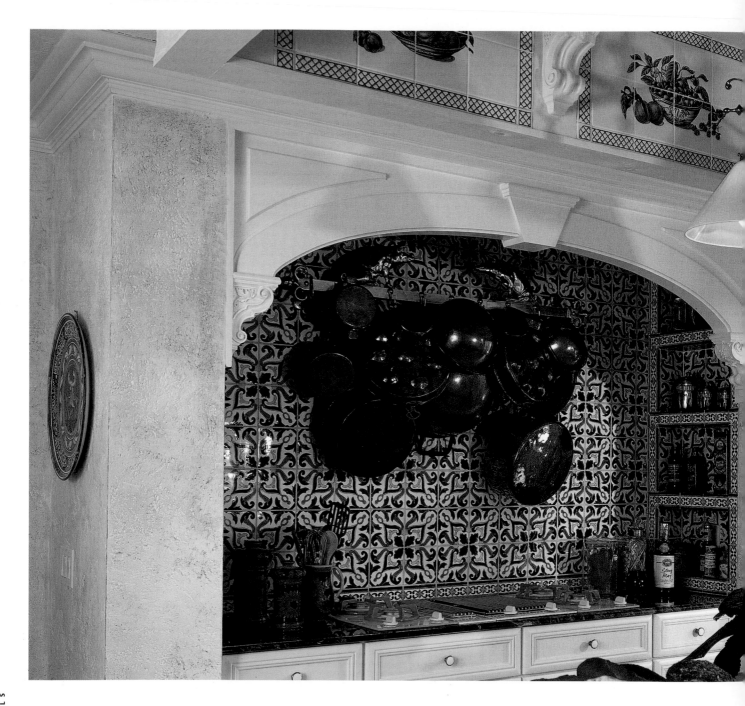

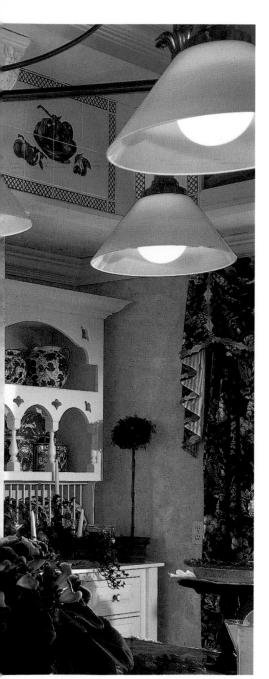

(left) There is no need to hang photos in this magnificent, high-detail kitchen. Let colorful mural tiles work their way around your ceiling edge, each within their own wood frame. Around the stovetop, allow repeating patterns to create a stunning storage area for a cluster of copper pans and racked spices. Tile: Country Floors. (below) Introduce decorative tiles to your fireplace and make that an integral part of your design and color theme. Tile: Country Floors.

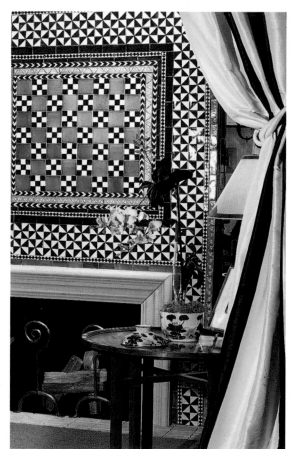

(right) Mosaics can be the design focal point in a room and set the palette for furnishings. Tile: Artistic Tile. (below) Create an old-world feel with a wall of mosaics and a vessel sink. Tile: Artistic Tile. (opposite) This arts-and-crafts–style border forms a mural that works well with the pedestal sink and metal mirror frame. Tile: Walker Zanger; Photo: Stuart Watson.

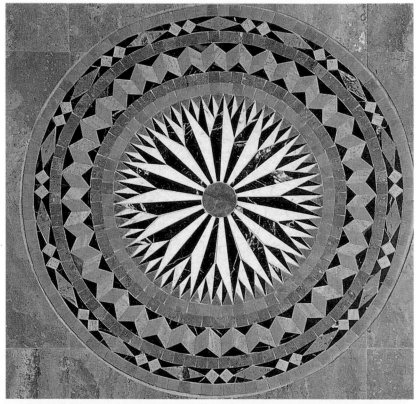

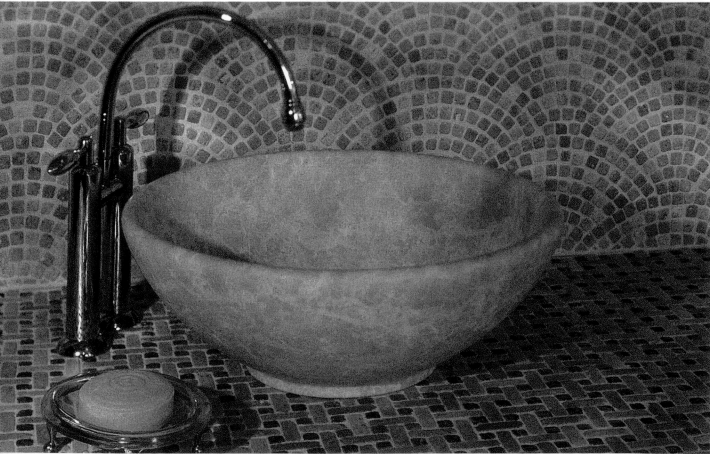

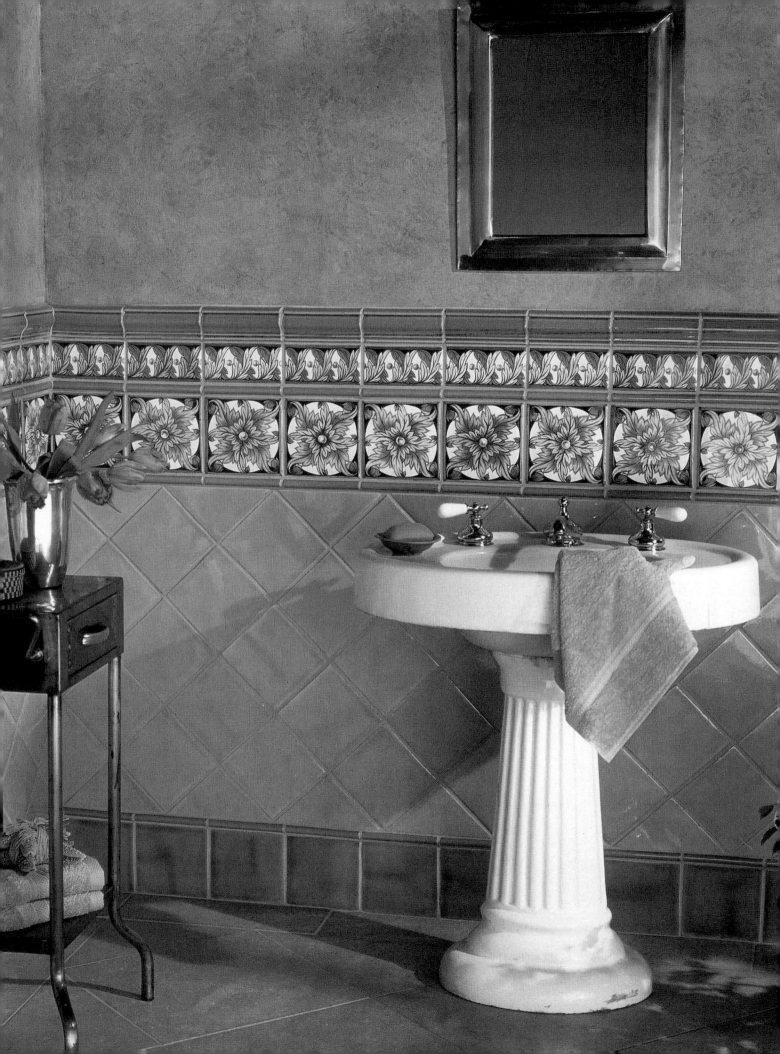

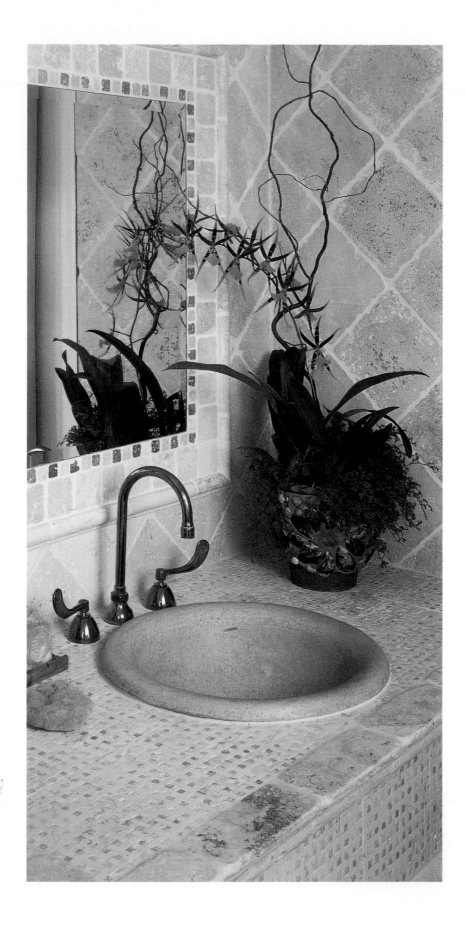

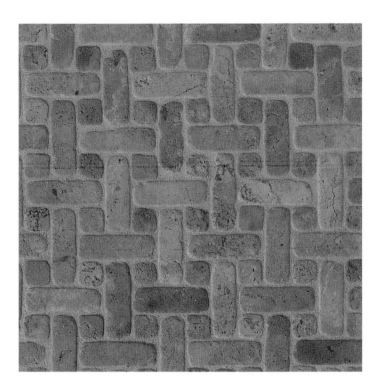

(left) Encase a bathroom sink with basketweave mosaic tiles that resemble a soft fabric cover. The small tiles contrast well with the mosaic-bordered mirror and the diamond and square-shaped stones on the walls. Tile: Country Floors. **(above)** Tile: Artistic Tile.

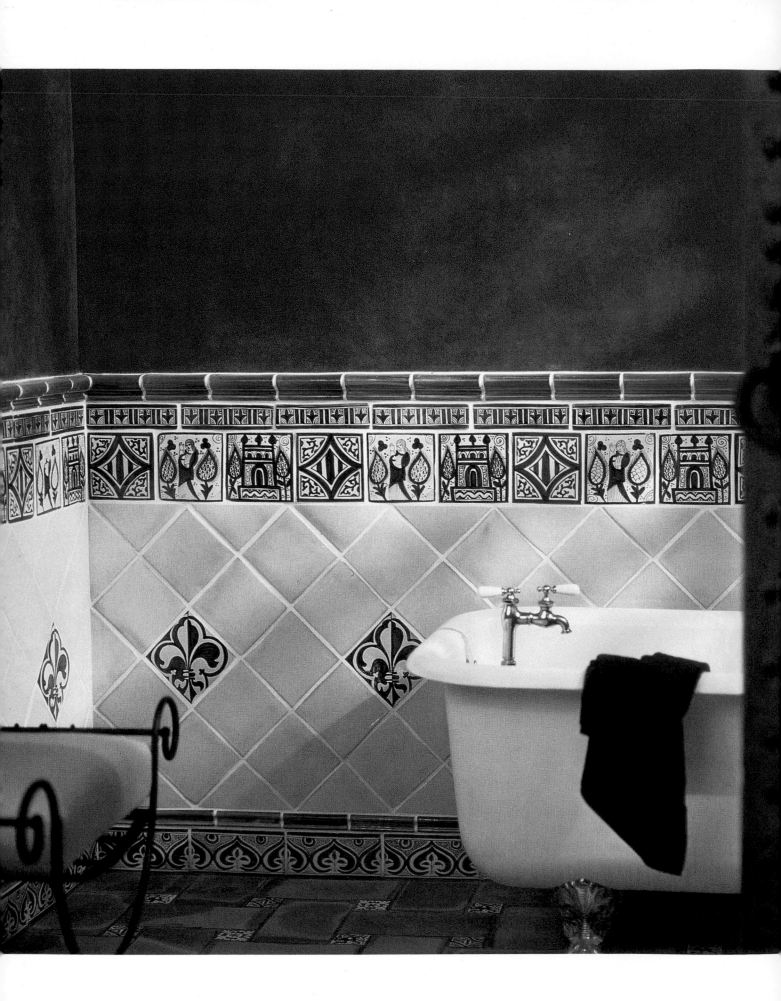

(left) **Study the choices carefully before selecting tile for murals; decide how great a part they should play in the overall design. These beautiful ceramic mural tiles are functional at splash level and provide colorful, engaging scenes that are abstractly repeated in the bottom wall border and on the floor.** Tile: Walker Zanger; Photo: Stuart Watson. **(below) Introduce a new art form in a room with a mix of mosaic and decorative relief stone.** Tile: Country Floors.

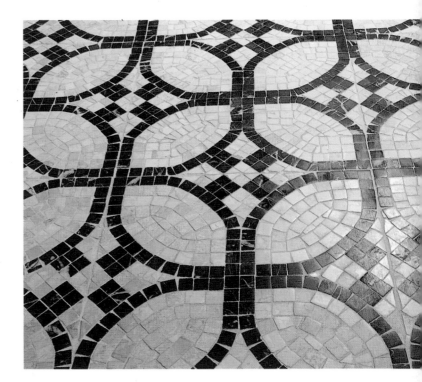

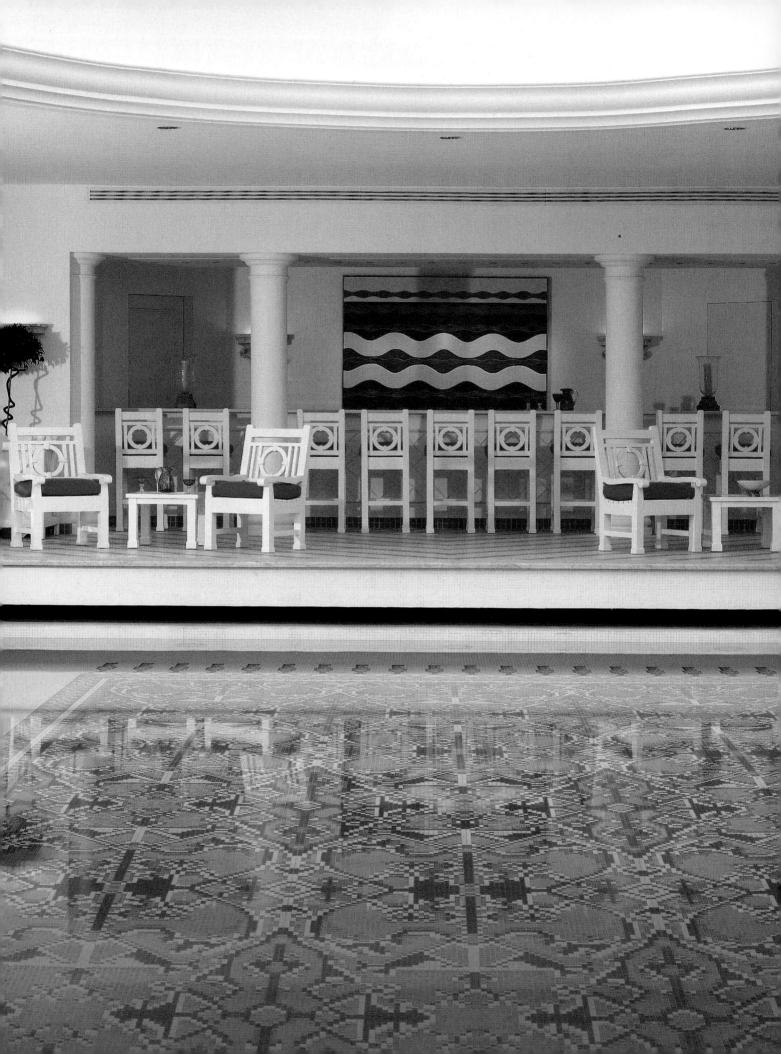

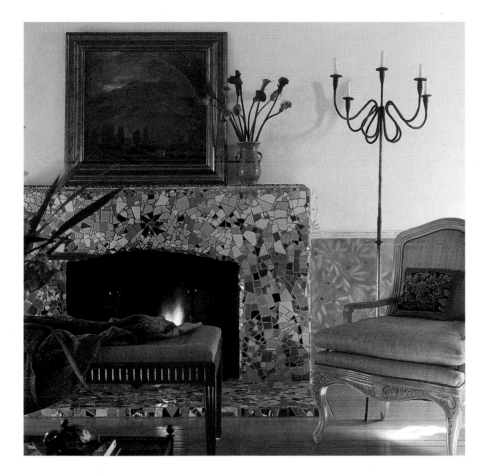

(opposite) **Consider laying an elegant underwater mosaic carpet for an indoor pool. Cool blue and warm yellow tiles create patterns that work well with natural light.** Palace in Riyadh, Saudi Arabia; Design: Erika Brunson Design Associates. **(left) Detail a fireplace in colorful mosaic tiles to secure its role as the focal point of a sitting room—with or without the flames.** Photo: Tim Street-Porter.

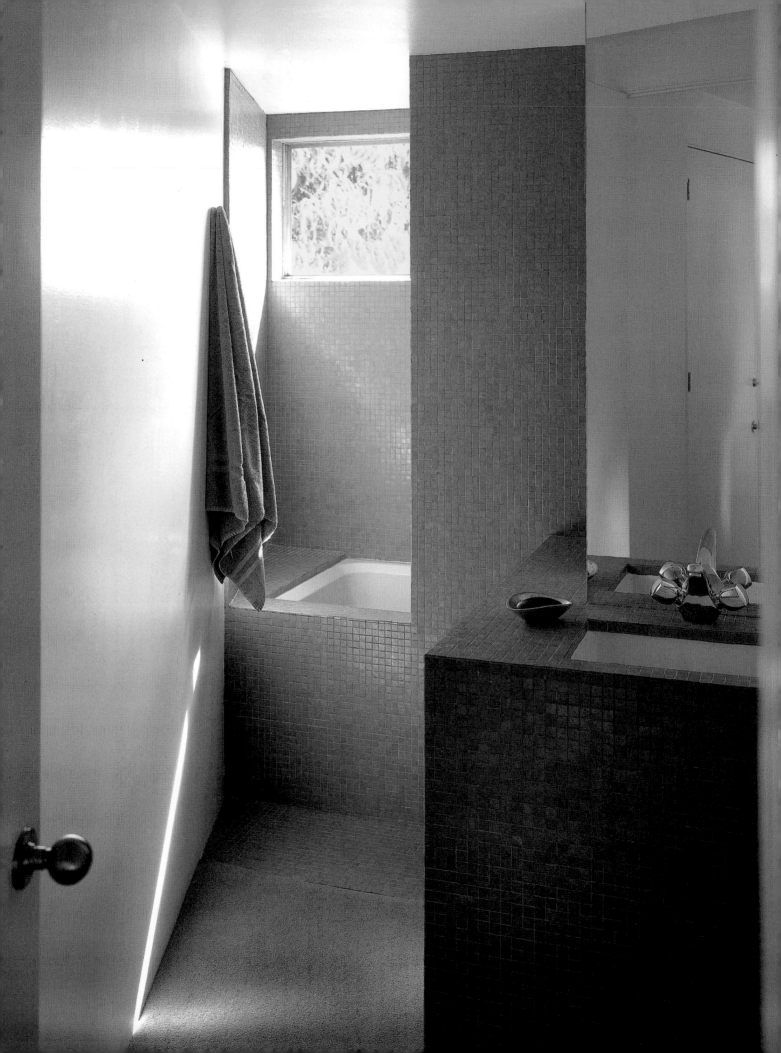

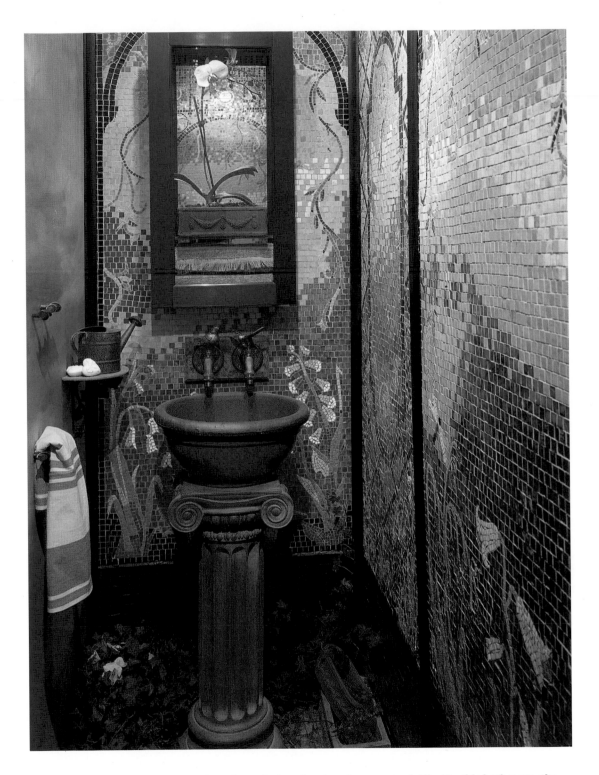

(opposite) Convey an elegant look with earth-toned and cool gray mosaic tiles. In this bathroom, the neutral colors meld into a complex, interesting texture off which light is free to play. Interior Design: Scott Johnson; Photo: Tim Street-Porter. (above) A windowless powder room is transformed into a Victorian conservatory by latticework, vines, and flowers of glass mosaics, highlighted with eighteen-carat gold chips. A terra-cotta planter for the sink completes this charming indoor garden. Design: Michael R. Golden Design; Photo: Tim Lee.

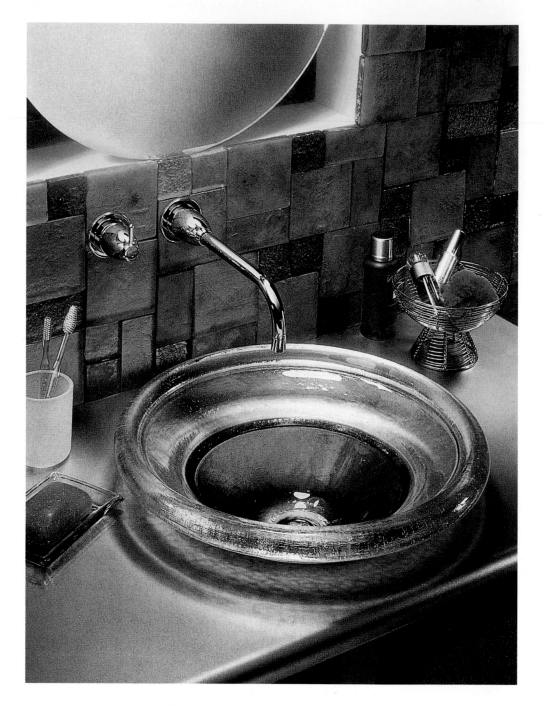

(above) Go all out with gorgeous iridescent tiles that look as though they've been shaken off the wings of butterflies. Complete the look with a crystal sink cradled on what appears to be a floating silver tray. This is drama at its best. Tile: Kohler Company. (right) Line a shower stall with shimmering glass mosaics to create a color extravaganza. Tile: Bisazza.

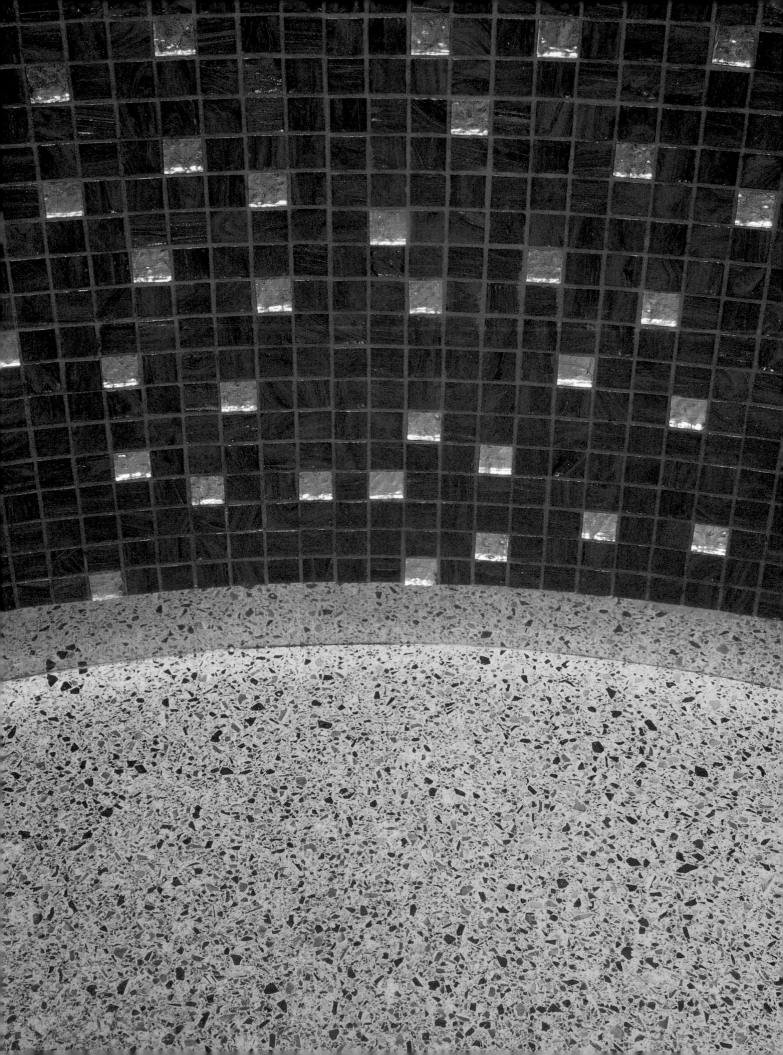

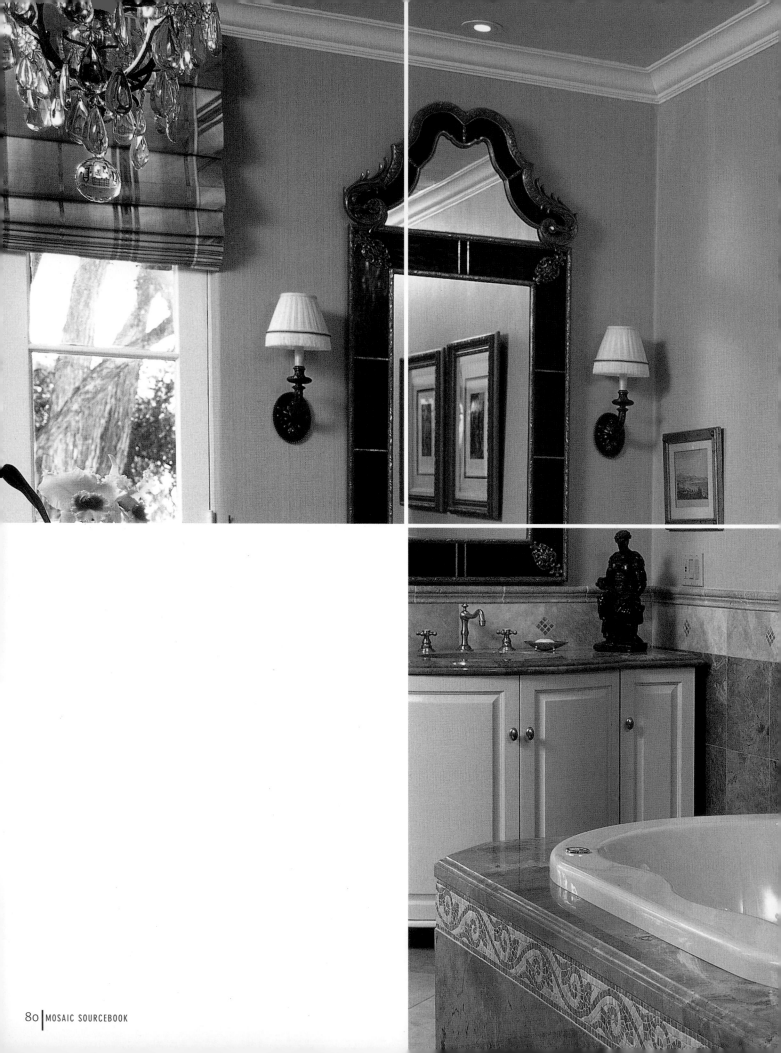

Mosaics Outside

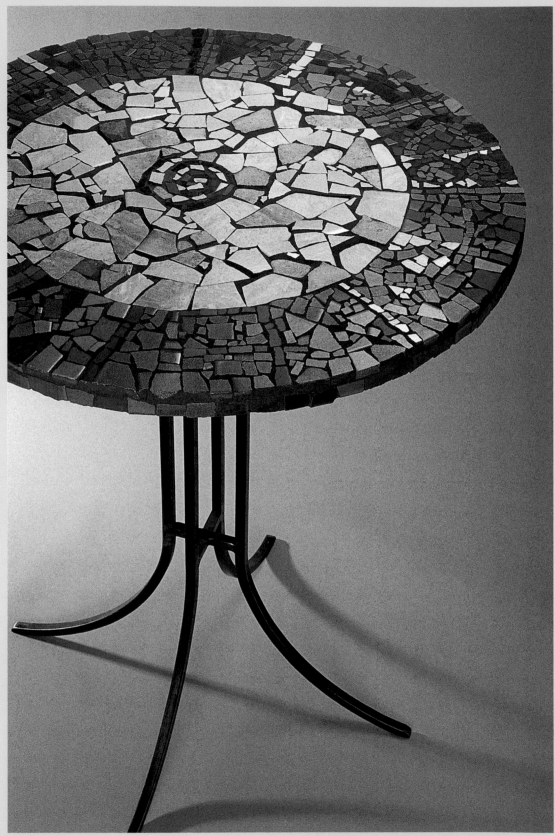

**Artist: Linda
Benswanger/Mozayiks
Photo by Allen Bryan**

Materials

marine board

wrought iron base

broken ceramic pieces

palette knife

hammer

tile nippers

cement

natural gray or dark gray sanded grout

acrylic admixture

grout sealant

kitchen scrubbing pad

safety goggles

latex gloves

filter mask

mixing bowls for cement and grout

Wrought Iron Patio Table

This elegant wrought iron table is a welcome addition to the garden, creating an ideal place to sit, eat, or just reflect. Sketch out ideas and plan the design on paper first, using colors, themes, or plantings from the garden as inspiration. Since this is a large project, tailor the design to fit skill level as well as personal taste so that it doesn't become overwhelming. The custom table here is made from a marine-board top and a separate base. Marine board, which resists warping, can be found at home-improvement centers. A whole wrought iron or metal patio table with a solid top can also be used for this project.

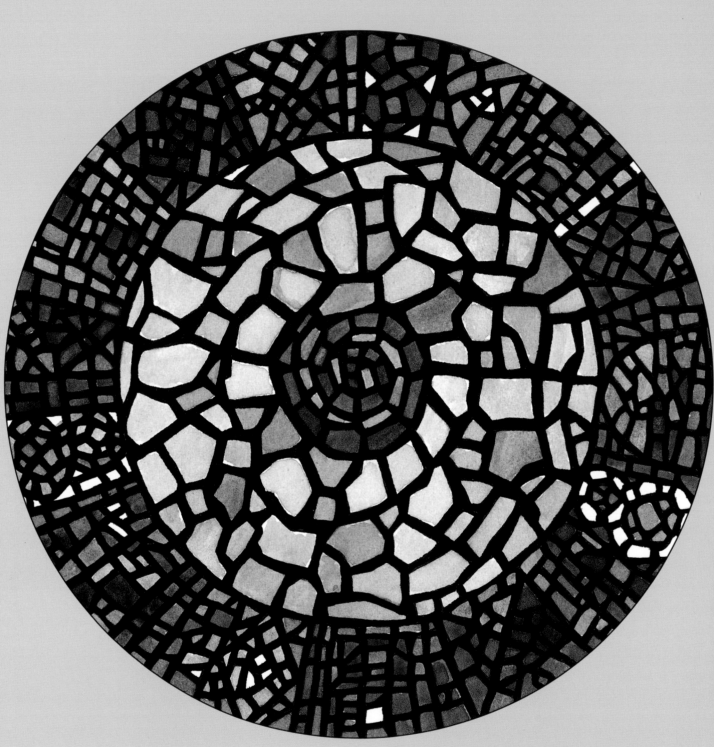

Artist: Linda Benswanger/Mozayiks

Photo by Allen Bryan

Attach the marine-board tabletop to the base before beginning the mosaic, because it will be much lighter and easier to manipulate. First, cut the board with a jigsaw or have a piece custom cut at a lumberyard or home center. Then, drill holes through the board that correspond with screw holes in the table base. Holes can be drilled into the base, if necessary, with a metal-cutting drill bit. Prepare a pattern by sizing the illustration to your selected tabletop. You can enlarge the pattern in sections using a copier, or sketch or photocopy the illustration onto graph paper to determine scale.

STEP 1

First, trace the pattern onto the marine board with a pencil or marker. Then, wearing safety goggles and protective gloves, break the ceramics to be used into shards using a hammer (see page 14 for guidance). Small to medium-size pieces, about 1/2 inch (1 cm) or 2 inches (5 cm), will work well for this project. Keep colors separated for quicker and easier application. Use tile nippers to refine the size and shape of the shards as necessary.

Tip: Use flat tiles to ensure that the tabletop has an even surface. Tile stores will often sell broken or discontinued merchandise at a discount.

STEP 2

Prepare the cement for outdoor use (see page 9). Use a flexible palette knife to apply a 1/8-inch (3-mm) layer of cement over a 6-inch (15-cm) -square area. Begin applying tiles, and continue until the entire horizontal surface is covered. Then, apply tiles to the vertical edges of the table. Let it dry for twenty-four hours.

Tip: Code each section of the pattern with a colored marker or numbering system, then complete one section before moving on to the next. This will eliminate confusion and make the process quicker.

Prepare grout for outdoor use (see page 9), then apply a small amount to the table with glove-protected hands. Work the grout completely into the crevices between the tiles using a circular motion. Keep wiping excess grout off the surface of the tiles. When the grout has dried enough to become powdery, no more than fifteen to twenty minutes, use a damp sponge to clean the tiles. Rinse the sponge frequently, and wipe the tiles until all the grout film is gone. Let it dry, then buff with a rag. When the grout is completely dry, which will take a few days, depending on humidity, apply grout sealant according to the manufacturer's directions.

Tip: When grouting the sides of the table, be sure to cover the bottoms of the tiles to conceal any sharp edges.

Tip: To prevent the table's horizontal surface from collecting snow or ice, bring it inside in winter or cover it with a tarp.

VARIATION

Play with the colors for this geometric design by spreading out several ceramic samples, then freely mix and match them. For an outdoor table such as this one, choose a sunny location for viewing the samples, because indoor lighting can cause certain colors to appear warmer or cooler than they really are. Be sure to follow the directions for the main project to ensure the durability of your outdoor table.

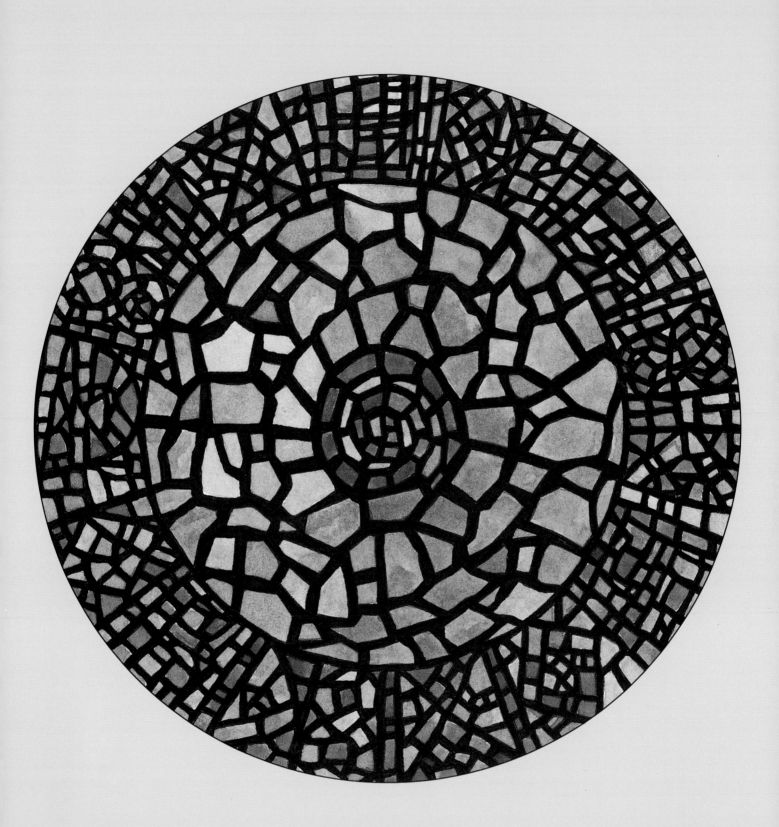

Illustrator: Mary Newell DePalma

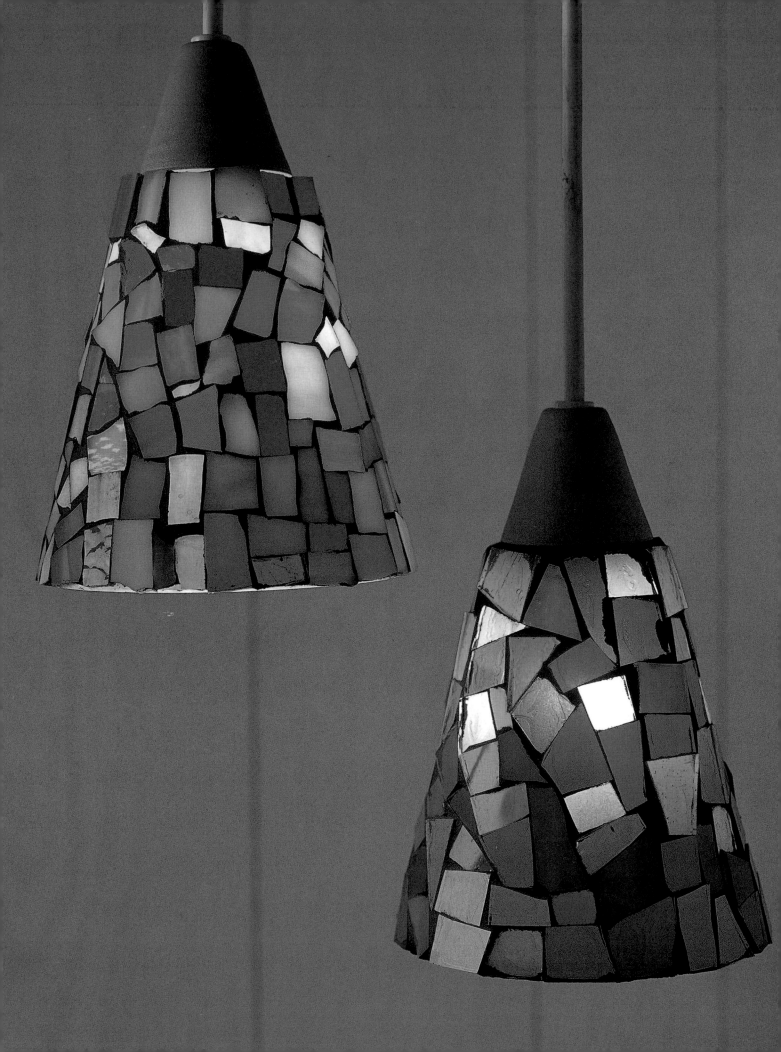

Materials

hanging light with glass shade

opaque and translucent stained glass

wooden craft stick

glass cutter

grease pencil

craft knife

sand paper

clean cotton rags

clear adhesive for bonding glass to glass

navy or black sanded grout

acrylic admixture

safety goggles

latex gloves

filter mask

mixing bowls for cement and grout

Glass Patio Lights

Reminiscent of stained-glass lamps, these glass patio lights can set a

festive, romantic, or soothing mood, depending on the color of the tiles that

cover the shade. Use only glass shades to ensure the most brilliant,

**Artist: Linda
Benswanger/Mozayiks**

sparkling light. A variety of prewired shades, such as the ones seen here,

can be found at home centers and lighting stores. The easy-to-cut custom

tiles used in this project are made from sheets of stained glass using

one simple tool.

STARTING OUT   Since both the shade and the tiles are transparent, it is very important to use adhesive specially made for bonding glass to glass that dries clear. Ask for it at the local hardware store.

STEP 1   Wearing safety goggles and sturdy work gloves to protect hands from sharp edges, cut the glass into square and rectangular tiles using a glass cutter. First, use a ruler and a grease pencil to measure and mark the glass for cutting. Then, use firm, even pressure to score the glass with the cutter along the first line. Next, lightly tap the glass along the scoring with the end of the cutter, and gently snap the glass into two pieces. It should break along the scored line. Repeat the procedure until all the tiles are cut. After cutting the glass, it is helpful to sort the pieces by color.

STEP 2   Squeeze some glass adhesive on a piece of cardboard or a plate. With a wooden craft stick, spread a 6-inch (15-cm) area of the shade with adhesive, and spread a small amount on the back of the tile. Begin applying the tiles. Cover the entire shade, fitting the pieces together very tightly to ensure maximum luminosity and a minimum of grout. Let it dry for twenty-four hours.

Tip: Use opaque or semi-opaque glass tiles for this project, which will conceal any grout that may have settled behind them.

Tip: If the glue is runny or very wet, let it dry to tackiness on the shade before applying the tiles.

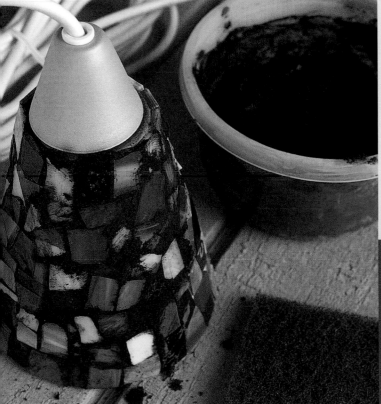

VARIATION
Shades of all shapes can be decorated using the same technique described for the main project. Glass tiles in pastel colors were used on this shade to create a softer look.

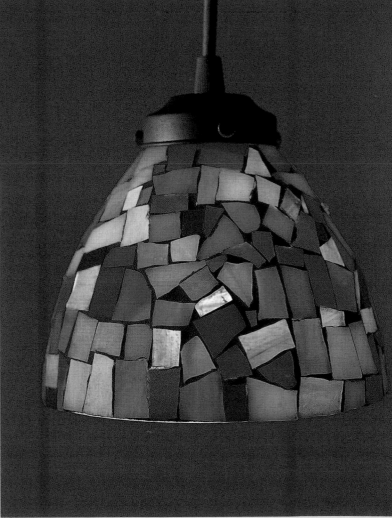

STEP 3   Prepare grout for outdoor use (see page 9), then spread a small amount on the shade with rubber glove – protected hands. Work the grout completely into the crevices between the tiles using a circular motion. Be careful to continually wipe excess grout off the tiles. Continue until all the spaces between the tiles are filled. Once the grout has dried enough to form a powdery film on the top of the glass tiles, use a dry rag to wipe off the film. Let the shade dry for twenty-four hours, then buff the glass with a clean cotton rag.

Tip: If there are any sharp edges sticking out of the grout after the project is completed, use a medium-grade sandpaper to remove them.

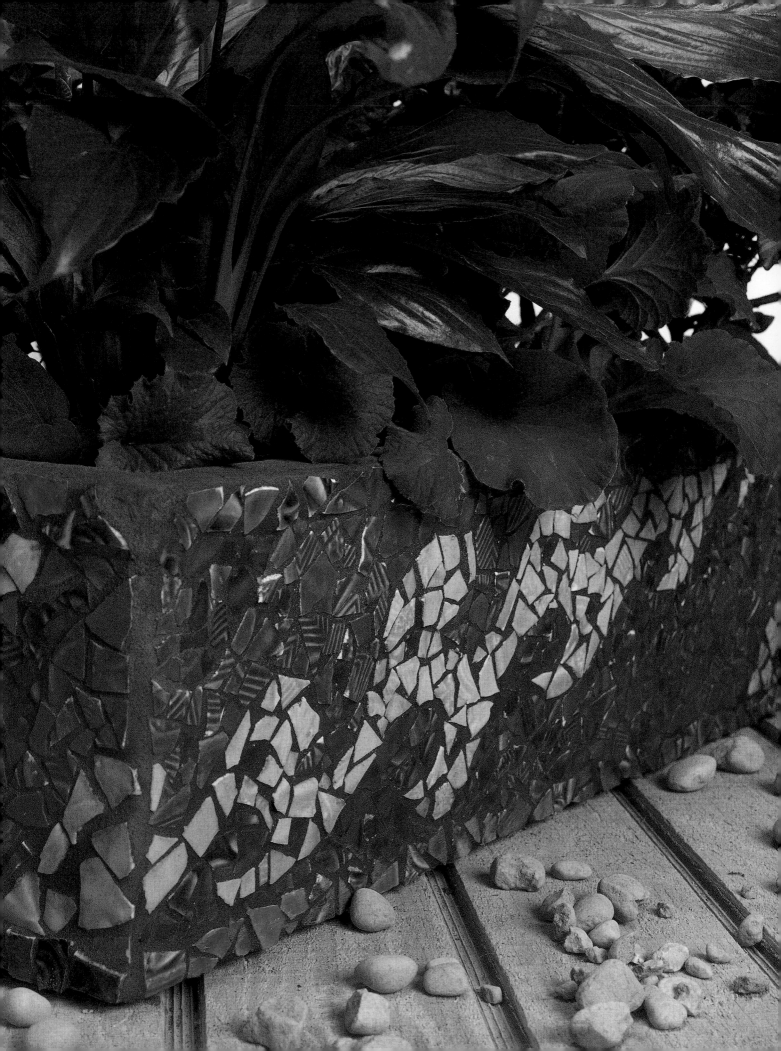

Materials

wooden window box

ceramic shards in earth tones

craft stick or plastic knife

hammer

tile nippers

tile mastic

rust-colored sanded grout

acrylic admixture

kitchen scrubbing pad

safety goggles

latex gloves

filter mask

mixing bowls for cement and grout

Three-Season Window Planter

Artists: Bruce Winn and Doreen Mastandrea

Undulating bands of color continue all the way around this planter, creating a dynamic design that keeps the eye moving without being distracting. The key to creating a harmonious design such as this one is to keep the pattern simple and distinct. Resist the temptation to add more detail – the completed mosaic will be greater than the sum of its parts. The base for this project is a simple pine window box, which can be purchased at home centers and garden stores. These planters should be sheltered in the winter to prevent splitting or cracking of the wood.

STARTING OUT   Earth tones, such as the moss green, butter yellow, and golden brown used here, enhance lush foliage and flowers alike. The red accents, reminiscent of berries, are sprinkled throughout the design to brighten up the planter.

STEP 1

Wearing safety goggles and protective gloves, break the ceramics to be used for the design and the border into shards using a hammer (see page 14 for guidance). Small pieces will work best for this intricate design. Separate the shards by color in bowls. Use tile nippers to refine the size and shape of the shards as necessary. Also nip very tiny accent pieces like the red ones used here.

STEP 2

Draw continuous, wavy lines around the planter to define the spaces for each color. Try sketching the design first, then finalizing it with a permanent marker. Mark spots for the red dots in an orderly pattern. Number each section of the pattern, and use this as a guide for applying the tiles in alternating bands of color. Each number should correspond to a different color. Then, with a palette knife, spread an area about 6 inches (15 cm) wide with a 1/8-inch (3-mm) -thick layer of tile mastic. Apply the blue border tiles to the top and bottom of the planter first, then apply tiny accent pieces. Next, begin filling in the wavy pattern, starting with color number one and continue until the planter is completed. Let dry for twenty-four hours.

Tip: It is easier to apply accents like these red dots first and work around them, rather than trying to fit them in last.

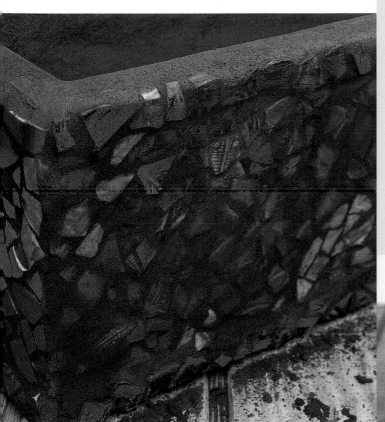

This whimsical, geometric planter uses black grout to make the brightly colored design pop. Use embellishments in the corners, like these ceramic spheres, to give the piece dimensionality. Follow the directions for the main project, but when adding the corner embellishments, be sure to use plenty of tile mastic for a strong, durable bond.

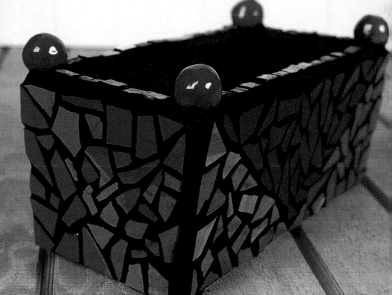

Artists: Michelle Fino, Carole Martin, and Doreen Mastandrea

STEP 3 | Prepare rust-colored sanded grout for outdoor use (see page 9 for guidance), then apply a small amount on the planter with glove-protected hands. Work the grout completely into the crevices between the shards using a circular motion. Fill all the spaces between the shards. Continue wiping excess grout off the surface of the shards. When the grout has dried enough to become powdery, no more than fifteen to twenty minutes, use a dry kitchen scrubbing pad to sand excess grout off the surface of the shards. Wear a filter mask while sanding. If the scrubbing pad scratches the glaze, wipe off excess grout while it is wet with a damp sponge, let it dry, then buff with a lint-free rag.

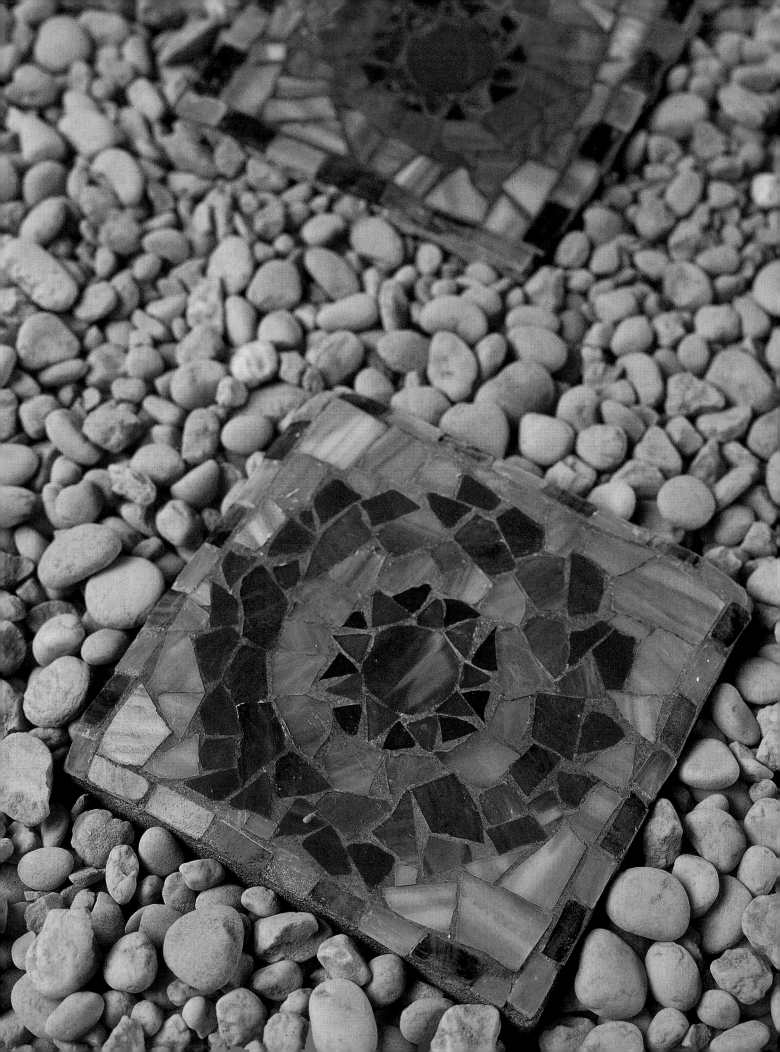

Materials

square cement garden paver

stained glass, preferably opaque

palette knife or craft stick

tile nippers

combination scorer and pliers for cutting glass

cement

acrylic admixture

natural sanded grout

kitchen scrubbing pad

latex gloves

filter mask

mixing bowls for cement and grout

Sunshine Stepping Stones

Artist: Linda Benswanger/Mozayiks

For almost immediate satisfaction, try making quick-and-easy stepping stones like these. Precast cement shapes for paving and edging are available at nearly any home-and-garden center and are relatively inexpensive. Use brightly colored glass tiles to keep the stones from fading into the background in an outdoor setting; they will sparkle in the sun. Make multiple stones and vary the images for a playful patio walkway, or use them as focal points in the garden – and even indoors as trivets or decorative accents!

Wash the paver thoroughly to guarantee a strong bond with the cement adhesive. When dry, draw the pattern directly on the stone to eliminate guesswork when applying tiles.

STEP 1

Cut the glass tiles using a combination scorer and pliers tool. First, score the section of glass to be cut, applying firm, even pressure. Then, grasp the glass with the tool and align the scoring with the guide mark. Press firmly, and the glass should snap off along the scoring. Keep the pieces organized as they are cut for easy installation by laying them out on a sketched paper pattern.

STEP 2

Prepare cement for outdoor use (see page 9 for guidance). Next, use a palette knife or craft stick to apply a 1/8-inch (3-mm) -thick layer of cement over a small area of the paver. Begin applying tiles, starting with the border. A simple alternating pattern of two colors was used here. Then, continue applying tiles, working from the center of the paver toward the border. Let it dry for twenty-four hours.

Tip: For a small, flat project such as this one, cut all the tiles needed before starting to apply them. Cut a few extra pieces, though, to avoid coming up short.

Tip: The defining, striped border here is highly visible in a garden setting. However, a looser pattern would still read well from a distance.

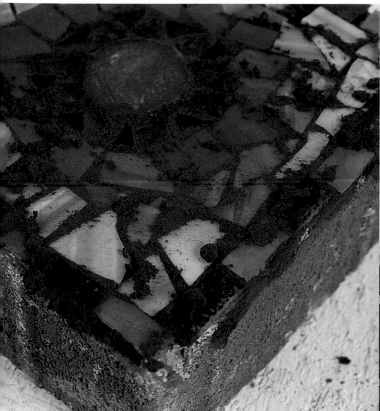

Cement borders, stepping stones, and pavers come in a variety of shapes and sizes. This scalloped border piece, intended to edge a flower bed, features a glass-tile floral pattern. The scalloped shape is a perfect accent for the soft, curving shape of many flowers. To make it, simply follow the directions for the garden paver. Experiment with simple and more intricate designs, and use colors that will complement nearby plantings.

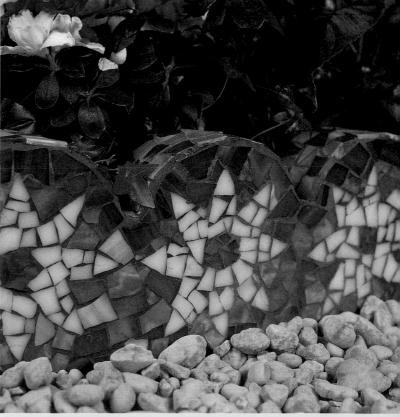

STEP 3 | Prepare natural sanded grout for outdoor use (see page 9), then apply a small amount to the paver with glove-protected hands. Work the grout completely into the crevices between the tiles using a circular motion. Continue until all the spaces between the tiles are filled. Keep wiping excess grout off the surface of the tiles. When the grout has dried enough to become powdery, no more than fifteen to twenty minutes, use a damp sponge to clean the tiles. Rinse the sponge frequently and wipe the tiles until all the grout film is gone. Finally, buff the glass with a dry cloth when the grout is completely dry.

BITS & PIECES: WORKING WITH FOUND OBJECTS

Virtually anything can be used for mosaic work. Mosaic artists see the possibilities in everything around them, and often collect odds and ends such as buttons, mirrors, beads, jewelry, pendants, coins, and bottle tops to incorporate into their projects. These are just some of the unusual items that can be transformed into tesserae. The only limit is the artist's imagination. Collecting strange or striking objects becomes a habit for the adventurous mosaic enthusiast who delights in creating the unexpected! To spark ideas for how to create a picture using a random assortment of bits and pieces, play with them – sort them by color, shape, and texture.

1 METAL
Cast metal pieces such as the grapes seen here add dimension to a mosaic. One uniquely shaped item can serve as the focal point of a piece, and inspire an entire project.

2 POTTERY SHARDS
Pottery shards offer a wide array of colors and motifs to choose from. Painted details can be broken apart and rearranged, or simply extracted and used whole.

3 GLASS BEADS
Inexpensive, flatbacked glass jewels are available in many colors, and the round shape is a pleasing contrast to traditional glass tesserae. They are especially fun to use on outdoor pieces that will be displayed in sunny spots.

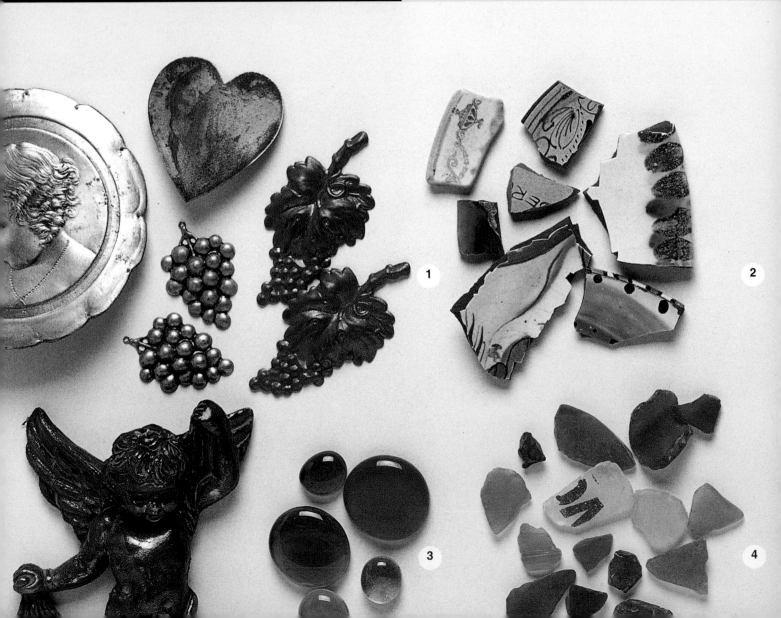

4 SEA GLASS
Frosted sea glass provides a softer alternative to reflective glass tiles. Shards can be found at the beach, or purchased in bulk from a mosaic supply store.

5 DECORATIVE BUTTONS
Many buttons offer a smooth, intricate shape that would be impossible to cut from glass or ceramic, and they can have unusual details like the ones shown here.

6 FABRIC FLOWERS
Fabric flowers are usually used to decorate garments or other sewn items, but when used in a mosaic, they add a delicate, tactile element.

7 SHAPED BUTTONS
Sewing notions suppliers often sell novelty buttons in every imaginable shape, making it easy to find something suitable for nearly any theme.

8 WOOD
Wooden pieces like these dominoes are perfect for repeating patterns.

9 PLASTER
Plaster is available in a multitude of shapes, both intricate and simple, and is easily painted, gilded, or stained. You can even mold your own customized shapes.

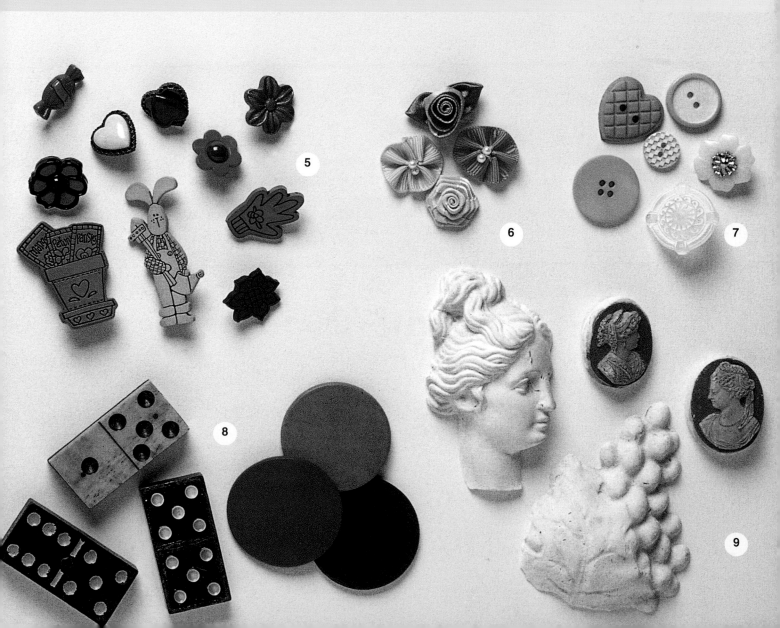

Materials

wood-backed frame

vitreous glass tiles

sea glass

clear, flat-backed glass beads

palette knife

tile nippers

soft, lint-free cloth

cement

natural gray sanded grout

acrylic admixture

grout sealant

kitchen scrubbing pad

safety goggles

work gloves

latex gloves

mixing bowls for cement and grout

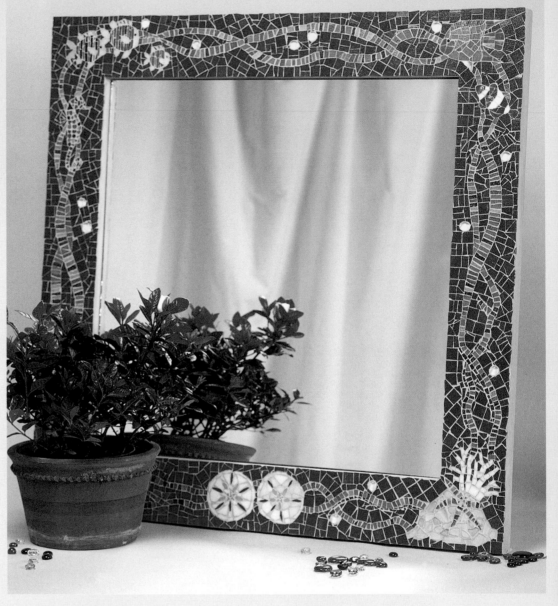

Artist: Aimee Southworth

Seascape Mirror

The vitreous glass tiles used in this mosaic shimmer beautifully in an outdoor setting. When planning an ocean-themed design such as the one here, the boundless variety and colors of sea life are sure to be inspiring. Refer to photographs of favorite sea creatures or seascapes, and use them as starting points for creating a simplified mosaic version. When selecting a frame, make sure it has a flat, wide border that will accommodate the design.

STARTING OUT

An intricate design such as this one requires planning. First, sketch out a pattern to the scale of the frame, making notes of the colors to be used in each area. Then, transfer the drawing to the frame using graphite paper. Use the lines as a guide when applying tiles.

STEP 1

Wearing safety goggles and sturdy work gloves to protect hands from sharp edges, nip an assortment of blue and green vitreous glass tiles into various shapes and sizes for the background and seaweed border of the frame. Keep the colors separated. Custom cut the colors for the images, such as the fish and sand dollars, as they are needed.

Tip: Remove the mirror before beginning the mosaic to prevent it from getting scratched.

STEP 2

Prepare the cement for outdoor use (see page 9). Using a flexible palette knife, spread a 1/8-inch (3-mm) -thick layer of cement on the back of the glass bead bubbles and place them randomly around the frame. Next, apply the tiles for each image, custom cutting tiles as they are needed. Then, use several shades of green tiles to create the undulating reed border. Randomly alternate the shades of green tiles when applying them to produce a naturalistic effect. When everything else is completed, spread cement over a 6-inch (15-cm) -square area on the frame using a palette knife, and begin applying the blue tiles to fill the background. Continue until the background is filled. Cut pieces as needed with nippers for the hard-to-fit areas around the images and the reeds. Let it dry for twenty-four hours.

Tip: The closer the tiles are to each other, the more unified a mosaic will look after grouting. This also makes the colors in a piece appear more intense.

Tip: Try incorporating items such as shells and sea glass to enhance an ocean-inspired design.

STEP 3

Prepare grout for outdoor use (see page 9), then apply a small amount on the frame with glove-protected hands. Natural gray sanded grout was used here. Work the grout completely into the crevices between the tiles using a circular motion. Continue until all the spaces between the tiles are filled. When the grout has dried enough to become powdery, no more than fifteen to twenty minutes, remove residual grout with a wet sponge. Be sure to clean the sponge often. Then, take a soft, lint-free cloth and buff the tiles. When the grout is completely dry, which will take a few days, depending on humidity, apply grout sealant according to the manufacturer's directions. Finally, replace the mirror in the frame and secure it with epoxy or weatherproof adhesive suitable for bonding glass and wood.

Tip: A thin layer of grout will finish the edges of a frame nicely. Add water to the grout mixture until the consistency is soupy, then use your hands or a paintbrush to apply it.

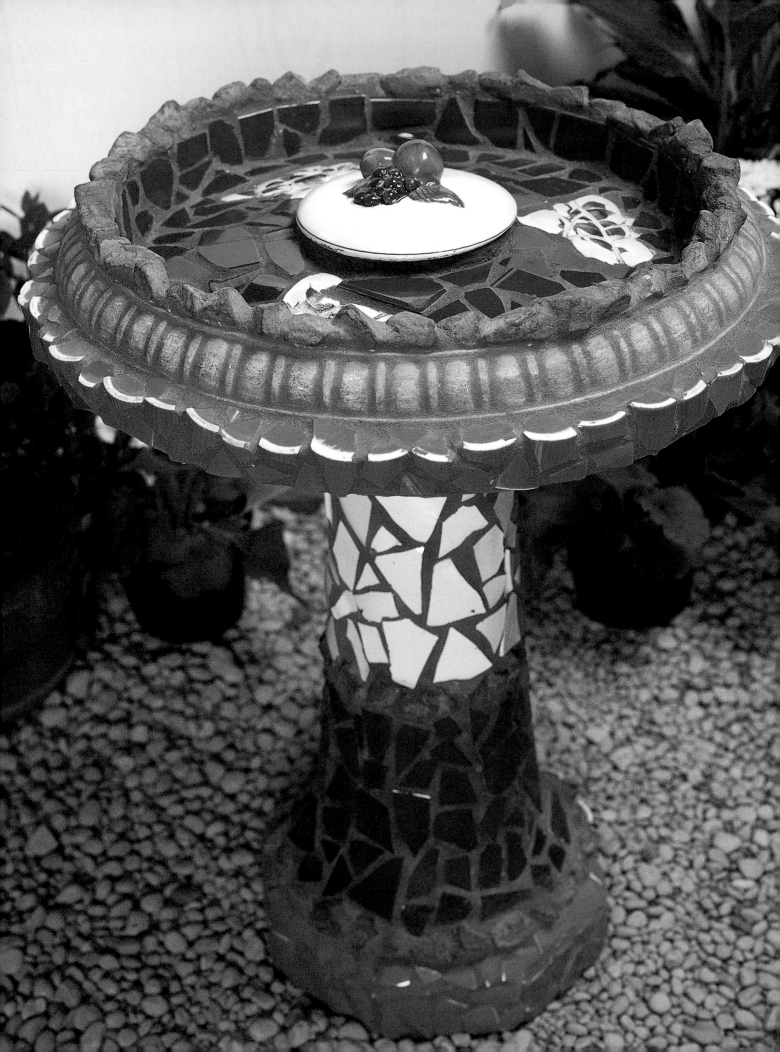

Materials
cement birdbath

broken ceramic tiles and dishes

china casserole cover

small rocks for borders

palette knife

hammer

tile nippers

cement

dark blue or charcoal grout, tan grout

acrylic admixture

grout sealant

kitchen scrubbing pad

safety goggles

latex gloves

filter mask

mixing bowls for cement and grout

Mixed-Tile Birdbath

This piece incorporates different types of tiles and grout colors and is a fun way to expand mosaic skills. Solid and patterned ceramic shards, small rocks, and a three-dimensional ceramic focal point make a striking combination, and are challenging to fit together in a pleasing way. Begin with a pedestal or tabletop cement birdbath, found at home-and-garden centers.

Artist: Susan Strouse/Artful Gardens

Make sure it is designed for practical use. Follow the instructions for weatherproofing exactly to ensure that the bath lasts for years to come.

Several different colors of grout were used to accentuate the various ceramic pieces on this birdbath. A dark grout, such as navy blue or charcoal, blends well with the maroon shards used on the pedestal and basin. A lighter grout, such as tan, works well with the mustard and white shards seen here.

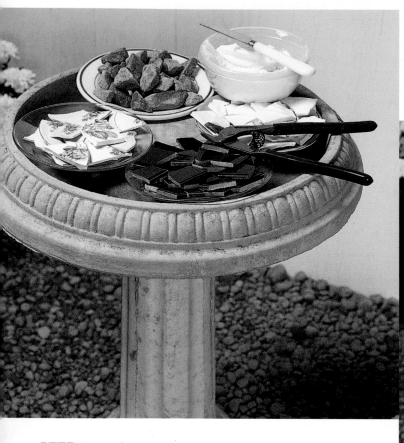

STEP 1

Wearing safety goggles and protective gloves, break the ceramics to be used into shards using a hammer (see page 14 for guidance). Medium-size pieces, about 1 to 2 inches (3 to 5 cm), will work well for most of this project. Use tile nippers to refine the size and shape of the shards as necessary. Sponge the surface of the birdbath to remove any dust or dirt.

STEP 2

Prepare the cement for outdoor use (see page 9). Starting with the base of the birdbath, use a flexible palette knife to apply a 1/8-inch (3-mm) -thick layer of cement over a 6-inch (15-cm) -square area. Press the shards into the cement one at a time, applying more cement as needed. If the base is heavily textured or uneven, apply the cement to the back of the shards instead.

Next, apply curved shards along curved areas of the basin. The white bottom ridges of mugs were used here to create the continuous line around the bath. Then, place rocks one at a time using a thicker layer of cement around the top edge of the basin. To finish the interior of the bath, first apply three reconstructed china plate images and a dimensional center piece. A casserole cover was used here. Then, fill in the rest of the space with solid colored shards. Let it dry for twenty-four hours.

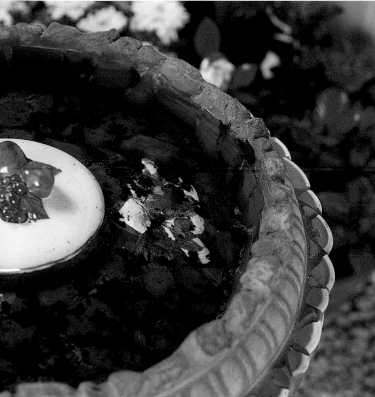

Coordinate the colors and motifs of the mosaic with the area the birdbath will be placed in. The blue-and-green color scheme of the bath here will look beautiful nestled in a wooded space or surrounded by lush foliage. Experiment with several color themes before deciding what to use. An easy way to do this is to spread out possible tiles against a neutral background in the area where the birdbath will be installed.

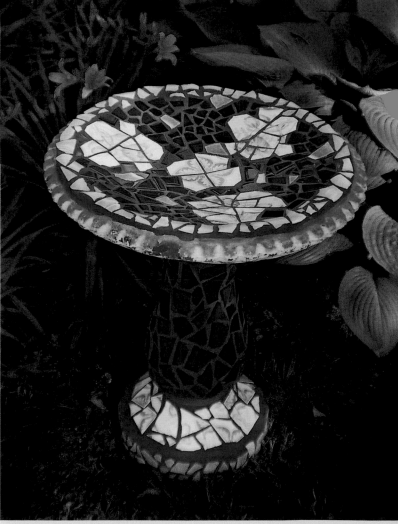

STEP 3 — Prepare grout for outdoor use (see page 9), then apply a small amount on the bath with glove-protected hands. Work the grout completely into the crevices between the shards using a circular motion. Continue until all the spaces between the shards are filled. Keep wiping excess grout off the surface of the shards, because it will be difficult to sand off once dry. When the grout has dried enough to become powdery, no more than fifteen to twenty minutes, use a dry kitchen scrubbing pad to sand excess grout off the surface of the ceramic shards. Wear a filter mask while sanding. If the scrubbing pad scratches the glaze, wipe off excess grout while it is wet with a damp sponge, let it dry, then buff with a lint-free rag. When the grout is completely dry, which will take a few days, depending on humidity, apply grout sealant according to the manufacturer's directions.

Photo by Susan Strouse

Tip: Grout sealers may not be enough to prevent some china pieces from frost damage. To be on the safe side, cover the birdbath with a tarp during winter or take it inside.

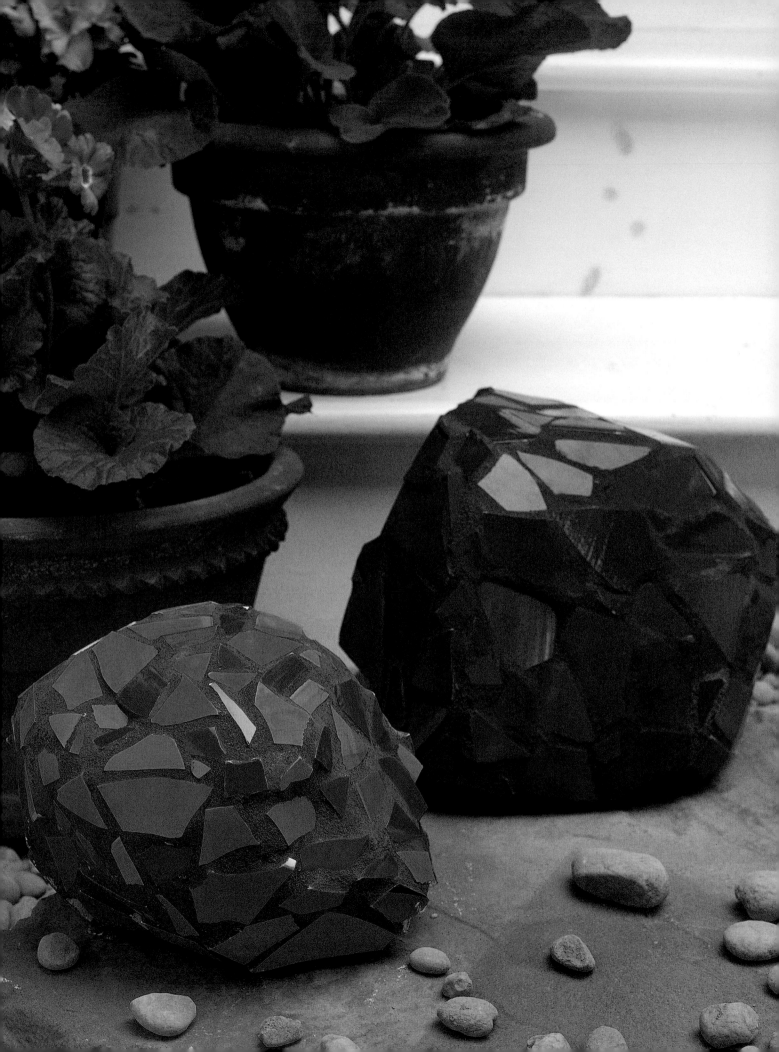

Materials

rocks

broken ceramic pieces

palette knife

hammer

tile nippers

cement

grout

acrylic admixture

grout sealant

kitchen scrubbing pad

safety goggles

latex gloves

filter mask

mixing bowls for cement and grout

Ornamental Garden Rocks

Artist: Susan Strouse/Artful Gardens and Doreen Mastandrea

These playful garden accents are the perfect showcase for ceramic shards. Any rock can be used—egg-shaped or multifaceted rocks work especially well. Since the pattern is free-form, odd bits and pieces can be used without much preparation, making this a great way to use a handful of collected shards that aren't appropriate for other projects. Choose colors that complement the ornamental plantings in your garden.

Use brightly colored shards to create striking, monochromatic garden gems.
Choose ceramics in several shades of the same hue for maximum impact,
and select a grout color that will enhance the color scheme.

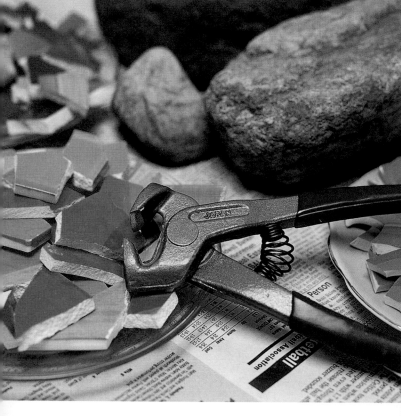

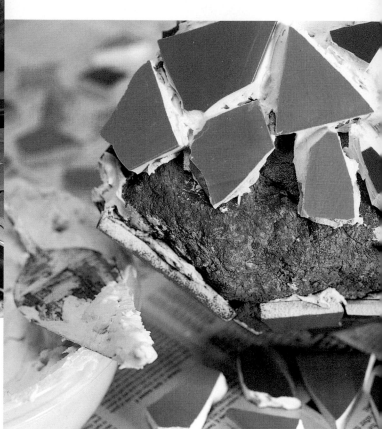

STEP 1

Wearing safety goggles and protective gloves, break the ceramics to be used into shards using a hammer (see page 14 for guidance). Use tile nippers to refine the size and shape of the shards as necessary.

STEP 2

Prepare cement for outdoor use (see page 9) and apply a 1/8-inch (3-mm) -thick layer to a small area of the rock. Press the shards into the cement one at a time, applying more cement as needed. Cover the entire rock. Let it dry for twenty-four hours.

Tip: Always use a dry kitchen scrubbing pad when sanding grout. A wet pad will moisten the grout, creating a film on the shards as you sand.

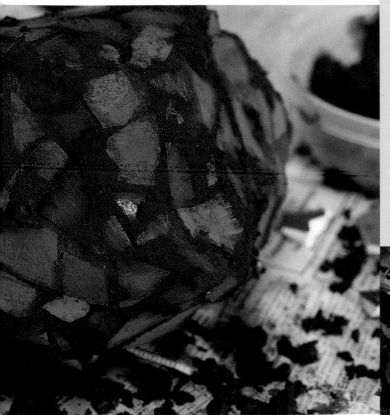

VARIATION

Softer shades like the blue of these "robin's eggs" have a subtle charm. Rather than using only smooth pieces, the ridged bottoms and edges of dishes were whimsically incorporated into this design, calling attention to the previous use of the shards.

Artist: Susan Strouse/Artful Gardens

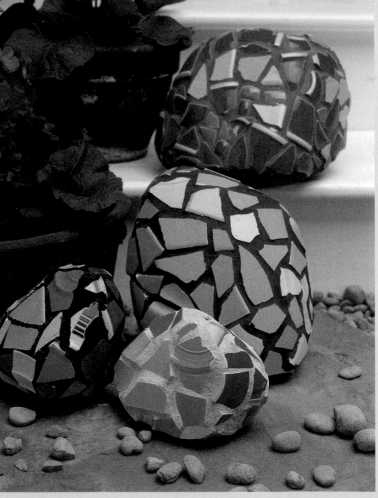

STEP 3

Prepare grout for outdoor use (see page 9), then apply it over a large area of the rock with glove-protected hands. Work the grout completely into the crevices between the shards using a circular motion. Continue until all the spaces between the shards are filled. Keep wiping excess grout off the surface of the shards, because it will be difficult to sand off once dry. When the grout has dried enough to become powdery, no more than fifteen to twenty minutes, use a dry kitchen scrubbing pad to sand excess grout off the surface of the ceramic shards. Wear a filter mask while sanding. Test the scrubbing pad on an extra shard first. If the scrubbing pad scratches the glaze, wipe off excess grout while it is wet with a damp sponge, let it dry, then buff with a lint-free rag. When the grout is completely dry, which will take a few days, depending on humidity, apply grout sealant according to the manufacturer's directions.

Tip: Any remaining sharp edges can be filed down using medium- to large-grit sandpaper or a metal file.

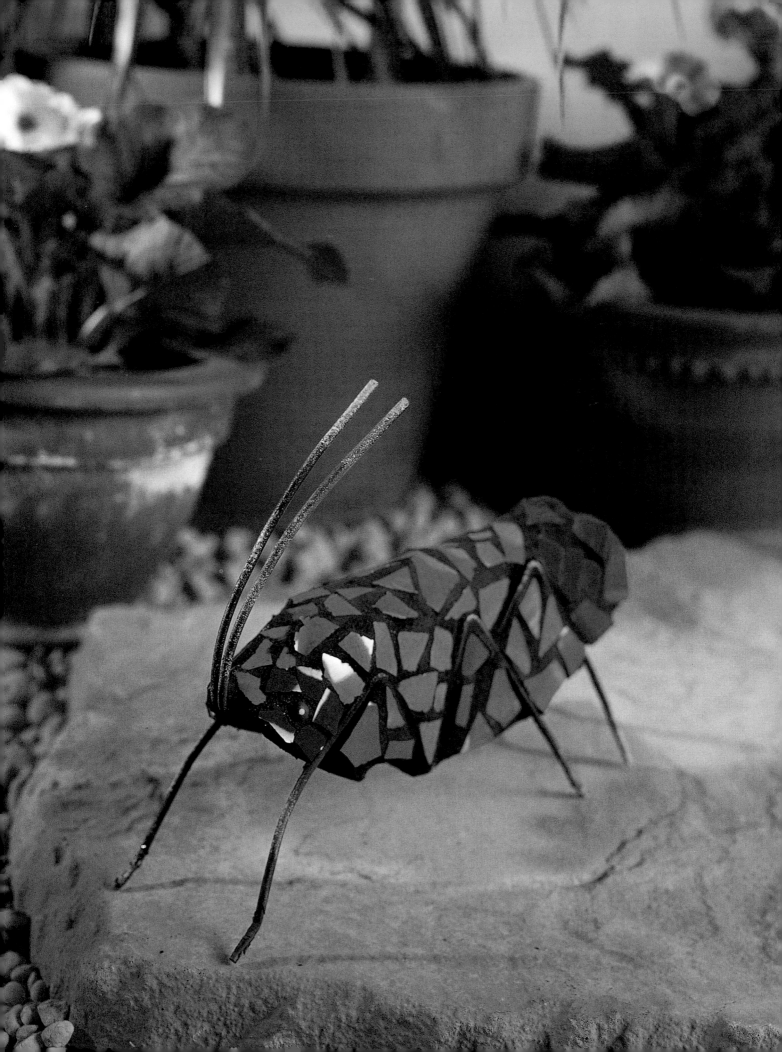

Materials

animal form

broken ceramic pieces in bright, solid colors

hammer

tile nippers

cement

dark gray or black grout

acrylic admixture

grout sealant

kitchen scrubbing pad

safety goggles

latex gloves

filter mask

mixing bowls for cement and grout

Garden Animals

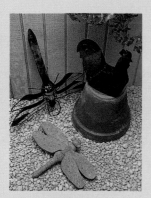

Any one of the forms seen above is a perfect candidate for this project, because nearly every surface is suitable for mosaic work.

Artist: Doreen Mastandrea

These charming creatures are a fun way to liven up any outdoor space, especially a garden. A search of local yard sales, thrift stores, or home-and-garden centers is sure to yield a treasure trove of interesting and unique outdoor sculpture. Collect the tesserae for this project from broken, orphaned, or found ceramic dishware and tiles to give them new life.

When selecting a form, be sure it will weather well and consider how difficult it will be to cover any crevices or tight areas with tesserae.

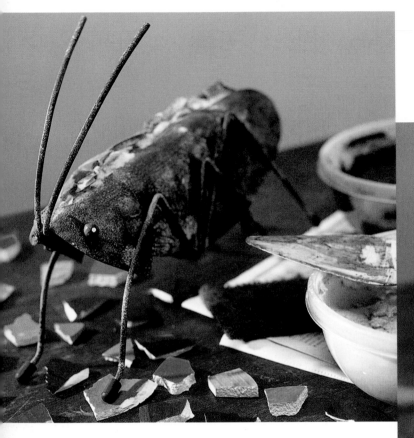

STEP 1

Wearing safety goggles and protective gloves, break the ceramics to be used into shards using a hammer (see page 14 for guidance). Use tile nippers to refine the size and shape of the shards as necessary. Clean and dry the animal form to be used.

STEP 2

Prepare cement for outdoor use (see page 9), and apply a 1/8-inch (3-mm) -thick layer to a small area of the animal. Press the shards into the cement one at a time, applying more cement as needed. Cover the entire animal. Let it dry for twenty-four hours.

Tip: In tight spots, it may be easier and neater to apply the cement to the back of the tile rather than to the form.

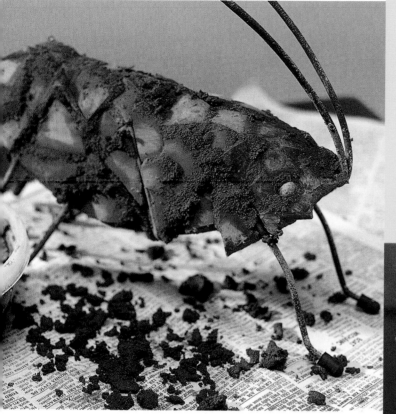

The fluid lines of this wire rooster are the perfect complement to ceramic tile work.

VARIATION

In this project, the shards are laid in a pattern reminiscent of a real bird's markings, but the colors used are whimsical rather than realistic. Consult photographs of animals to plan the placement of shards, but use your imagination when deciding on a color scheme. This combination of techniques is sure to create a striking design.

Artist: Susan Strouse/Artful Gardens

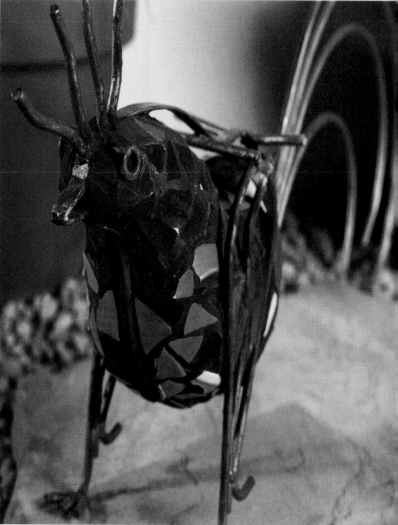

STEP 3

Prepare grout for outdoor use (see page 9), then apply it over a large area of the animal with glove-protected hands. Work the grout completely into the crevices between the shards using a circular motion. Be careful not to leave too much grout on the surface of the shards, because it will be difficult to sand off. When the grout has dried enough to become powdery, use a dry kitchen scrubbing pad to sand excess grout off the surface of the ceramic shards. Wear a filter mask while sanding. When the grout is completely dry, which will take a few days, depending on humidity, apply one coat of grout sealant.

Tip: When sanding grout, be sure to use a light-duty kitchen scrubbing pad that is safe for ceramic surfaces.

Tip: Use cups to create curved shards that fit perfectly on rounded surfaces.

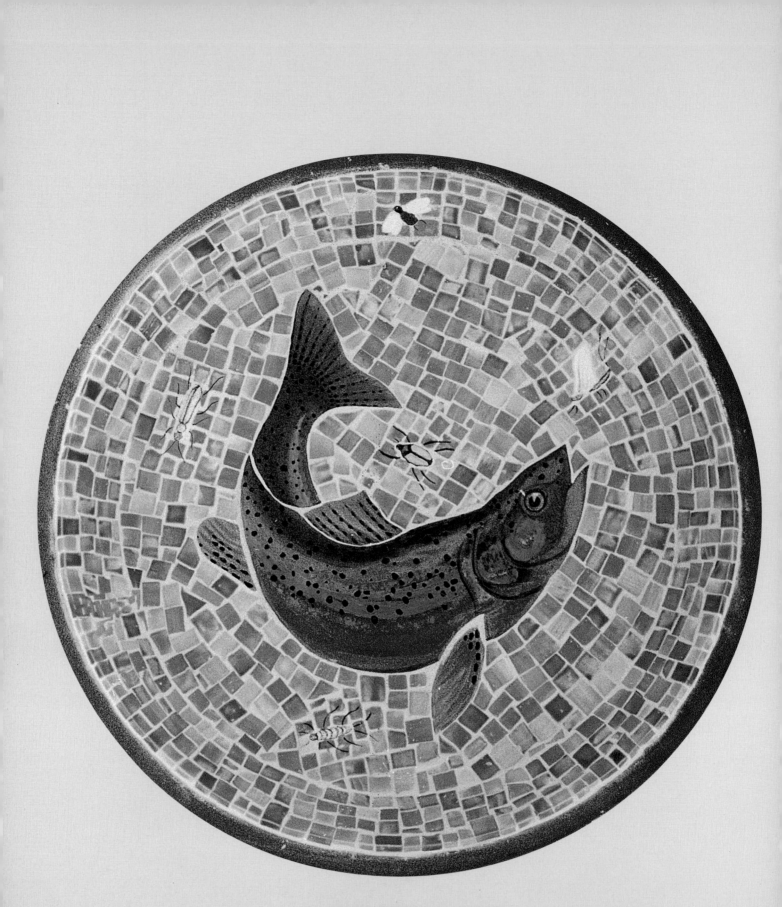

Artist: Melissa Glen/Melissa Glen Mosaics
Photo by Melissa Glen

Materials

terra cotta saucer

stoneware clay

canvas

ceramic underglaze and overglaze paint in various colors

brushes

rolling pin

paring knife

tracing paper

cement

premixed white unsanded grout for outdoor use

acrylic admixture

safety goggles

latex gloves

filter mask

mixing bowls for cement and grout

Trout Rain Catcher

This mosaic is built on a terra cotta saucer, using handmade tesserae.

Stoneware clay, access to a kiln, and some simple handbuilding techniques

are all you need to start making specialized, custom tiles in any shape or

size. Many pottery studios offer a firing service for a small fee, eliminating

the need to buy a kiln or learn how to use one. Just be sure to bring in the

manufacturer's firing information for the clay and glazes used, so that the

kiln master can properly fire the pieces.

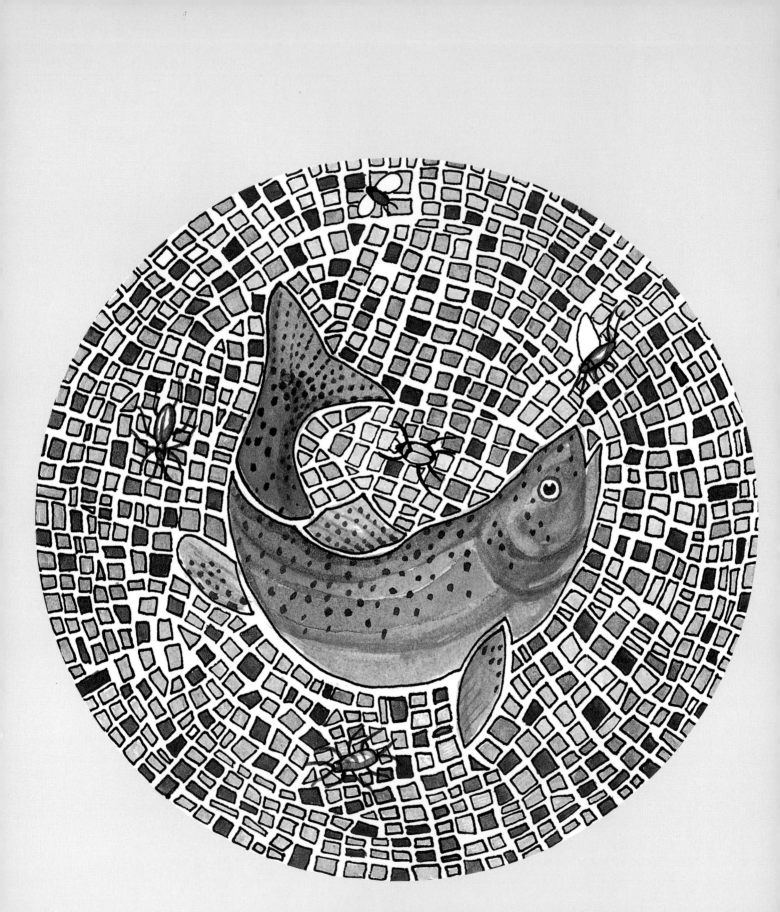

Illustrator: Mary Newell DePalma

STARTING OUT
Draw the outline of a fish on a piece of tracing paper to make a pattern. Field guides or photographic marine-life books are great sources of inspiration, both for the shape of the fish and for the color scheme. Prepare a pattern by sizing the illustration to your selected tabletop. You can enlarge the pattern in sections using a copier, or sketch or photocopy the illustration onto graph paper to determine scale.

STEP 1
On a piece of canvas secured to a work table, use a rolling pin to flatten a piece of stoneware clay approximately 1/4 inch (7 mm) to 1/2 inch (1 cm) thick. Let that clay rest for about thirty minutes. Place the fish pattern on top of the slab of clay, then cut it out using a paring knife. Cut the remainder of the slab carefully into small squares and rectangles. These will be used to fill the area around the fish. Do not pick up or move the fish or tiles until the clay has dried enough to become rigid. At this point, they can be handled without deforming them.

Next, paint the trout using ceramic underglazes. Then, cut the fish into several tiles. The tail and fins were cut into separate tiles on this fish. Let the clay dry completely, which will take several days, then fire the fish and tiles to cone 2.

Finally, paint a clear overglaze on the once-fired trout, and paint a colored overglaze on the tiles. Apply the paint according to the manufacturer's directions. Fire all the pieces according to the manufacturer's recommendation, usually cone 06 to cone 2.

STEP 2
Prepare the cement for outdoor use (see page 9). Using a flexible palette knife, apply an 1/8-inch (3-mm) layer of cement to the saucer. Beginning with the fish, press the tiles into the cement one at a time, applying more cement as needed. Then, fill in the background leaving the edge exposed to show off the natural terra cotta. Let it dry for twenty-four hours.

With glove-protected hands, apply a small amount of premixed unsanded grout for outdoor use on the rain catcher. Work the grout completely into the crevices between the tiles using a circular motion. Keep wiping excess grout off the surface of the tiles. When the grout has dried enough to become powdery, no more than fifteen to twenty minutes, use a damp sponge to clean the tiles. Rinse the sponge frequently, and wipe the tiles until all the grout film is gone. Let it dry, then buff with a rag. When the grout is completely dry, which will take a few days, depending on humidity, apply grout sealant according to the manufacturer's directions.

VARIATION

The Idea of a central custom tile can be applied to an unlimited number of themes and is the perfect way to further personalize a mosaic. Create a reusable cardboard pattern if making more than one tile, or try using specialty cookie cutters for quicker tiles.

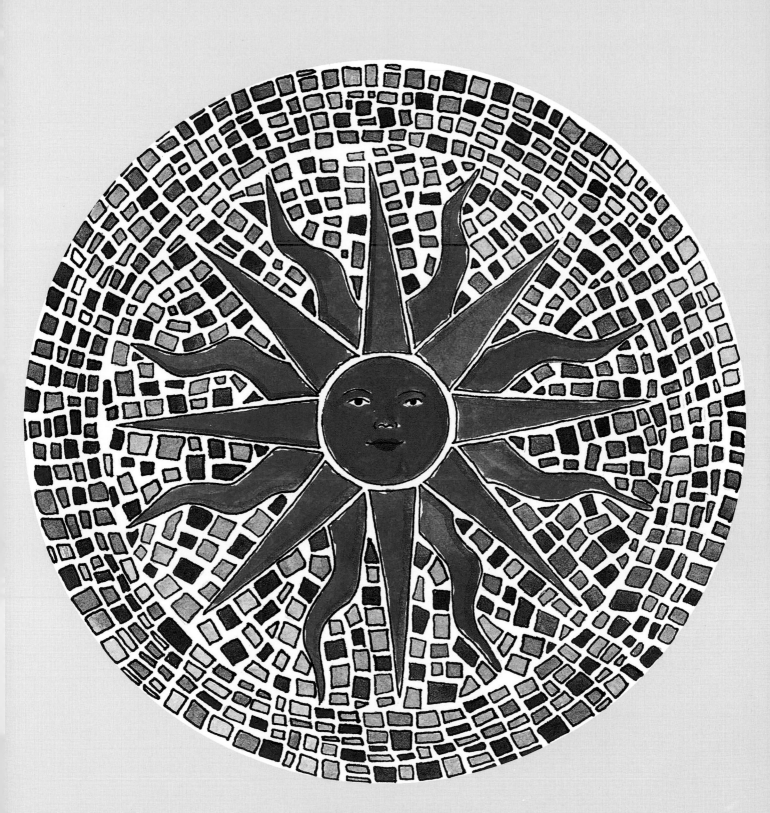

Illustrator: Mary Newell DePalma

BITS & PIECES:
TESSERAE FROM NATURE

The inherent range of colors and patterns in natural materials such as marble, pebbles, rocks, and shells can be inspiring to work with. Marble is a classic material for floors and will lend an air of sophistication and history to a project. Stones of all kinds are perfect for outdoor pieces because they are durable and blend easily into a natural setting. Seashells come in such a gorgeous array of textures and intriguing forms that they can be used exclusively in endless ways. While all these materials are widely available for purchase, a leisurely scavenger hunt around the countryside or the seashore is the most enjoyable way to discover and collect natural tesserae.

1 MARBLE

Marble is available in a range of beautifully variegated earth tones. It can be used to make striking and unusual mosaics by combining several contrasting colors and by taking advantage of interesting streaks and patterns. It can be polished to a glasslike finish or to a more natural, matte finish. Since the shinier finish reflects more light and attracts the eye, try using both kinds within the same mosaic to call attention to specific areas.

1

2 METALLIC ROCKS

A stone mosaic doesn't necessarily have to be neutral. These rocks have streaks of vibrant metallic color running through them, which will add sparkle and depth to a piece. Try combining especially beautiful or bright rocks with subtle, uniformly colored pebbles and stones so that they stand out.

3 RIVER ROCKS

Smooth, naturally polished pebbles like these river rocks are perfectly at home in an outdoor space. Try using them to pave an area of the garden or to make stepping stones. The subtle, comforting shapes and colors of the stones here would make a serene, subtle, but inviting mosaic. The early mosaics of the ancient Greeks consisted of pebbles. For inspiration, try looking at photographs in art history books of these classic designs.

4 SHELLS

Shells of all shapes and sizes make a perfect mosaic component. Use them whole or broken, depending on the planned design. Tiny shells of the same variety can be used whole to make simple, linear patterns. Small shards created from very large shells can be used to fill a background without having to worry about matching colors. Many shells also have an iridescent sheen, especially when polished. Use these for an opulent, jeweled effect.

5 LARGE ROCKS

Rocks like these were used to make the border around the birdbath on page 80. Bulky rocks add an organic dimension to a mosaic, and their natural shape is often full of character. Rocks with bands of color provide an additional design element that can be used to delineate an area, make a simple pattern, or even spell something out. Be sure to partially submerge rocks like these in a liberal amount of adhesive cement to secure them.

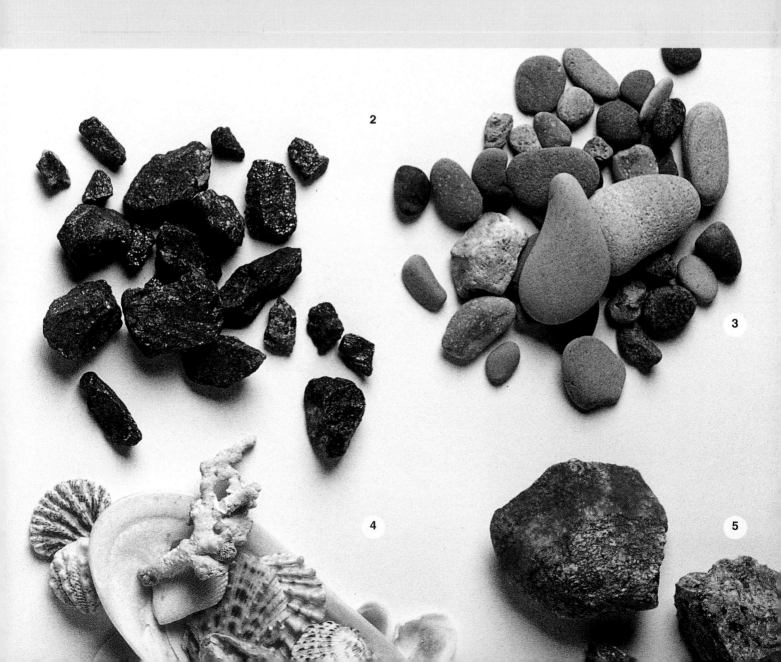

Materials

1/2-inch (1-cm) -thick plywood cut to desired shape

2 eye screws

picture-hanging wire

sandpaper

assorted china plates

stained glass shards

assorted found objects for accent pioeces

palette knife or craft stick

hammer

tile nippers

combination scorer and pliers

cement

grout

acrylic admixture

kitchen scrubbing pad

safety goggles

latex gloves

filter mask

mixing bowls for cement and grout

dry, lint-free cloth

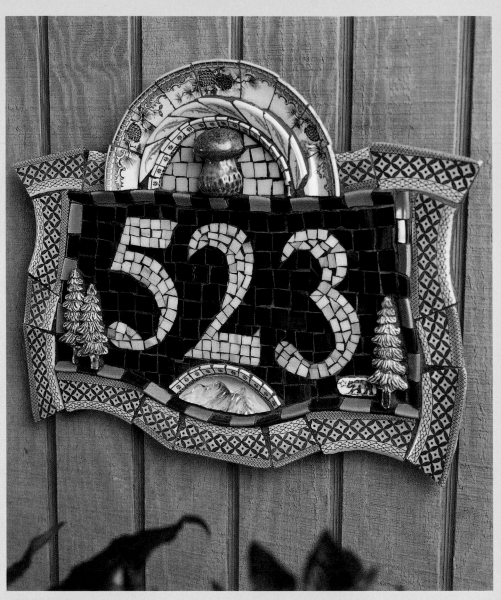

Artist: Sara Curtis

House-Number Plaque

This mixed-media plaque combines glass and china tiles for a unique, fun, flea-market feel.

The numbers are made of stained-glass shards, and the borders and dimensional pieces

are ceramic. First decide on a theme or color scheme, then accumulate pieces that fit

within that framework. Seek out plates with interesting borders, images that share similar

colors, and three-dimensional pieces that relate to one another. The mushroom on the top

of this plaque is an antique salt shaker!

STARTING OUT   Custom cut a piece of plywood for this plaque using a jigsaw, or order a piece to the desired specifications from a lumberyard. It's extremely helpful to draw or trace the entire design on the plywood before beginning to apply tiles.

STEP 1

Wearing safety goggles and protective gloves, break the ceramics to be used into shards using a hammer (see page 14 for guidance). Use tile nippers to refine the size and shape of the shards as necessary. To cut the glass pieces for the numbers, use a combination scorer and plier. First, score the section of glass to be cut, applying firm, even pressure. Then, grasp the glass with the tool and align the scoring with the guide mark. Press firmly, and the glass should snap off along the score mark. Keep the pieces organized as they are cut for easy installation by laying them out on a sketched paper pattern.

Tip: Use a stencil for the numbers or create one using computer fonts and a printer, then trace them on the board.

STEP 2

Prepare cement for outdoor use (see on page 9 for guidance). Starting with the numbers, use a palette knife or craft stick to apply a 1/8-inch (3-mm) -thick layer of cement on the wooden board. Begin applying the glass pieces, custom nipping the tiles as needed to fit them within the number stencils. Fit the glass tiles closely together. Next, fill in a solid-colored background behind the numbers so they will read clearly. Apply cement over a 6-inch (15-cm) -square area at a time. Be sure the adhesive doesn't squeeze into the crevices between the tiles. Next, begin applying the border pieces along the edges of the plaque and add any additional elements. Let it dry for twenty-four hours.

Tip: If a design calls for a lot of intricate cutting around images or three-dimensional pieces, look into renting a wet saw from a home center for the day. It will make the process quicker and easier. Carefully follow the manufacturer's instructions for use.

STEP 3

Prepare grout for outdoor use (see page 9), then apply a small amount to the plaque with glove-protected hands. Work the grout completely into the crevices between the tiles using a circular motion. Continue until all the spaces between the tiles are filled. Keep wiping excess grout off the surface of the tiles. Once grouting is completed, use a damp sponge to wipe off any excess. Let it dry, then buff with a lint-free rag. Finally, apply hardware such as eye screws and picture-hanging wire for installation.

Tip: Let the border pieces extend off of the plaque. This is an easy and effective way to conceal the unfinished edges.

Materials

metal mailbox

flat-backed glass beads in various colors

palette knife or craft stick

cement

acrylic admixture

black sanded grout

grout sealant

kitchen scrubbing pad

latex gloves

filter mask

mixing bowls for cement and grout

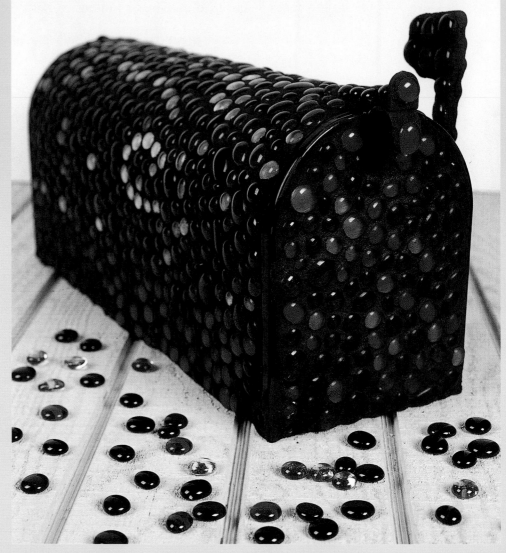

Artist: Robin Millman

Tool Mailbox

A plain, purely utilitarian metal mailbox from a home center was covered with flat-backed glass beads to make this outdoor toolbox — a beautiful solution for keeping tools organized and protected from the elements after a busy day of gardening. It can also be used as a fun, funky alternative to a traditional mailbox. Black grout was used to make these ordinary glass beads pop out, transforming them into glistening gems as they catch sunlight.

STARTING OUT

Flat-backed glass beads in various colors and sizes can be purchased from stained-glass or craft supply stores. Use contrasting classic colors such as the red, green, yellow, and blue seen here for a dramatic, vibrant effect. Be sure to rough up the surface of the metal to ensure good adhesion.

STEP 1

Prepare cement for outdoor use (see page 9 for guidance). Lay the mailbox on one side. Starting on the bottom edge, use a craft stick or flexible palette knife to spread a 1/8-inch (3-mm) -thick layer of mortar over a small area. Begin applying the beads closely together. Green and yellow were used here to create a border pattern. Continue until the edge is complete. Let the mortar set up for ten to fifteen minutes. Then, stand the mailbox upright and begin applying beads to cover the top and sides. Let the finished side dry completely, then lay the mailbox on that side and cover the other bottom edge with beads. Next, apply beads to the front and back ends of the mailbox. Finally, apply accent beads to the front latch and the flag. Blue, green, red, and yellow beads were used here. Let it dry for twenty-four hours.

Tip: It can be difficult to secure beads to a plastic flag. If possible, use a mailbox with a metal flag.

Tip: Make sure the consistency of the mortar is thick enough to hold the beads in place securely, so that they won't slide on the mailbox's curved surface.

STEP 2

Prepare grout for outdoor use (see page 9), then apply a small amount on the mailbox with glove-protected hands. Work the grout completely into the crevices between the beads using a circular motion. Continue until all the spaces between the beads are filled. Keep wiping excess grout off the surface of the beads, so that the glass can be easily cleaned once the grout is dry.

STEP 3

When the grout has dried enough to become powdery, no more than fifteen to twenty minutes, use a dry kitchen scrubbing pad to sand excess grout off the surface of the beads. Wear a filter mask while sanding. Try to uncover as much of the beads as possible. Then, use a soft, dry cloth to buff the beads. When the grout is completely dry, which will take a few days, depending on humidity, apply grout sealant according to the manufacturer's directions.

Materials

birdhouse form

broken china pieces

palette knife

hammer

tile nippers

cement

white sanded grout

acrylic admixture

grout sealant

kitchen scrubbing pad

safety goggles

latex gloves

filter mask

mixing bowls for cement and grout

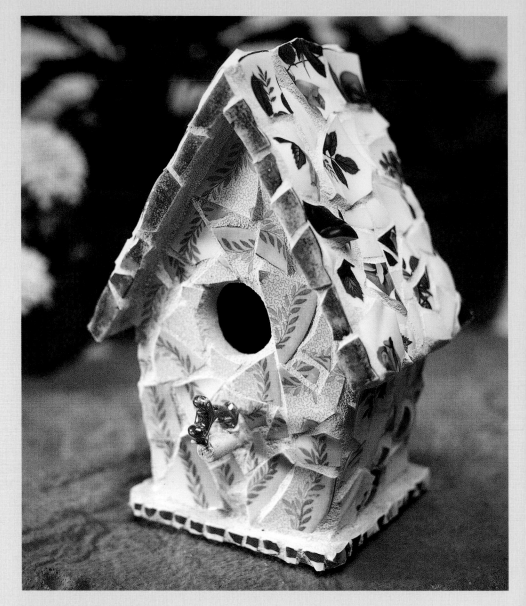

Artist: Doreen Mastandrea

China Birdhouse

China dishware provides an unlimited resource for patterns that can be used in mosaic work. Before adhering the shards, play with the placement possibilities of the design elements on the plates and cups. A running vine or repeating floral pattern can be put back together or rearranged in a new way. Here, a cup handle was used for the bird perch, and a gold-rimmed saucer was used to delineate the edge of the roof.

STARTING OUT   Choose cups and plates that share many of the same colors, but have different patterns. This helps to unify the piece when using mismatched china. The colors used here are predominantly red, pink, pale yellow, various leaf greens, and white.

STEP 1   Wearing safety goggles and protective gloves, break the china plates and cups to be used into shards using a hammer (see page 14 for guidance). Use tile nippers to refine the size and shape of the shards as necessary.

Tip: Keep the tile nippers handy to custom cut pieces for hard-to-fit areas, and to cut out flowers or other interesting patterns from the plates.

STEP 2   Prepare the cement for outdoor use (see page 9). Using a flexible palette knife, apply a 1/8 -inch (3-mm) -thick layer of cement over a small area on one side of the birdhouse. Press the shards into the cement one at a time, applying more cement as needed. Be careful to keep the cement off the top of the china. It will be difficult to clean off once the mixture dries. Continue until all the sides are covered. Let it dry for twenty-four hours.

STEP 3   Prepare grout for outdoor use (see page 9), then apply a small amount over one side of the birdhouse with glove-protected hands. Work the grout completely into the crevices between the shards using a circular motion. Continue until all the spaces between the shards are filled. Keep wiping excess grout off the surface of the china because it will be difficult to sand off once dry. Be careful in delicate places such as the perch and roofline. When the grout has dried enough to become powdery, no more than fifteen to twenty minutes, use a dry kitchen scrubbing pad to sand excess grout off the surface of the ceramic shards. Wear a filter mask while sanding. Test the scrubbing pad on an extra shard first. If the scrubbing pad scratches the glaze, wipe off excess grout while it is wet with a damp sponge, let it dry, then buff with a lint-free rag. When the grout is completely dry, which will take a few days, depending on humidity, apply grout sealant according to the manufacturer's directions.

Tip: Always use a dry kitchen scrubbing pad to sand excess grout, because moisture and grout dust create a film on china that is difficult to clean.

BITS & PIECES:
PIQUE ASSIETTE

Pique assiette, a French term that literally means stolen from plate, is a mosaic style that transforms into works of art broken or orphaned ceramic pieces such as china plates, teacups, figurines, and other odds and ends that are otherwise destined for the trash. Part of the fun of this addictive, recycling-oriented form of mosaic is cruising flea markets, antique stores, yard sales, and even the attic, looking for unique ceramics. For an especially personal "memoryware" mosaic, try using those chipped or damaged family heirlooms that you just can't part with to create something new.

Some ceramics can be damaged by frost, so take this into consideration before planning an outdoor project. Always weatherproof a china mosaic, and to be on the safe side, bring the piece indoors or cover it with a tarp during winter.

1 METALLIC GLAZES
China often features beautiful metallic glazes that can be used to great effect. The edges of these cups could be reassembled to make a glittering border for a mosaic image.

2 BLUE-AND-WHITE WARE
Try using only two colors to create a harmonious, understated design. One traditional and popular pairing in ceramics is blue and white. Incorporating a range of shades in a single hue will lend interest and elegance to a piece.

3 CERAMIC ORNAMENTS
Ceramic ornaments like this bird can be used as the focal point for a mosaic.

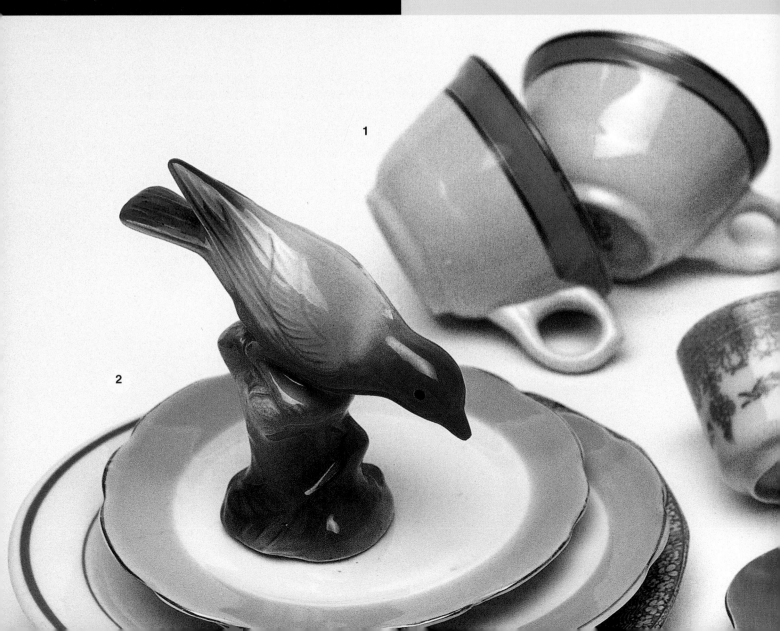

4 CERAMIC BOXES

In addition to dishware, look for other ceramic items such as vases, planters, lamp bases, or boxes like the heart-shaped one here. Small to medium-sized box covers can be used almost like tiles and need very little, if any, preparation.

5 PATTERNED DISHWARE

China is often covered with gorgeous patterns that can be creatively reassembled for a mosaic (see the birdhouse project on page 104 for tips on how to do this). Elements of a pattern, such as the flowers on this cup, are easy to trim out of delicate china using tile nippers. Take advantage of small-scale elegant floral designs to create a set of traditionally sized tiles.

6 TEACUP HANDLES

An ornate teacup handle, such as the one here, was used to make the perch for the birdhouse on page 104. Take advantage of the open, delicate shape to create vinelike patterns.

7 PLATE EDGES

Plates can be used to make easy, continuous borders. The solid-colored, wavy edge of this one is simple but elegant – the perfect complement to a complex or ornately patterned design.

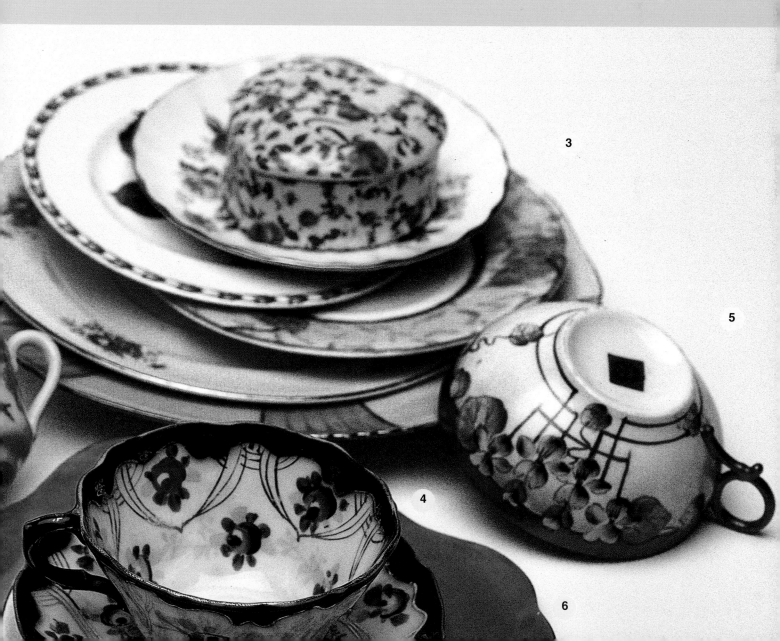

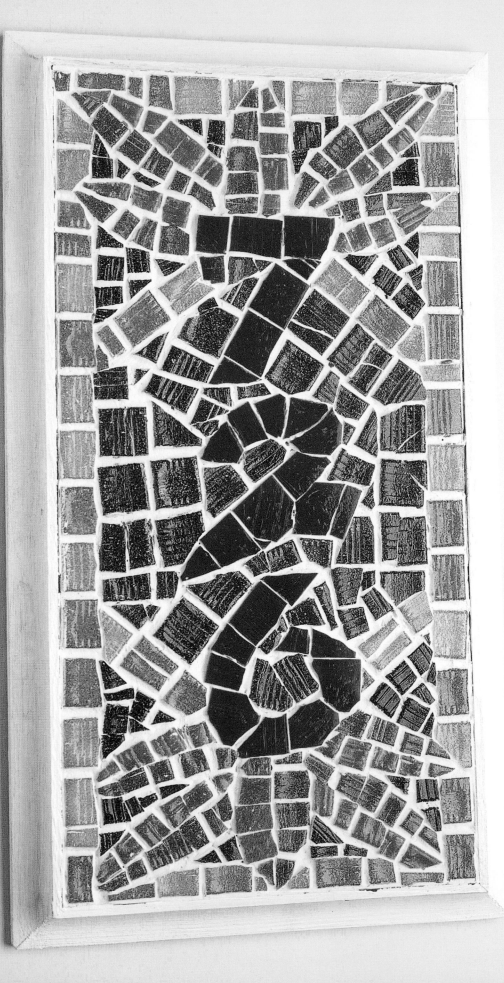

Mosaic has been a popular decorative art throughout the ages. Here's an easy way to create a charming address plaque using glass tiles and premixed latex grout. Mosaic tiles can be purchased in small, square pieces or cut into irregular shapes to add an artistic air to the final piece. If you don't have the woodworking tools to create a frame from plywood and molding, use a ready-made picture frame and have a woodworking shop cut a piece of plywood to fit the interior.

mosaic address plaque

Makes one plaque

1 Cut wood molding to size, miter corners, and attach to plywood base with finishing nails and wood glue. Paint or stain molding as desired.

2 Sketch your desired tile design on a sheet of tracing paper. With carbon paper, transfer the design to the plywood base. Using tile nippers, clip tiles to fit desired pattern, setting them on the tracing paper sketch to organize. Allow up to 1/8" (.32 cm) space between tiles.

3 Working in one small area at a time, apply tile adhesive to the wood surface with a v-notch trowel or glue spreader according to manufacturer's directions. Transfer the cut tile pieces, smooth side up, from the paper template to the adhesive. Set for 5–6 hours.

4 Protect the finished frame molding with quick release tape. Spread premixed grout over the tiles with a grout float or flat-blade spreader tool and work into open spaces until grout is level with tiles. Let set 20–30 minutes. Wipe away excess grout with a damp sponge. Let dry completely. Remove tape and polish tiles using a soft cloth or damp paper towel.

MATERIALS

- 5/8" (1.5 cm) thick plywood, cut to desired size
- wood molding for edging
- finishing nails
- wood glue
- paint or stain
- mosaic glass tiles
- tile nippers
- mosaic tile adhesive
- v-notch trowel or glue spreader
- premixed latex nonsanded grout
- grout float or flat-blade spreader tool
- grout sponge
- general craft supplies

VARIATIONS

Add a bit of acrylic paint to the grout to tint. Instead of tiling your address number, make a mosaic of your family name or initials, and hang on your front door.

TIPS

Wear safety glasses and gloves when cutting tile with nippers. Apply the tile adhesive to the wood base in areas delineated by the sketched design to facilitate transferring the tiled pattern from the paper sketch to the final project. Premixed, nonsanded latex grout is appropriate for grout lines that are 1/8" (.32 cm) or less. For wider grout lines, use sanded grout following manufacturer's instructions for preparation. To prevent warping of thinner wood substrates, prime wood first with mosaic tile primer.

ARTIST: BRIDGET HEIDI NEWFELL

133

Whimsical and unique, this embellished cowbell will be the perfect accent to your patio or garden. This mosaic is created from preshaped decorative tile pieces, available from craft distributors; or you can use stones, charms, or pieces of broken tile, china, or mirror. Because the area to be tiled is three-dimensional, work one face at a time, moving to the next section only when the previous surface is dry.

mosaic
chime

Makes one chime

1 Make a paper template of one side of the cowbell. Snip tile and china pieces into irregular shapes with tile nippers or use pre-shaped mosaic pieces, and place on template until area is filled. Apply tile adhesive with a v-notch trowel or flat-blade spreader to one face of the chime and transfer the cut tile and china pieces onto the tile adhesive. Let dry. Repeat for remaining sides, leaving joins uncovered.

2 Following manufacturer's directions, mix sanded grout with water in a disposable container until it has a fudgelike consistency. Wearing rubber gloves, spread grout into spaces between tiles with a grout float. Let set for 10–15 minutes, then brush away excess grout with a stiff brush such as an old toothbrush. Allow to dry for another 10 minutes. Wipe away remaining loose grout with a damp soft cloth or sponge, then polish tiles with a dry cloth to remove any leftover haze. Repeat for remaining sides.

3 Apply 2–3 coats of grout sealer according to manufacturer's recommendations.

MATERIALS

- metal cowbell
- tile and china pieces
- tile nippers
- tile adhesive
- v-notch trowel or glue spreader
- sanded grout
- grout float or flat-blade spreader tool
- grout sealer
- general craft supplies

TIP
Wear safety glasses and gloves when cutting tile with nippers.

ARTIST: CONNIE SHEERIN

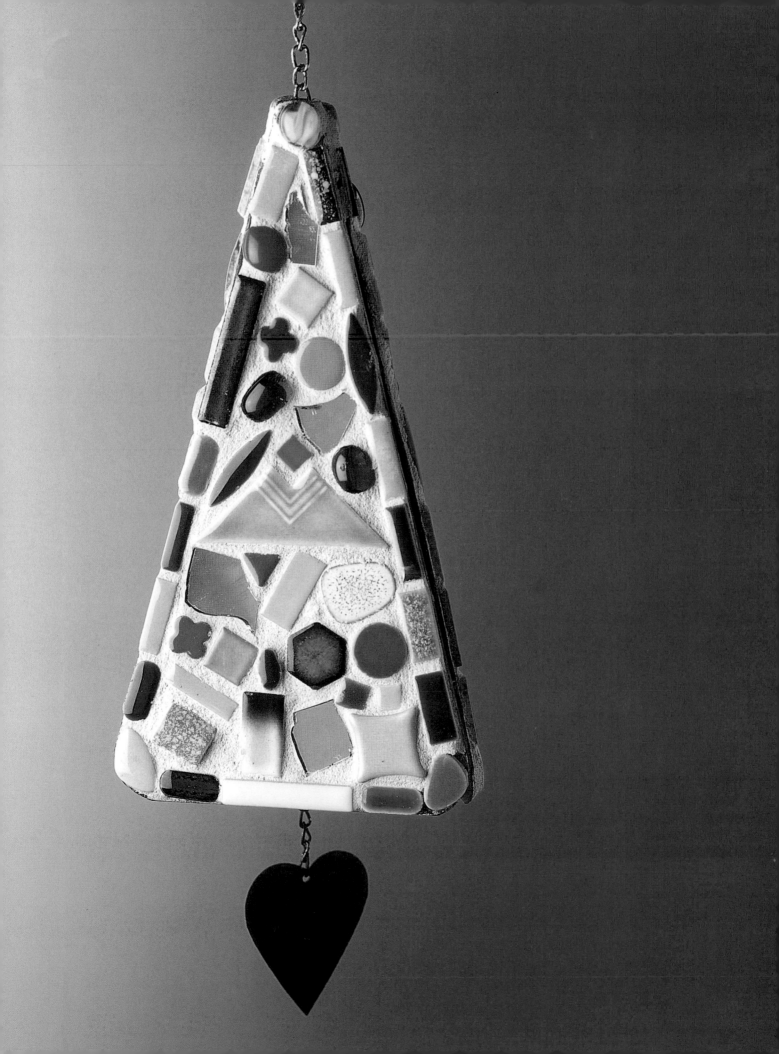

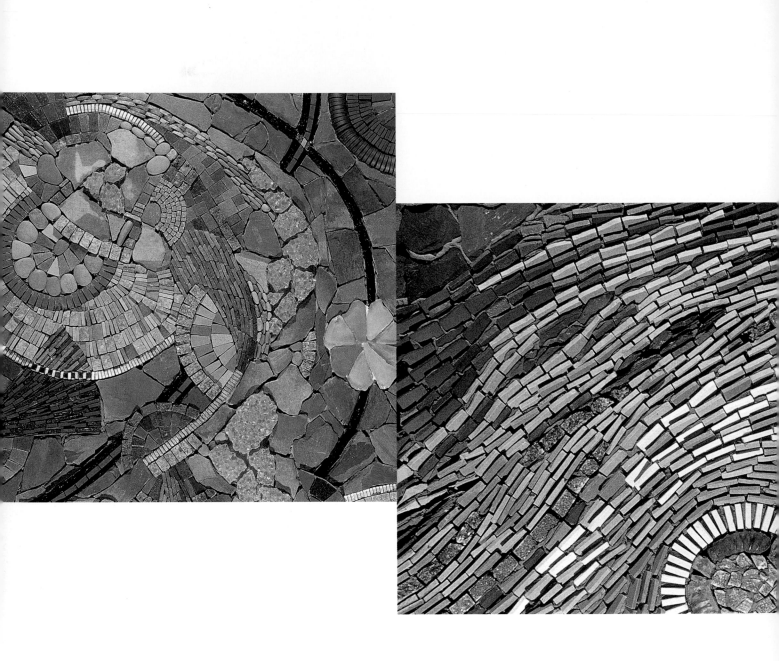

Artist's Gallery

The projects in this section can be completed by any beginner, and they provide all the know-how and practice you need to progress to the next step: the making of more challenging, personal, and expressive mosaics. The installations pictured in the Gallery were created by professional mosaic artists, and we include them in hopes that they will encourage your creativity. Use them as a starting point for designing your own original works.

The different style of each Gallery artist suggests new and distinctive ways to approach your personal mosaic efforts. Since you can use a multitude of materials to make a mosaic, and there are endless ways to arrange the tiles, designing a project from scratch can be overwhelming. A sure way to get focused is to look at beautiful, professional pieces and analyze how they are put together.

Finally, don't be intimidated by professional pieces – everyone starts somewhere. Desire and a little practice are all you need to make a good mosaic. Let the works of these fellow mosaic artists serve as both inspiration and motivation, and may the muses be with you.

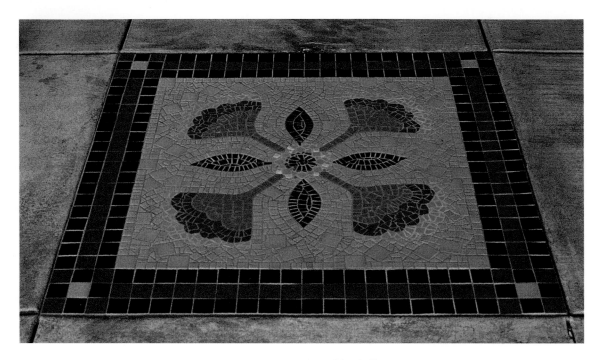

Porcelain tile; 10 feet (305 cm) by 4 feet (122 cm).

Title: Quilts

Artists: Twin Dolphin Mosaics, Stephanie Jurs and Robert Stout

These floor panels were inspired by quilts. Quilt patterns lend themselves to mosaic work because of their graphic shapes and focus on color. Look to other traditional artwork, such as stained glass, for more ideas and motifs.

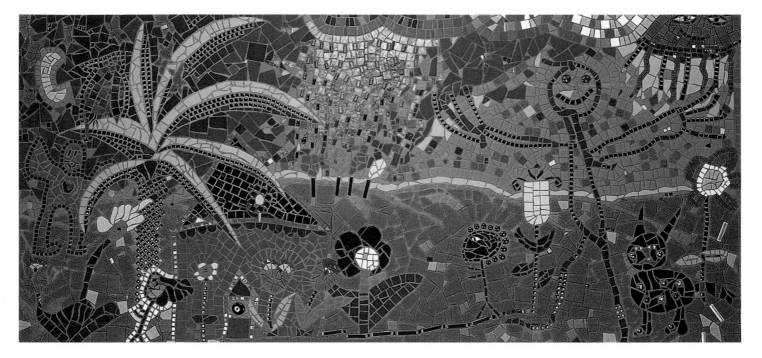

Broken ceramic tile; 8 feet (244 cm) by 4 feet (122 cm).

Title: Children's Clinic Mosaic

Artists: Twin Dolphin Mosaics, Stephanie Jurs and Robert Stout

Many mosaic artists are commissioned to do murals; this piece was commissioned by a children's health clinic. A successful mural starts with planning and a good design. The fanciful, childlike imagery here is both comforting and cheerful – just the thing to brighten a health care facility. By tailoring your design to suit the place where it will be installed, you make sure that the piece will be seamlessly integrated into its surroundings.

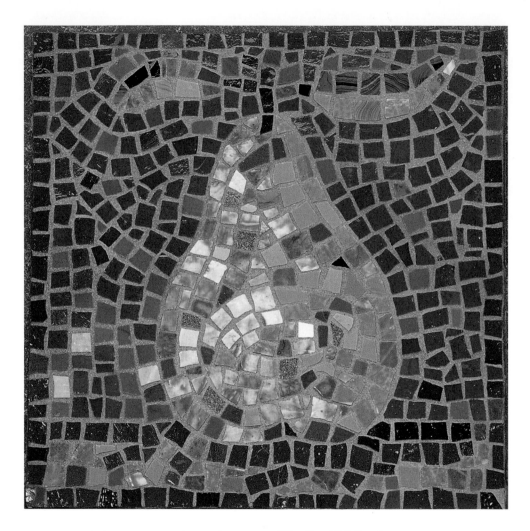

Broken ceramic tile; eight 4-foot (122-cm) by 4-foot (122-cm) panels.

Title: Pear Wall Hanging

Artists: Twin Dolphin Mosaics, Stephanie Jurs and Robert Stout

This simple image of a pear illustrates how any image can be translated into individual dots of color. Seen from a distance, the colors blend into one smooth image. A computer can help easily translate a photo into a mosaic template – just enlarge the image until each pixel, or dot, is evident. Historically, fruits appear in many mosaics. Look through books on historical mosaics for more inspiration.

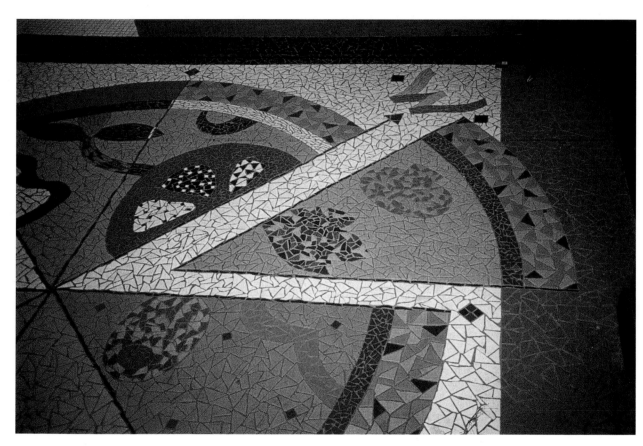

aBroken ceramic tile; eight 4-foot (122-cm) by 4-foot (122-cm) panels.

Title: Tile Floor Installation

Artist: Andrew Martin

This floor installation demonstrates how anything can be depicted in a mosaic. The scale of this architectural piece makes a huge impact, drawing the viewer into the work. The grout lines are spaced evenly to give the piece a clean look. An image of pizza or other foods would work well on the floor of a large kitchen.

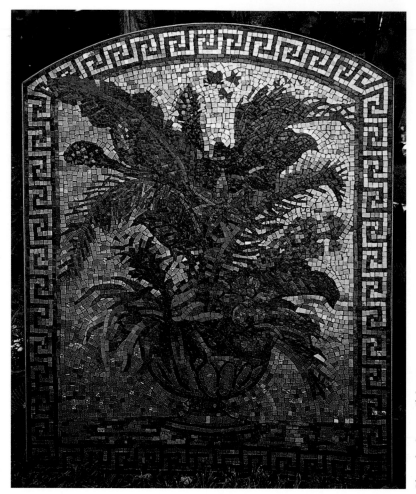

Glass smalti and gold.

Title: Tropical Bouquet II

Artist: George Fishman

This piece combines glass smalti and opulent gold tiles for a classic, traditional look. The materials used in a project are as important as the design, so consider the desired effect before selecting tiles. Imagine this mosaic made with ceramic shards; the overall piece would be looser and more casual.

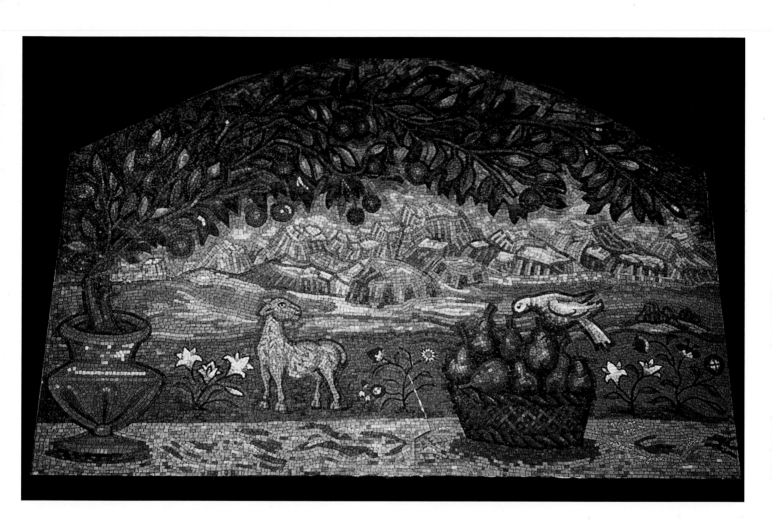

Broken ceramic tile; eight 4-foot (122-cm) by 4-foot (122-cm) panels.

Title: Byzantine Fantasy I

Artist: George Fishman

Since every picture can be broken into individual bits of color, mosaics are the perfect medium for illustrating scenes like this one. Reminiscent of an ancient tapestry, this mosaic shows how individual tiles can coalesce into one remarkably detailed image.

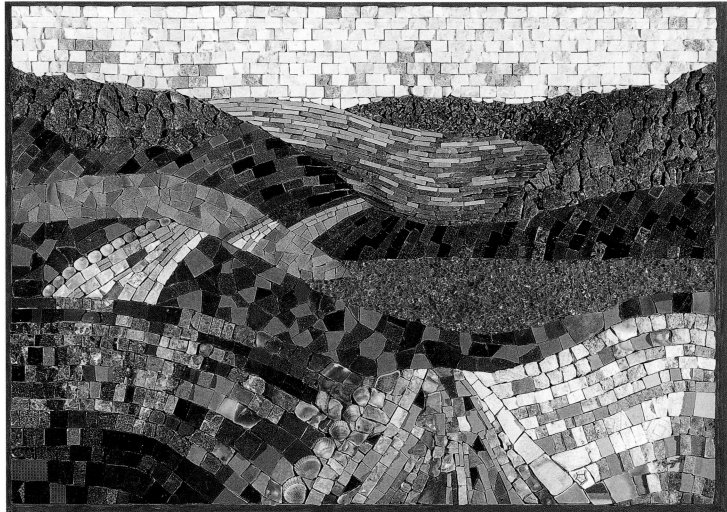

Slate, glass, marble, stone, aluminum, mirror, ceramic, and other materials; 27 3/4 inches (70 cm) by 20 1/2 inches (52 cm).

Title: Hill Country

Artist: Sonia King

This piece, crafted entirely of natural materials, transforms a simple linear pattern into a wonderfully detailed landscape. It's not necessary to begin with an intricate pattern to make a successful mosaic. Paying attention to each tile's color and texture adds depth to a piece like this one, making it easier to convey a complex design idea with a simple pattern.

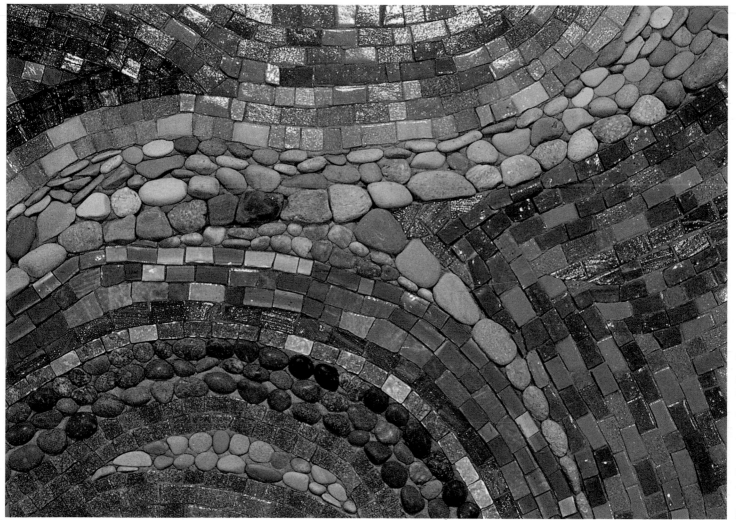

Slate, ceramic tile, marble, and fossils; 20 inches (51 cm) by 14 1/4 inches (36 cm).

Title: Riverscape

Artist: Sonia King

This work uses only a few simple shapes to successfully depict a river scene. The key to getting a design idea across in a mosaic is to identify the elements that will make it recognizable. Simplify an image, such as a photo, as much as possible, and try to figure out which lines and shapes are crucial.

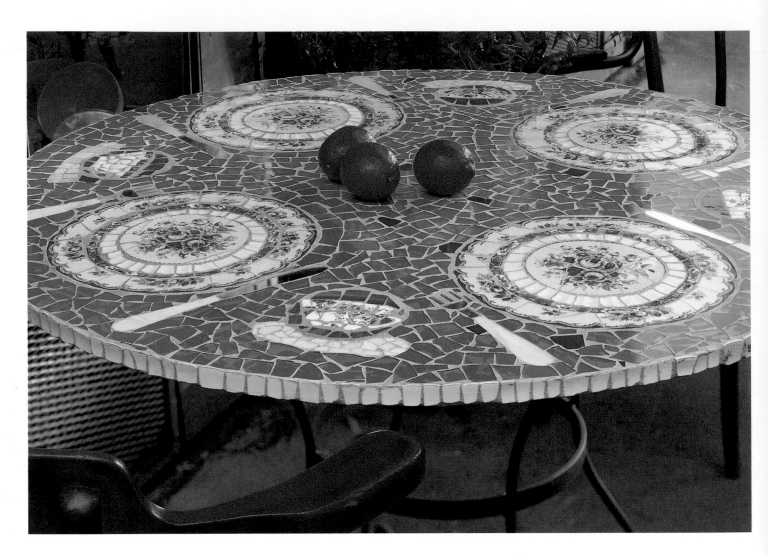

Broken ceramic tile, china, and glass.

Title: Patio Table

Photo: Picture Press: Schöner Wohnen

This patio table is a perfect example of how to use your favorite plates or family heirlooms to create a dynamic new piece of mosaic furniture. Each place setting includes a fork, knife, and coffee cup adding whimsy to a sophisticated design.

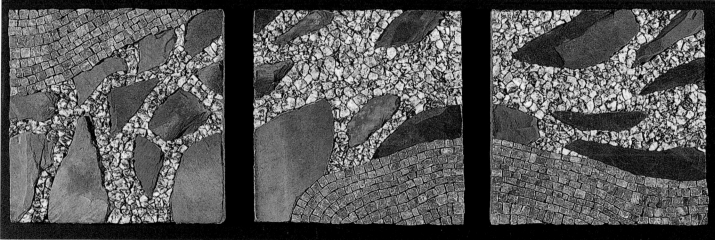

Slate, marble, and granite; 8 inches (20 cm) by 26 inches (66 cm).

Title: Rio de la Roca

Artist: Sonia King

Mosaic design can be representative or abstract. This triptych shows the "movement" of a river through the placement and size of the stones. Playing with these elements you can create different types of effects. Using color to "shape" the formal elements also works in an interesting way to create movement.

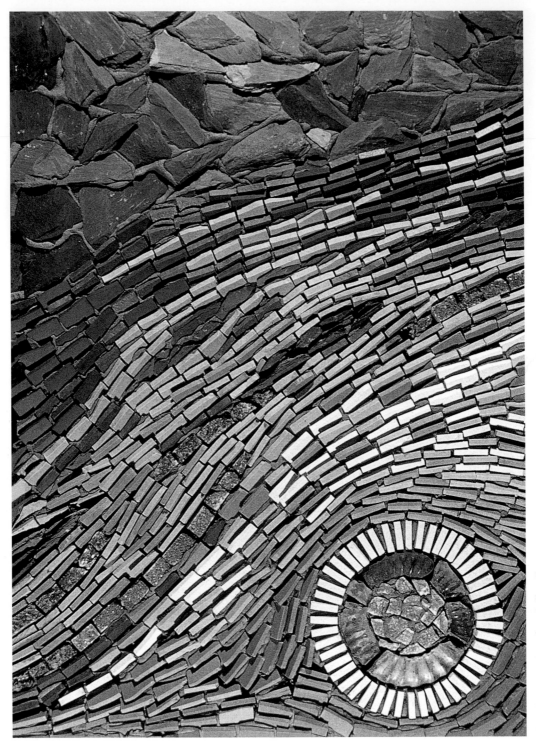

Vitreous glass, limestone, ceramic, and shell; 16 inches (41 cm) by 23 inches (58 cm).

Title: Moon River

Artist: Sonia King

The narrow tiles used here to make undulating patterns suggest the currents and eddies of a river. Paired with subtle variations in color, these tiles accurately convey the feeling of gentle running water. When putting together a mosaic, try to use tiles with shapes that suggest certain emotions or sensations.

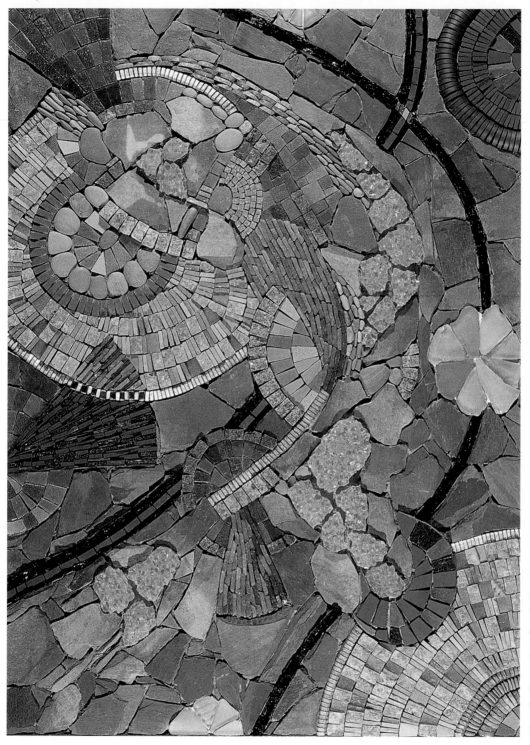

Marble, glass, ceramic, shell, soapstone, granite, and other materials; 18 1/2 inches (47 cm) by 26 inches (66 cm).

Title: Primeval

Sonia King

The combination of glazed ceramic tiles and pebbles in this piece creates an interesting interplay between shiny and matte surfaces. By using pieces with different surface textures, the artist keeps the viewer interested in all elements of the design.

GLASS MOSAICS

Glass mosaics date from around the second century B.C., and became widespread by the fifth century, but it wasn't until the mid-fifteenth century when smalti manufacturers in Murano and Venice learned to precut small, regular pieces known as *tesserae*. These small units could be produced in a multitude of reflective colors that offered more diversity and potential than the options found with stone. While stone mosaics were limited somewhat by the size they could achieve with the tools available before they fractured, glass did not suffer this restriction. Even minute pieces of glass *tesserae* were possible to cut from the malleable glass threads blown from molten glass before it vitrifies.

Artists Felice Nittolo, Erin Adams, and Lucio Orsoni all work with the vivid smalti that characterizes historic glass mosaic artistry, yet their styles are anything but traditional. Rather than the church, geometric forms, magic carpets, and computer chips are the prevailing influences for their art, fashioned in the late 1990s. Although Diana Maria Rossi does include religion and the church in her colorful glass sculptures, it is more a reference to the struggle of an immigrant culture to assimilate than direct devotion. As for Ellen Blakeley, it can only be said that she has moved beyond the church to exalt the new religion of the streets. Tied together solely by their medium, this group of artists each offers their unique vision of life at the birth of a new millennium.

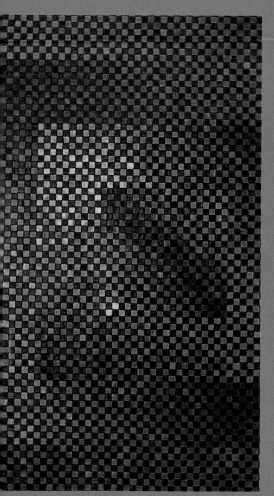

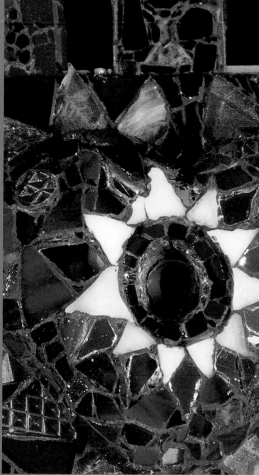

LUCIO ORSONI
Detail from
Black and Copper Gold

DIANA MARIA ROSSI
Detail from
Immigration 3: Donato

FELICE NITTOLO
Detail from
Sfera Rosa

ERIN ADAMS

Many of Erin Adams's glittering, glowing compositions of opaque, iridescent, and transparent glass are based on intricately patterned oriental rugs. As elements of interior design, these mosaic projects function just like their cloth counterparts—sometimes they act as area rugs, outlining a space; other times they dominate.

A childhood devoted to understanding the differences between good and bad art, under the hand of a very perceptive mother, eventually led Adams to pursue creative studies. While working on a master's degree from Pratt Institute, Adams focused on outsider art. After graduating, she opened a gallery of crossover art, then moved on to her own studio.

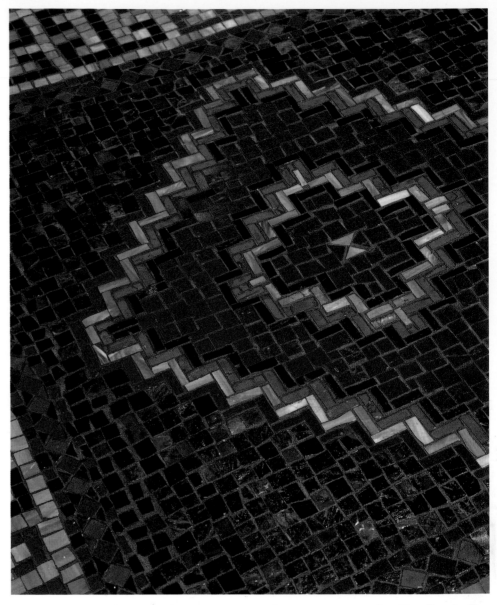

Detail from **Tapestry/Rug**
Radisson Empire Hotel, New York, New York

Detail from **Tapestry, Navajo Rug**

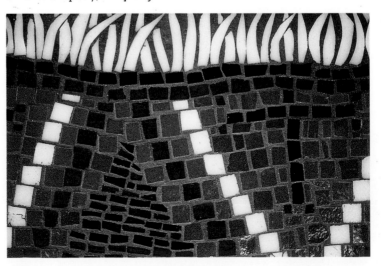

Erin Adams creates glass rugs patterned after kilim, Navajo, and oriental woven textiles. She designs each installation much like needlepoint: "While glass is as

TECHNIQUE

far away from fabric as possible, I try to make it seem malleable. A rug should look as though it's been walked on, so I shape the fringes to look as if disarranged, to have what we used to call 'toe hitches.' It is a visual joke, what I call 'vitreous humor.'" Her installations are also compatible with many types of flooring

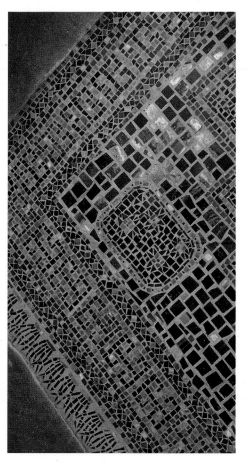

Detail from **Tapestry/Rug**
Cynthia Steffe Showroom, New York, New York

materials—they are typically surrounded by concrete, marble, or wood—and the gem-toned works catch and reflect all kinds of light.

The mosaicist's largest and most complex project to date is a *65,000-tesserae* installation in a New York City hotel restaurant. Because the glass she

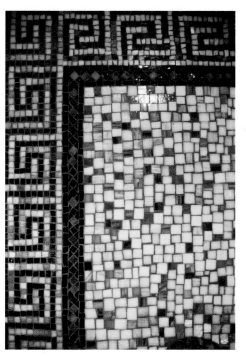

Detail from **Greek Key Table**

uses cannot be nipped into fragments smaller than .25 square inches (.5 square centimeters), this is a sizable project. Such elaborate projects are her passion. "I love the obsession of many, many parts making up a whole."

Detail from **Tapestry/Rug**, kitchen installation

153

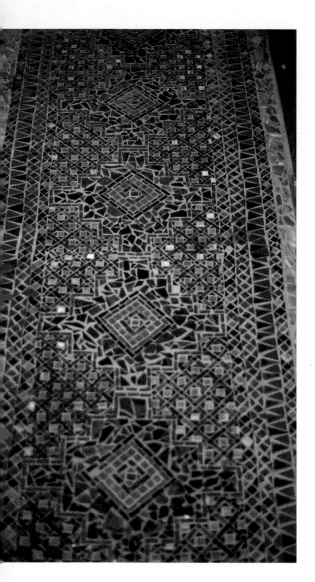

Tapestry/Rug, kitchen installation
glass mosaic
14' x 5' (4.3 m x 1.5 m)

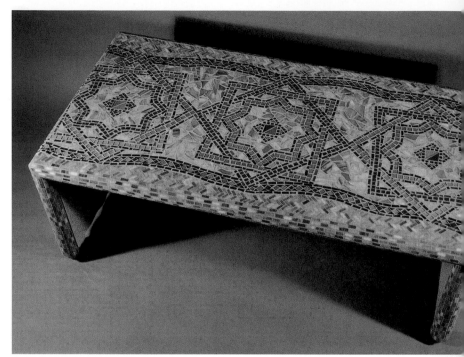

Bench (above)
glass mosaic
7' x 24" x 24" (2.1 meters x 60 cm x 60 cm)

Tapestry/Rug (below)
Radisson Empire Hotel, New York, New York
glass mosaic
16' x 6' (4.9 m x 1.8 m)

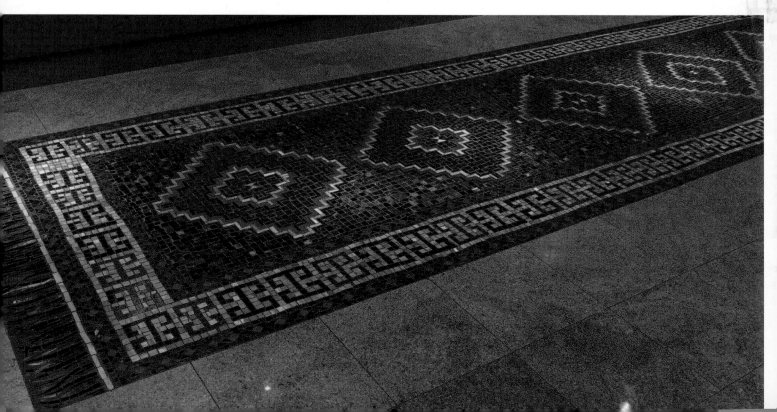

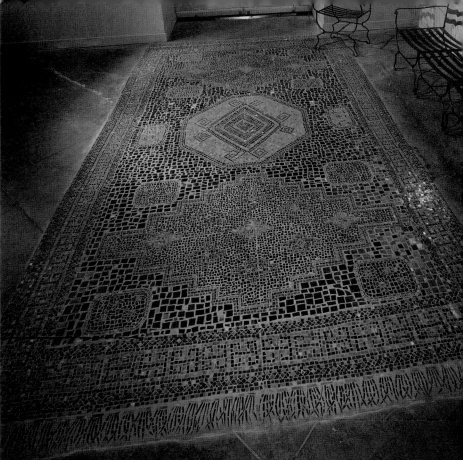

Tapestry/Rug
Cynthia Steffe Showroom, New York, New York
glass mosaic
10' x 6.5' (3 m x 2 m)

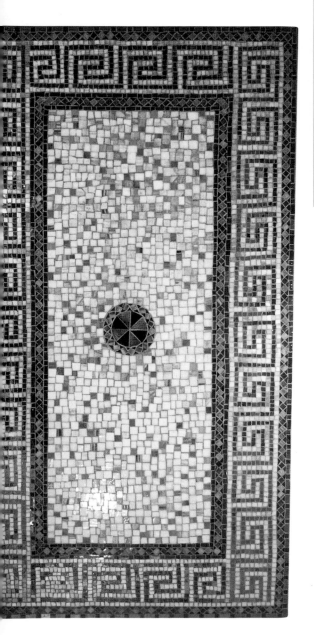

Greek Key Table
glass mosaic
x 5' (2.1 m x 1.5 m)

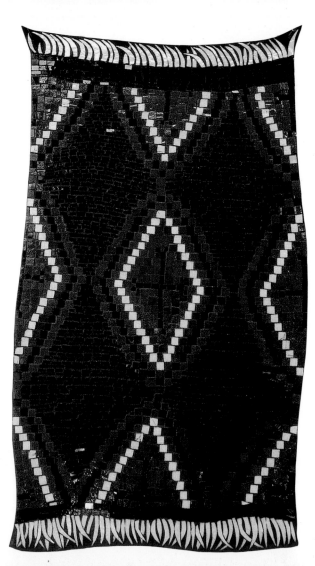

Tapestry, Navajo Rug
glass mosaic
36" x 20" (91 cm x 51 cm)

ELLEN BLAKELEY

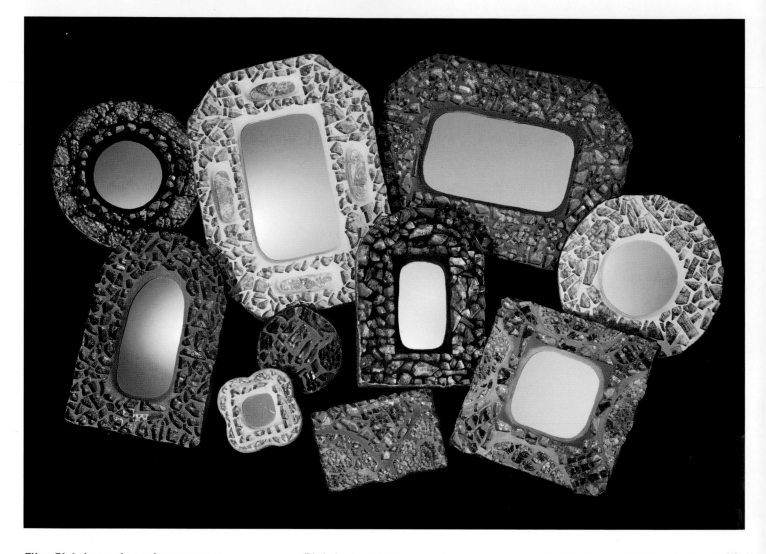

Ellen Blakeley makes urban mosaics using the grit of city life. Forget marble, gemstones, gold and silver smalti, and even ceramics. This San Francisco artist's preferred medium is shattered safety glass salvaged from vandalized bus shelters and store windows. These found raw materials give Blakeley's mosaics a street-smart sensibility.

Blakeley's artistic career has evolved from printmaking and painting to ceramic sculpture and vessels to her current foray into glass mosaics. She studied ceramics under Ron Nagle at Mills College in Oakland, California, for four years, then opened a small tile design business that she ran from 1985 to 1992. Blakeley developed her special glass mosaic technique in 1993, and since then she has found a ready market for a series of picture frames, tabletops, mirrors, and other household items. Her line of goods is being distributed in stores throughout the United States.

Collection of Mirrors
glass and collage, various sizes

Referring to her work as "recycled vandalism," the artist gives glass shards center stage in her projects. She discovered her inventive shattered glass technique about

TECHNIQUE

five years ago, treating broken tempered glass as her *tesserae*. Rather than obliterating the surface below, the glass opens it up as another dimension within each artwork where colors and patterns sparkle.

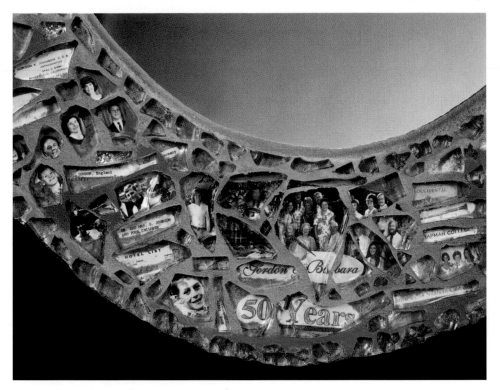

Fragments are the basic mosaic building blocks, but they also act as unobtrusive lenses to view collage images that lie beneath them. Bits of patterned paper, colored foil, drawings, photographs, and printed text are used to create different effects. Because thick pieces of glass often contain webs of internal fractures, the compositions have extraordinary refractive qualities. "The information that goes under the glass, along with the pureness of the glass itself, keeps me endlessly intrigued with the play between surface and depth," she says.

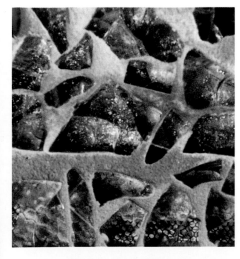

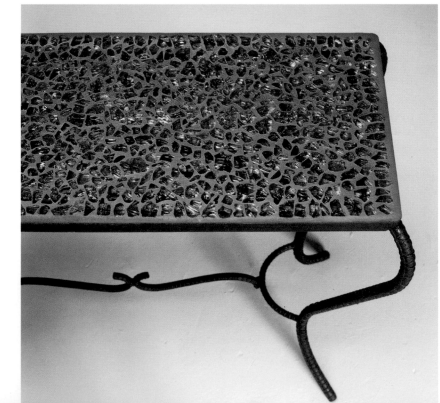

Details from **Rebar Console Table** (above and right)

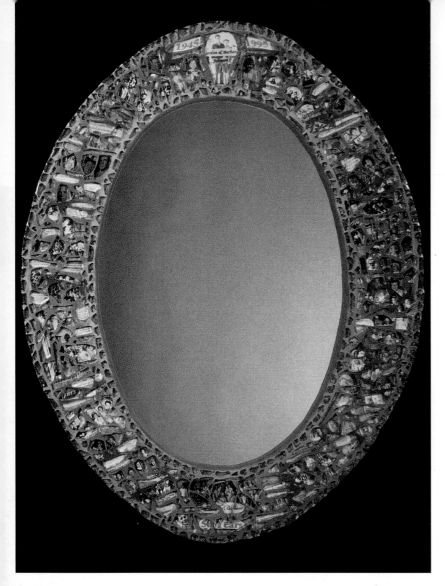

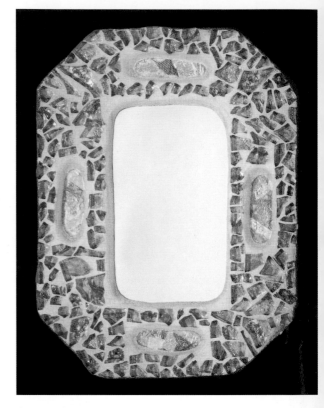

Oval Mirror
glass and collage
36" x 27" x 1" (91 cm x 69 cm x 3 cm)

Octagon Mirror
glass and collage
12" x 8" (30 cm x 20 cm)

Men, Women, and Money
glass and collage
9" x 17" x 1" (23 cm x 43 cm x 3 cm)

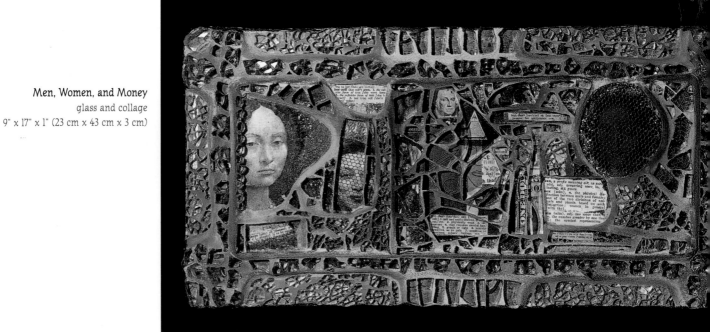

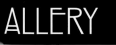

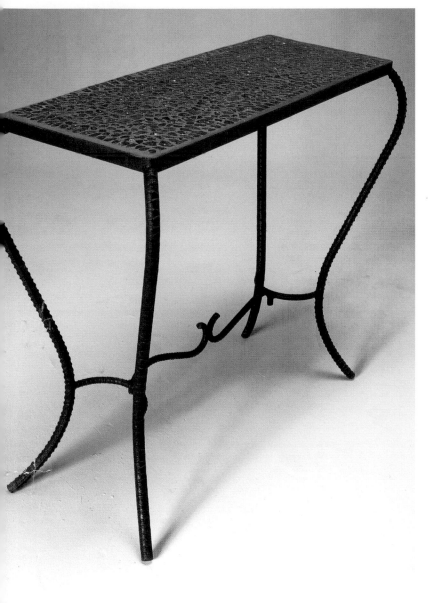

bar Console Table
ass and collage
' x 3.8' (1 meter x 1.1 meters)

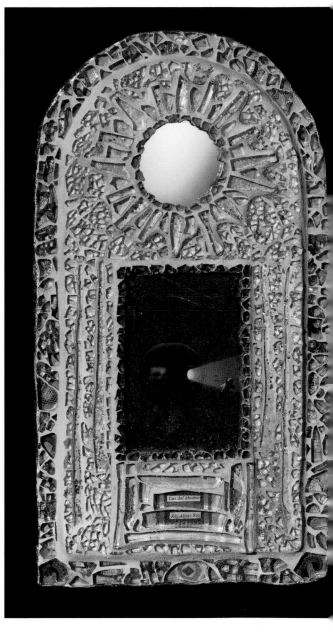

River under the Glass
glass and collage
18" x 10" x 1" (46 cm x 25 cm x 3 cm)

FELICE NITTOLO

Mosaic artist and sculptor of wide renown, Felice Nittolo maintains his studio in Ravenna, Italy, considered by many to be the classic source of traditional mosaics since the fifth and sixth centuries. However, Nittolo is focused on breaking the rules and creating a new tradition.

Nittolo's provocative sculptures are rendered as pyramids, cones, spheres, totems, and pillars. These innovative volumes are vibrantly glazed in Byzantine mosaic—the artist's trademark—highlighting shapes, materials, and colors. His unique viewpoint offers geometric speculation, a visual perception of space executed in terms of light and shadow.

He has taught mosaic art since 1982 at the Istituto Statale d'Arte in Ravenna, where he imparts his perspective on art. "We must transmit our time. Today we have to react to recent academic tradition in order to fit in with the needs of a society that has been changing at a faster and faster pace. We have to force a radical renewal in the very concept of art."

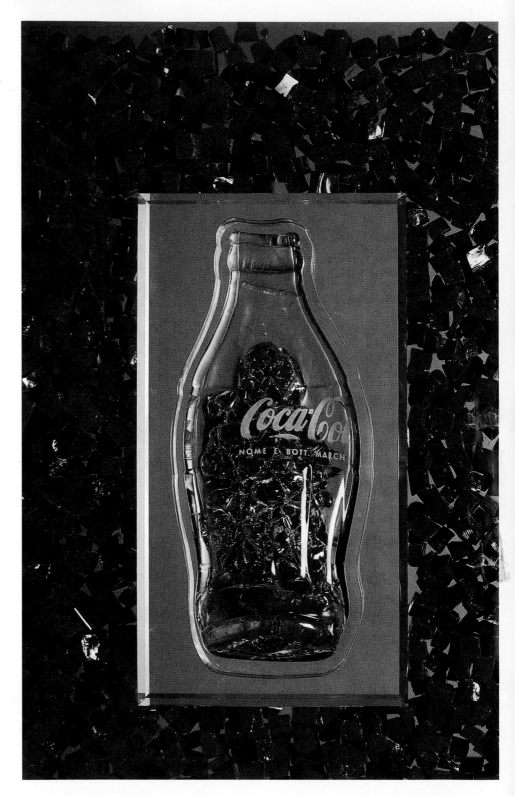

Detail from **Always Mosaic**

New ideas are few and far between in the contemporary art world, according to Felice Nittolo. "Mosaic has aesthetic value of great severity and innovation;

TECHNIQUE

the tesserae—each one of them—are unique. They cannot be replicated," says Nittolo.

True to this belief, the artist often manipulates the interstices between the tesserae in his pieces, sometimes exaggerating empty spaces so that the smalti suggests thin strands of beads lying across an expanse of sand. In other instances, he sets them together so tightly that they appear to be woven like fabric.

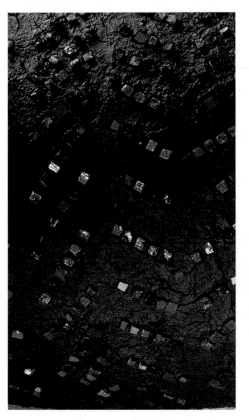

Detail from **Coperton**

These spatial explorations often go a step further and assume three dimensions; by using cardboard, plastic materials, or lightweight acrylic resins for the tile

armature, Nittolo is able to initiate yet another departure from conventional mosaic designs, while making his art very much of his own era. In his own words, "the mosaic *tessera* can do away with the present crisis of ideas since it

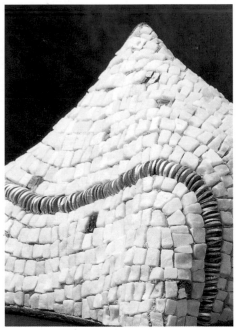

Detail from **Baco da Seta**

is . . . a tradition anew. Mosaic has aesthetic and artistic values of great severity and innovation; the *tesserae* are, each one of them, unique."

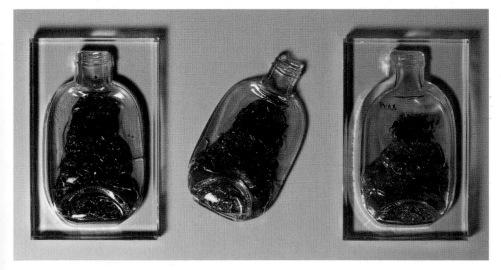

Detail from **Always Mosaic**

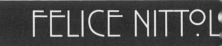

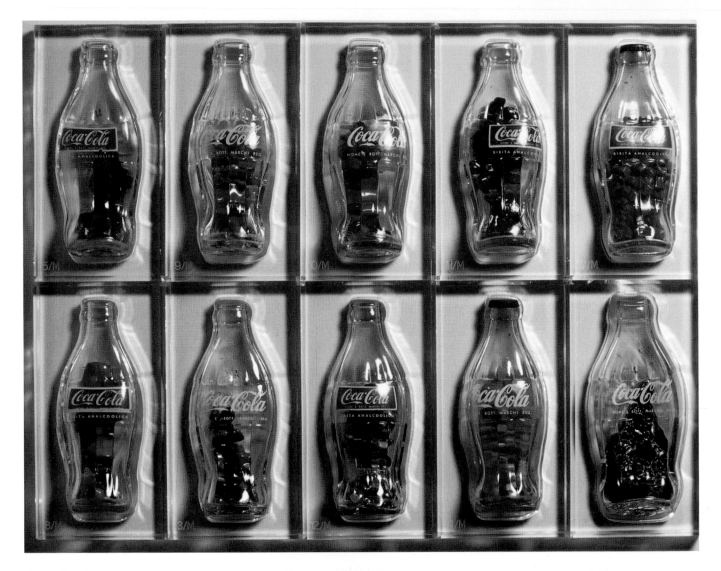

Always Mosaic
glass mosaic and glass
29" x 19" (73 cm x 48 cm)

Baco da Seta
glass mosaic and marble
17" x 7" x 7" (45 cm x 18 cm x 18 cm)

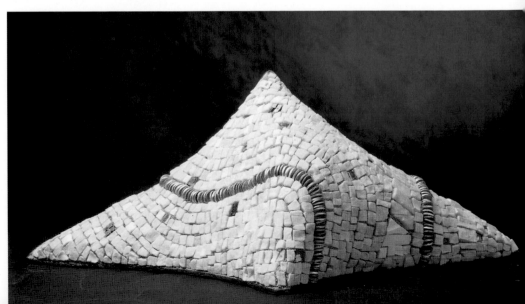

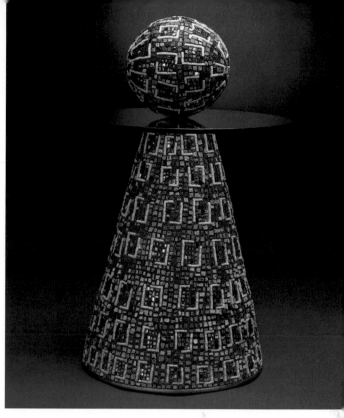

Coperton (below)
glass mosaic, gold, marble, and tar
19" x 16" x 10" (48 cm x 44 cm x 26 cm)

Omino (above)
glass mosaic, glass, marble, and mirror
35" x 23" diameter (89 cm x 57 cm diameter)

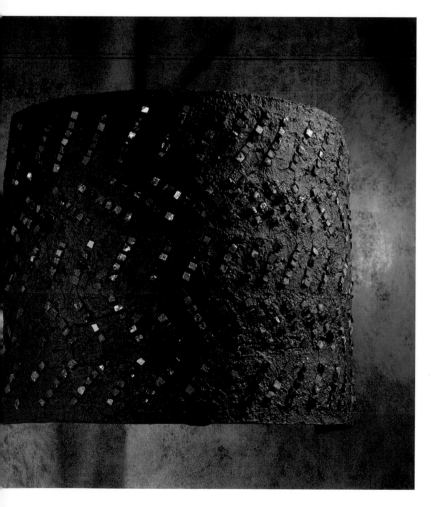

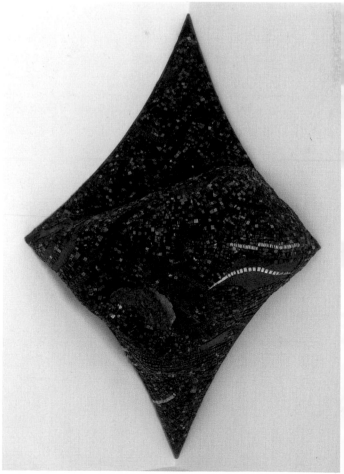

Bozzolo
glass mosaic, marble, and metal
4.8' x 24" x 24" (1.4 m x 60 cm x 60 cm)

Sella d'Argento
miope, silver, aluminum, and glass
12" x 6" x 5" (30 cm x 15 cm x 13 cm)

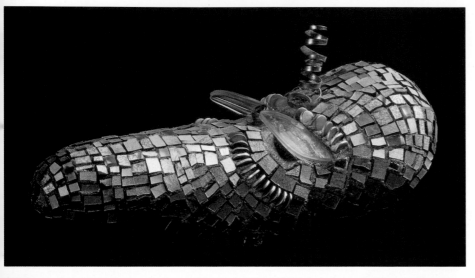

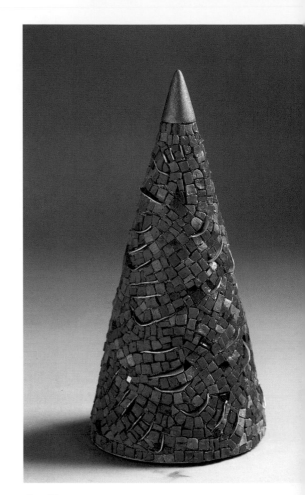

Cono Blu
glass mosaic, lead, and ceramic
7" diameter x 15" (18 cm diameter x 37 cm)

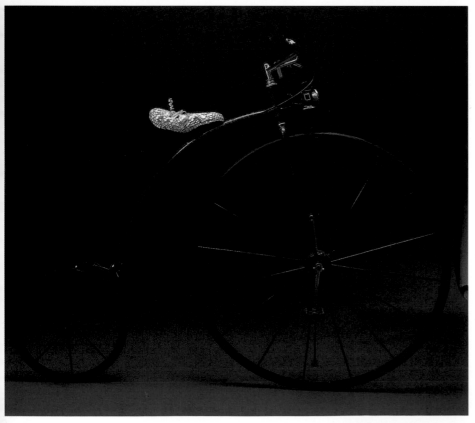

Biciclo con Sella (above)
miope, silver, aluminum, glass, and velocipede

Sfera Rosa
glass mosaic
11" diameter (28 cm diameter)

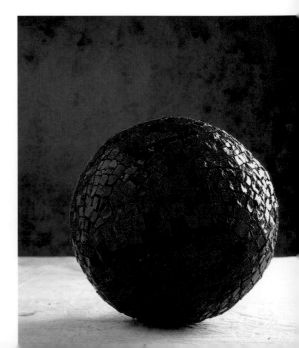

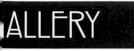
Sfera Nera
glass mosaic, marble, and gold
11" diameter (28 cm diameter)

Installazione
glass mosaic, wood, and steel
6.5' x 3.3' x 20" (2 m x 1 m x 50 cm)

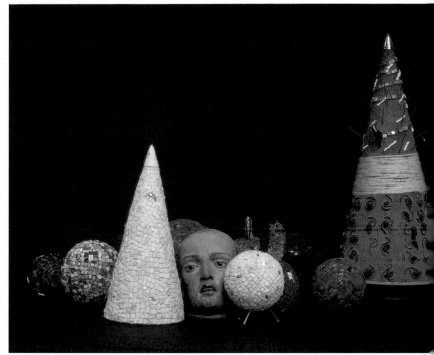

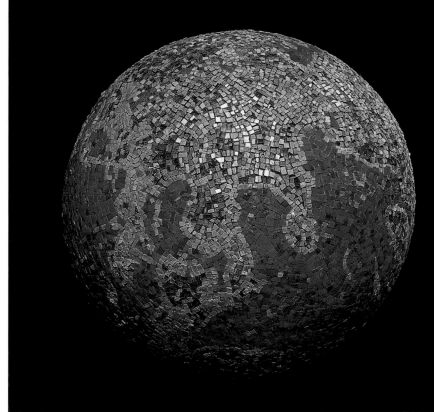

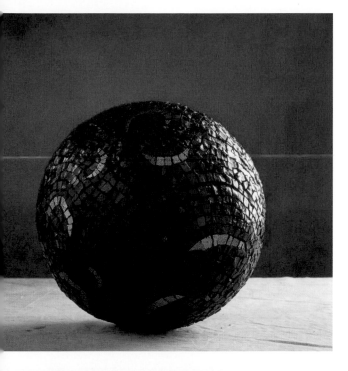

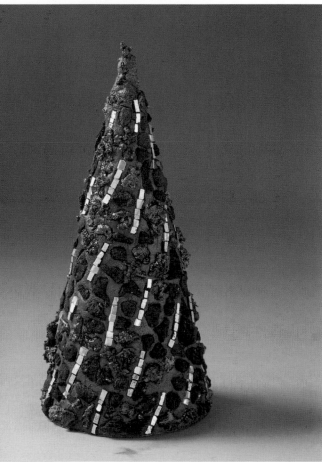

Cono Nero
glass mosaic, marble, coal, and lava
7" diameter x 15" (18 cm diameter x 37 cm)

Il Mondo
glass mosaic, marble, yellow terra cotta, and gold
34" diameter (85 cm diameter)

LUCIO ORSONI

Born in 1939, Venice artist Lucio Orsoni studied art in Venice, presented his works at numerous exhibitions, and then concentrated strictly on mosaics for the Angelo Orsoni family factory. For more than thirty years, in addition to his creative work, Orsoni has been deeply involved in the supply side of art. He has been producing *smalti e ori per mosaico* for the family business, which is one of the few remaining smalti manufacturers in the world.

With their saturated colors and deliberate, skillful shading, Orsoni's smalti mosaics echo the techniques and objectives of classical artistic precedent. His work then takes leave of that figurative tradition, with its exacting, ordered geometry. His compositions are similar to labyrinth tracings, and have been likened in appearance to computer microchips.

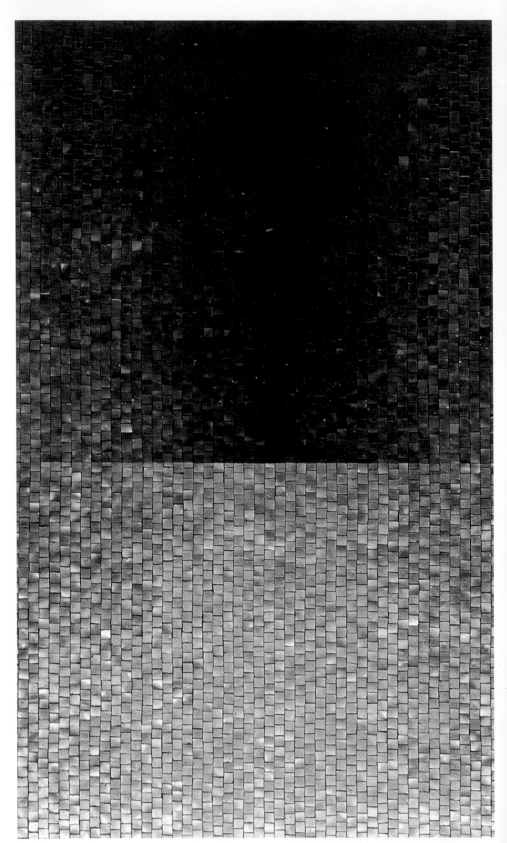

Detail from **Oro Ramino**

Among the most visually engaging of Orsoni's monochromatic studies are his gold-tinted pieces. The artist pairs black tesserae with a particular hue of gold—

TECHNIQUE

blue gold, grey gold, violet gold, or white gold—in a basic checkerboard pattern to create fields of graduated color that are literally vibrant. As the shapes formed by the smalti optically recede into, and grow out of, the plane of the image, a hypnotic visual effect takes place. A few of these installations

Detail from **As a Compliment to Constable**

are large; one piece, *Palazzo Ferro Fini*, measures 5.3 feet by 7.8 feet (1.6 meters by 2.4 meters) and was constructed in sections.

Disturbed by the decline of mosaic artistry over the centuries, Orsoni found little inspiration from most historical works. He now sees that the rebirth of

Detail from **Bianco E Oro**

mosaics as a fine art has come about at last, and he is grateful to those artists who have begun to create them again: ". . . thanks to the works of those artists who have begun again, and who continue, to think mosaic."

Detail from **Blue and Copper Gold**

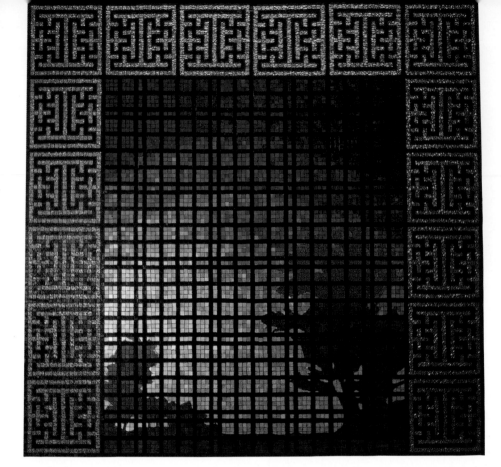

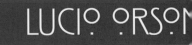

As a Compliment to Constable
Venetian glass smalti
4' x 4' (1.2 m x 1.2 m)

**Mane Nobiscum Domine Quia Vesperascit,
3 panels**
Venetian glass smalti
4' x 4' (1.2 m x 1.2 m) each

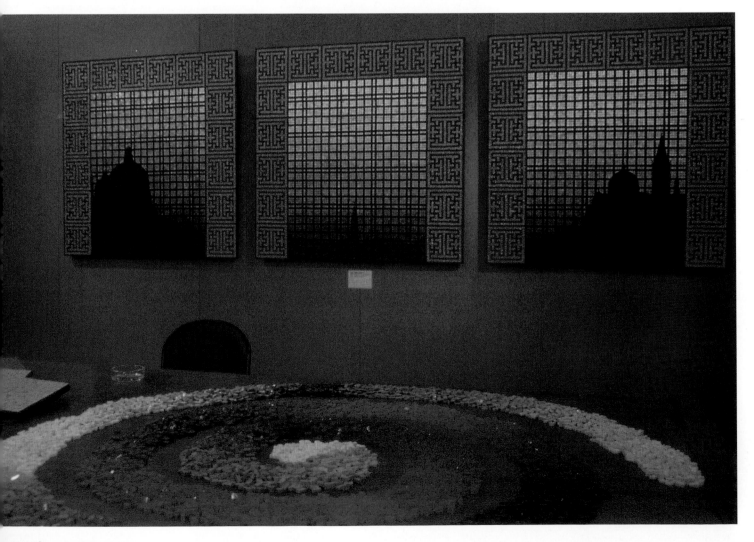

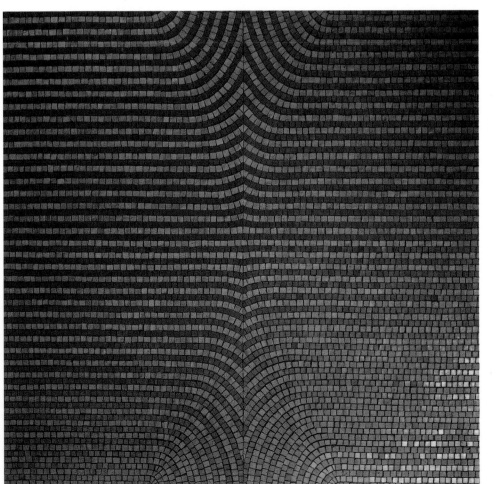

Oro Ramino
Venetian glass smalti
3.3' x 3.3' (1 m x 1 m)

Bianco E Oro
35th Biennale 1970
Venetian glass smalti
3.3' x 3.3' (1 m x 1 m)

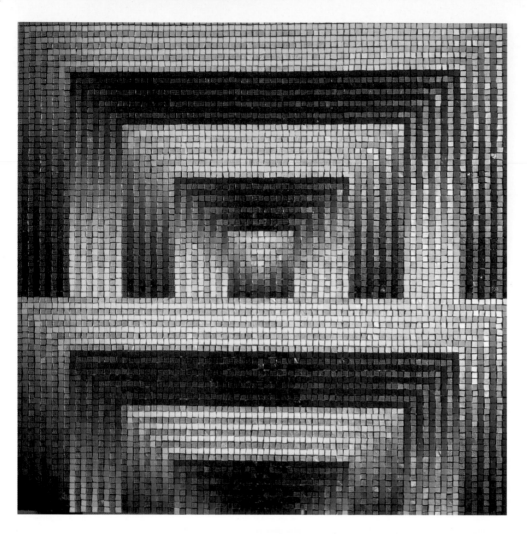

Blue and Copper Gold
Venetian glass smalti
20" x 20" (50 cm x 50 cm)

Black and Copper
Venetian glass sᵣ
35" x 35" (89 cm x 89

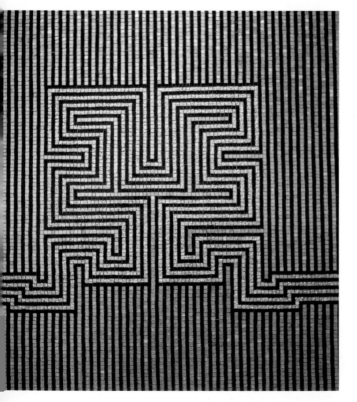

Black and White Gold
Venetian glass smalti
3.6' x 3.6' (1.1 m x 1.1 m)

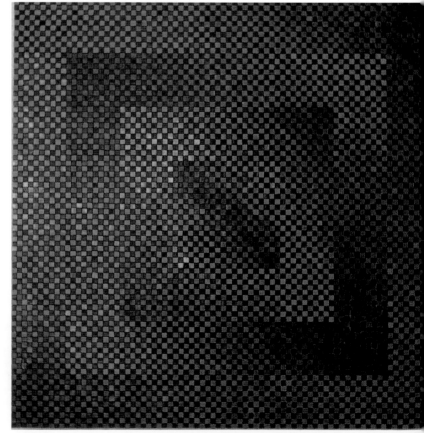

ze Gold
ian glass smalti
3.3' (1 m x 1 m)

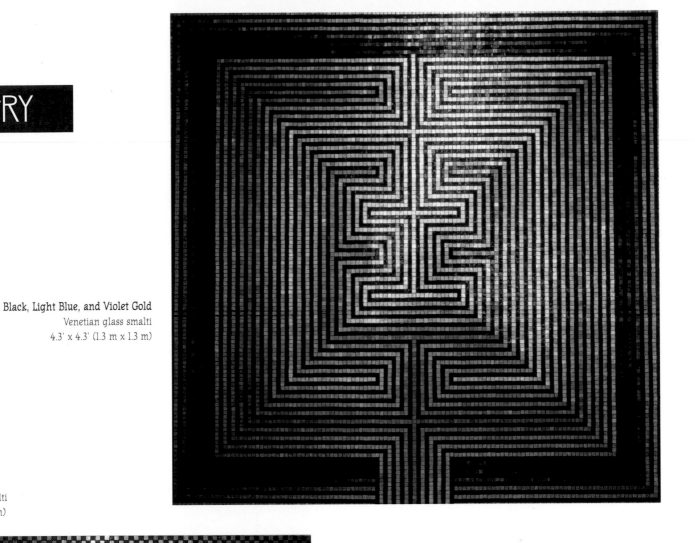

Black, Light Blue, and Violet Gold
Venetian glass smalti
4.3' x 4.3' (1.3 m x 1.3 m)

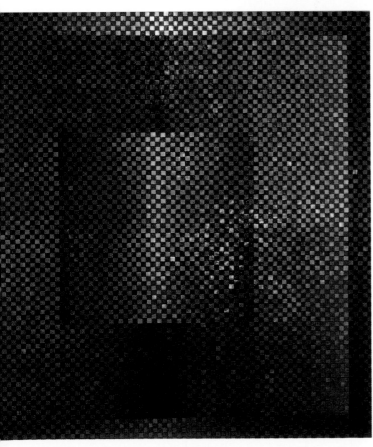

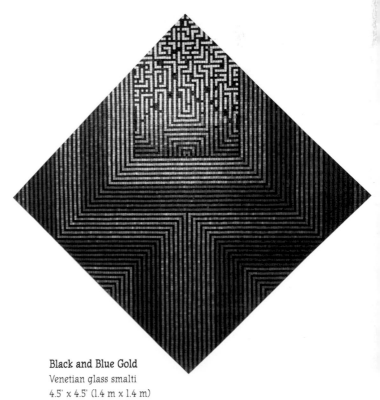

Black and Blue Gold
Venetian glass smalti
4.5' x 4.5' (1.4 m x 1.4 m)

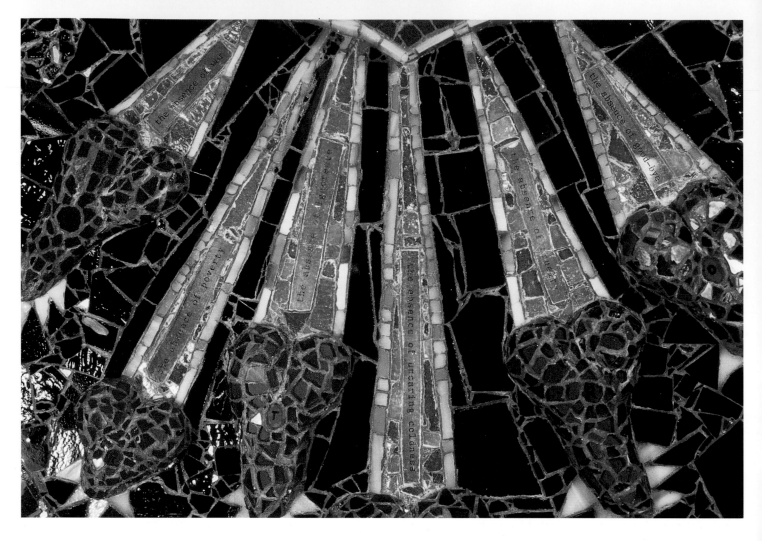

Diana Maria Rossi's glass mosaics create an emotional impact rarely experienced in this medium due to the social content of her work. As she explores thought-provoking themes such as the pain and dislocation of immigrants and home and homelessness, she creates vivid, iconographic images. For the last decade, Rossi has been making mosaics that unite her formal training in printmaking at the San Francisco Art Institute with her affinity for vivid colors and Italian-Polish-American heritage.

Her fascination with many of her subjects is likely due to the environment in which she was raised—Catholic churches and Italian-American living rooms. "Many of my sensibilities were cultivated in these places—ornate sanctuaries of rococo embellishment," she says. Quite a few of her mosaic portraits have been singled out for the substance they give to all kinds of faces, from peasant to prom queen.

Detail from **A Rebuttal for My Critics
(with Aunt Bea Watching)**

Portraits, hearts, and landscapes are the basic images Diana Maria Rossi utilizes, and her social consciousness and meaningful themes are expressed through mosaics.

Rossi has developed a technique that supports her vision. In her direct method of mosaic design, the *tesserae* are laid into mortar and then grouted, a process that joins glass chips of various thicknesses together into a highly faceted, reflective surface. "This technique allows

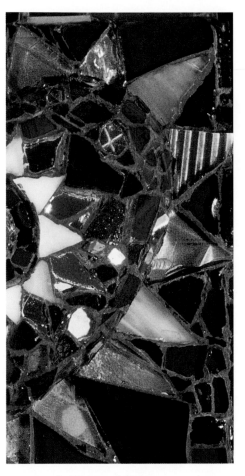

Detail from **Immigration 3: Donato**

me to pull out all the stops," states the artist, "to revel in the glittery, jewel-like nature of glass, to explore my idea of beauty. By working in this manner, I hope to show respect for the aesthetic qualities which comprise my cultural heritage." Of her portraits, Rossi says, "I want to make explicit the beauty in every face, the saint in each of us." She has also made hundreds of mosaic hearts in an attempt to give substance to a symbol that is often trivialized and cast aside as a cliché.

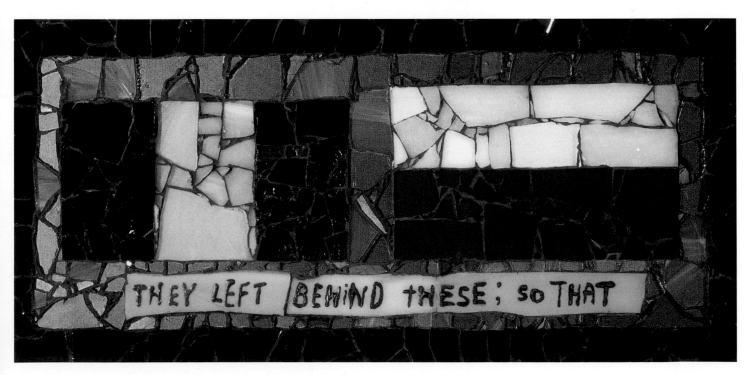

Details from **For My Grandparents: Assunta, Donata, Eva, and Jacob**

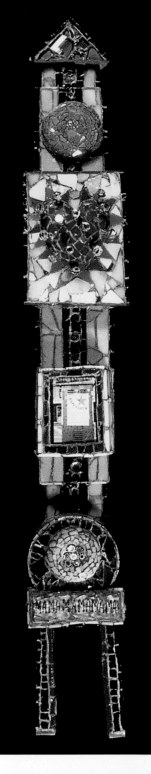

Modern Motherhood
glass mosaic on wood with nails and photographs
2.5" x 17" x 1.5" (6 cm x 43 cm x 4 cm)

**A Rebuttal for My Critics
(with Aunt Bea Watching)**
glass mosaic on wood
15.5" x 16.75" x .75" (39 cm x 42 cm x 2 cm)

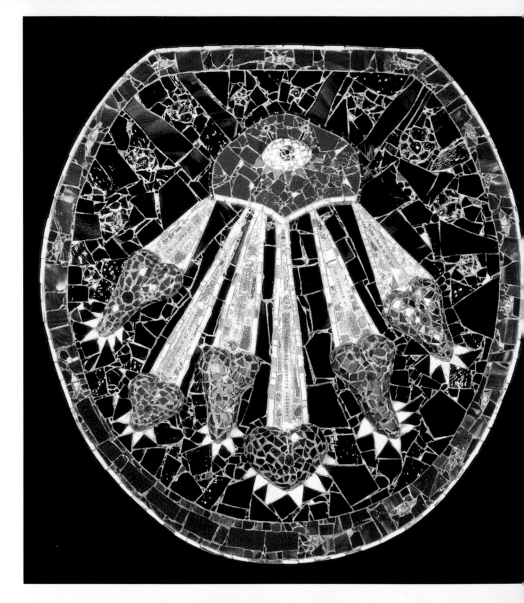

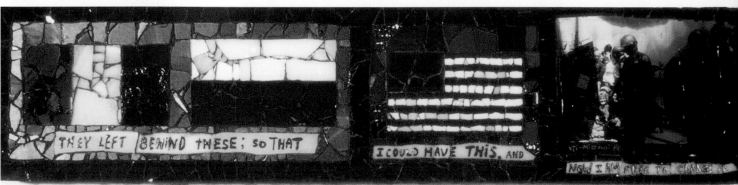

THEY LEFT BEHIND THESE; SO THAT

I COULD HAVE THIS, AND

NOW I AM FREE TO CHANGE

For My Grandparents: Assunta, Donata, Eva, and J
glass mosaic on wood with photogr
24" x 5.5" x .75" (60 cm x 14 cm x 2

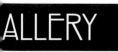

Immigration 3: Donato
glass mosaic on wood with photograph
4.25" x 5.5" x 1.5" (10 cm x 14 cm x 4 cm)

Angela di Cortile Cascino
glass mosaic on wood
12" x 12.75" x .75" (30 cm x 31 cm x 2 cm)

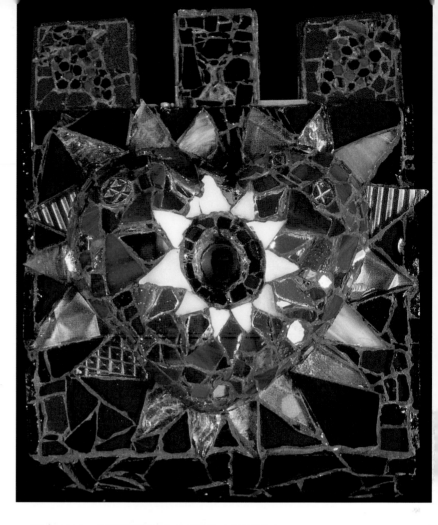

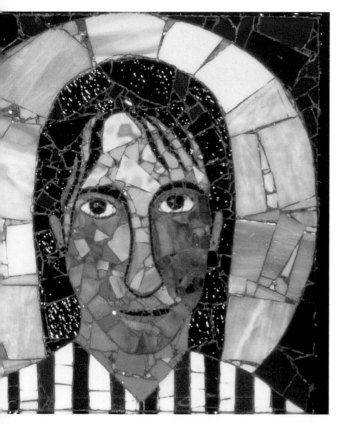

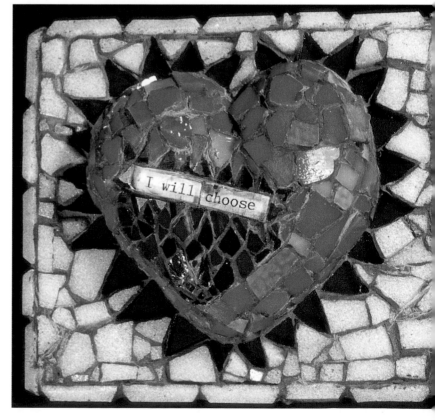

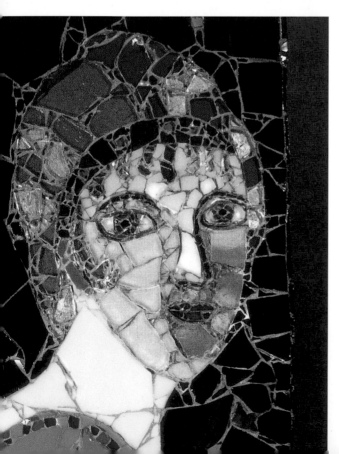

I will choose

Flavia
glass mosaic on wood
4.75" x 7.5" x .75" (12 cm x 19 cm x 2 cm)

To Be Female and Free
glass mosaic on wood
4.25" x 3.75" x 1.5" (10 cm x 9 cm x 4 cm)

175

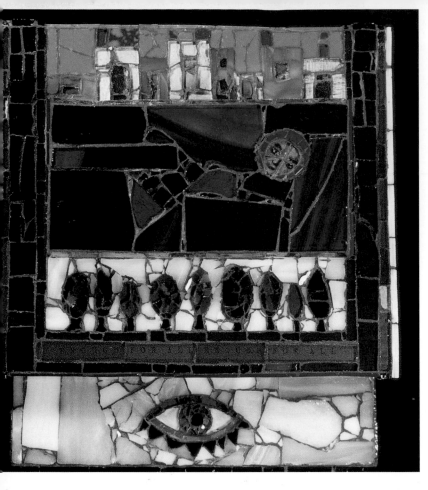

Lost Between the Present and the Past Imagining the Future
glass mosaic on wood with paint
7" x 9" x 5" (18 cm x 23 cm x 13 cm)

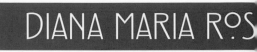

DIANA MARIA ROS

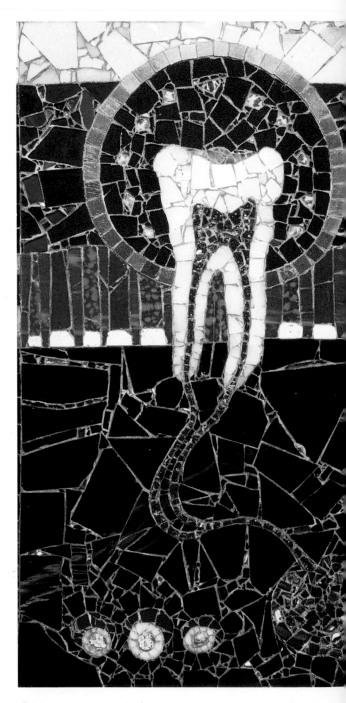

Destiny Takes Us to Strange Places (for
glass mosaic on
10.5" x 18" x .75" (27 cm x 46 cm x

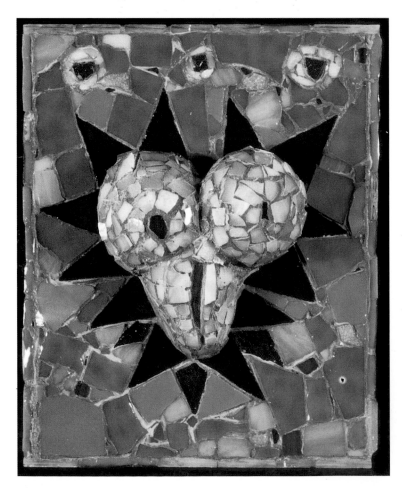

Delicious Bodies
glass mosaic on wood
4.75" x 5.75" x 1" (12 cm x 14 cm x 3 cm)

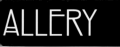

Truth
glass mosaic on wood
5.25" x 6" x 1.5" (13 cm x 15 cm x 4 cm)

Marcella
glass mosaic on wood
5.5" x 7" x .75" (14 cm x 18 cm x 2 cm)

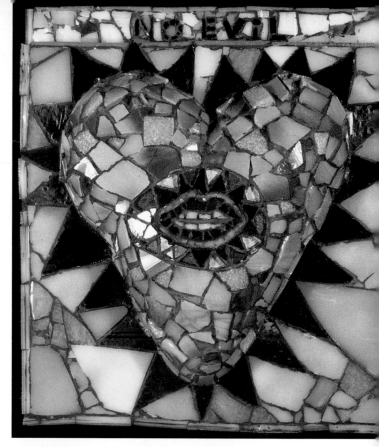

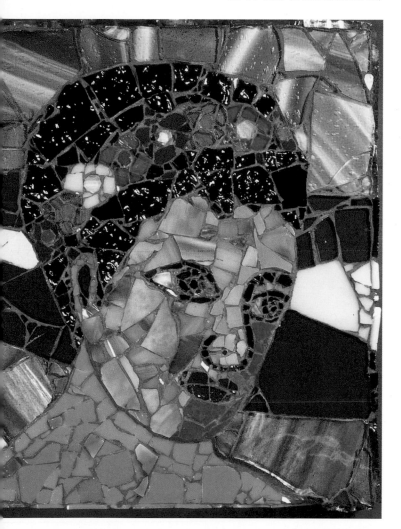

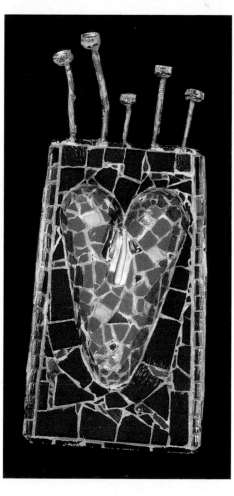

It's a Hard Full Life
glass mosaic on wood
with nails
3.5" x 6" x 1.5"
(9 cm x 15 cm x 4 cm)

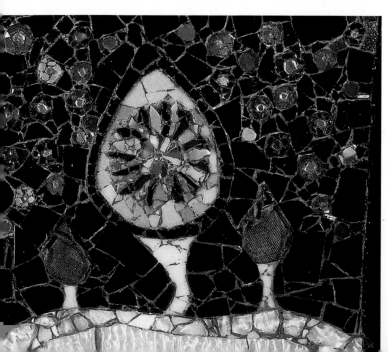

Starry Night (Thanks Vincent)
glass mosaic on wood
5.5" x 5.5" x .75" (14 cm x 14 cm x 2 cm)

177

The core of the turn-of-the-century Art Nouveau movement was a passion for decorative motifs; flowing patterns and stylized forms were to be found in architecture and the arts throughout Europe. Austrian painter Gustav Klimt produced mosaics in this style and took the medium to a new level through his murals. Architect/artist Antonio Gaudi, who had sheathed many of his fanciful structures in glazed ceramics, can also be credited for validating the medium.

Contemporaries, both Klimt and Gaudi set the stage for experiments in tactility and innovations in materials that the artists featured here all continue today.

Robert Stout and Stephanie Jurs, Joseph Blue Sky and Donna Webb, Gloria Kosco, Beryl Solla, and Gary Stephens have moved beyond the Art Nouveau style, yet their patterns are often stylized in flowing form. While their works are quite varied, these artists represent the latest thinking in ceramic mosaics. Like Gaudi, their works transcend the two-dimensionality of historic mosaics and pave the way for cutting-edge ventures into tactility.

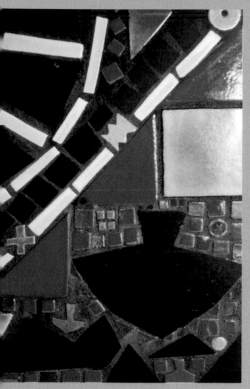

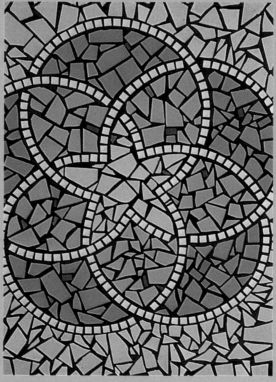

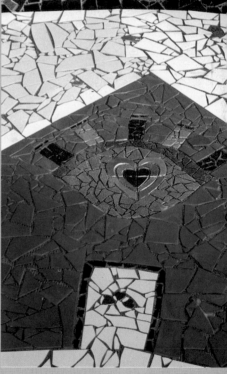

KOSCO
rom
Bathroom Installation

ROBERT STOUT AND STEPHANIE JURS
Detail from
The Pathway I

BERYL SOLLA
Detail from
Home of the Brave II, small fountain

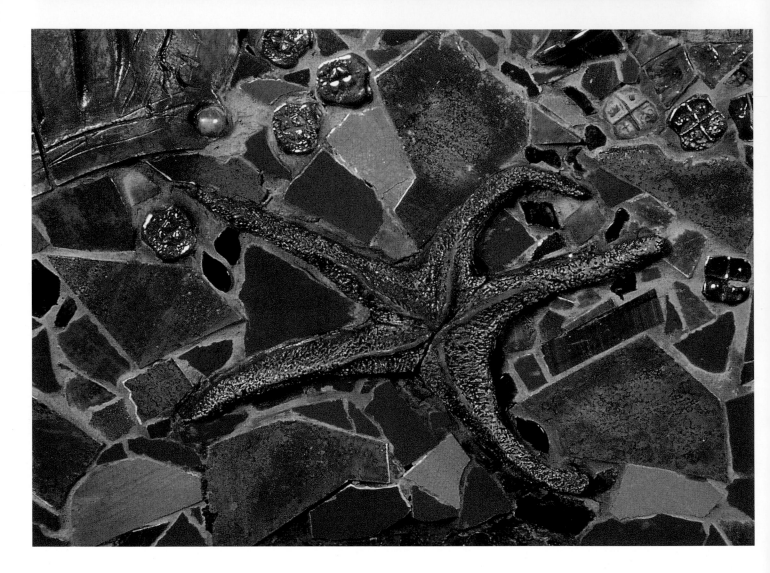

The art of Joseph Blue Sky and Donna Webb deals with the relationship of architecture to figures and other objects and the way they all combine to tell a story without words. Partners, they work together as one—each contributes their disparate talents to create a unified whole. Blue Sky is the model crafter and carpenter, while Webb brings a lively sense of color and a sure hand at the potter's wheel and kiln. Thus, their collaboration becomes synergistic.

In their installation for the University of Akron School of Art, a revealing collection of figures stylized in various ceramic arts applications emerges from the picture's plane. Blue Sky and Webb incorporate ancient pottery forms, classical statuary, formal portrait busts, and modern figurative sculpture into the mural. These elements are modeled in extreme relief and posed next to a towering kiln in this engrossing chronicle of the eras and styles of art history.

Detail from **King Triton and the Little Mermaid**, mural in collaboration with **Group See**

Bringing a well-rounded aesthetic to their mosaic projects, Joseph Blue Sky and Donna Webb claim, "We are not minimalists but more like maximalists,

TECHNIQUE

in that color, sculptural form, composition, function, and storytelling contribute meaning to our work."

The pair strives to equally develop a pictorial sense as well as a rich and varied surface treatment—narrative and dimension are among their prime concerns. "We like to explore the middle ground between painting and sculpture that tile occupies," they explain.

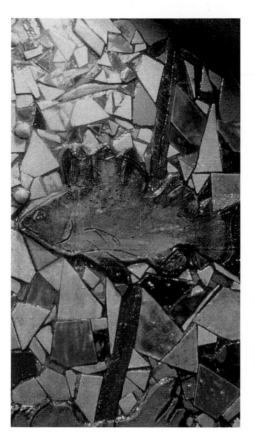

Detail from **Magic Fountain**

Historically, tile integrates easily with architecture. "It achieves a tactile materiality not possible with canvas painting,

yet it also allows exploration of color and composition. This combination suits our talents and our special kind of storytelling"—much, they feel, like Gaudi, Tiffany, and Michelangelo did before them in decorating walls, ceilings, and floors of churches and

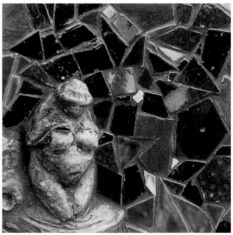

Detail from **Ceramic Mural**

public buildings. "In doing our work we take the roles of 'The Makers.' These characters are from a story we wrote about an old man and an old woman who are constantly renewing the world . . . . We believe that making art is a way of making ourselves and our world, and of defining our culture for future generations."

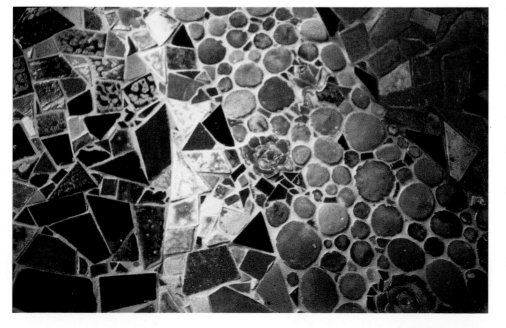

Detail from **Four Seasons Floor**

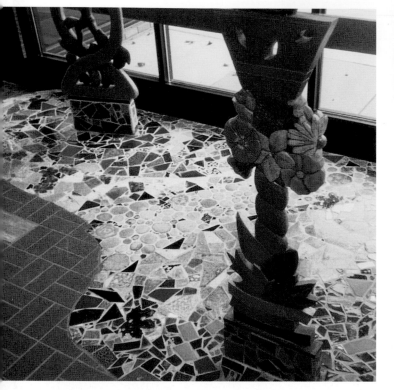

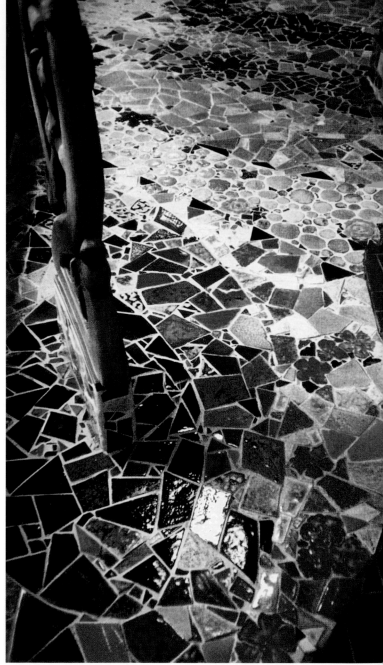

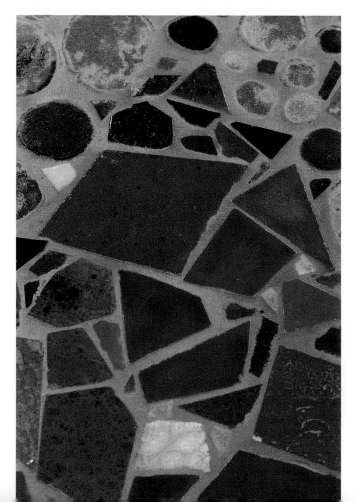

Details from **Four Seasons Floor**
Central Ohio Psychiatric Hospital
ceramic with wood sculpture by Charlotte Lees

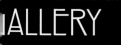

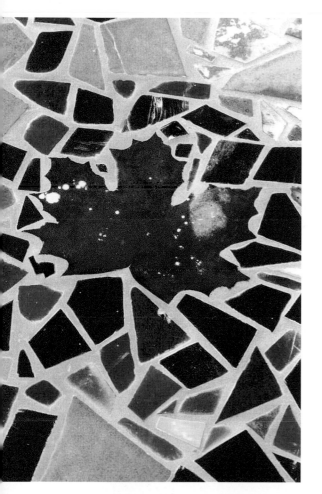

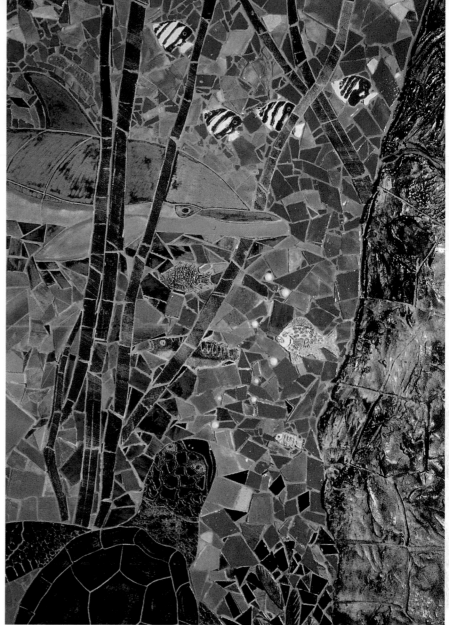

King Triton and the Little Mermaid,
mural in collaboration with Group See
(above) *Children's Hospital, Akron, Ohio*
ceramic
24' x 8' (7.3 m x 2.4 m)

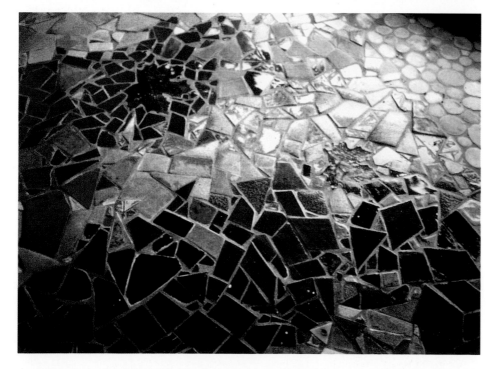

Details from **Four Seasons Floor**
(left and above left)
Central Ohio Psychiatric Hospital

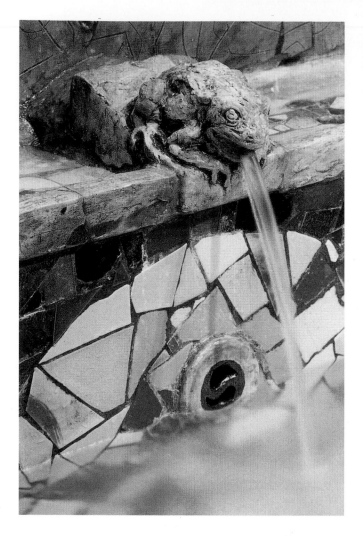

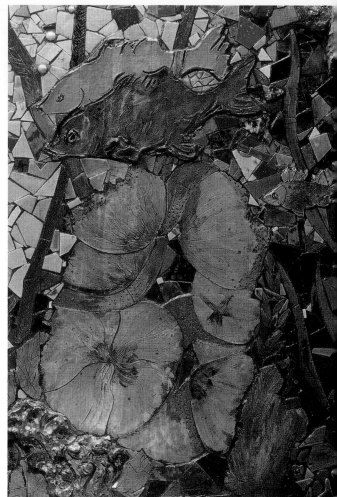

Details from **Magic Fountain**
*The Tree House, a children's room at
the Metro Health Center, Cleveland, Ohio*
ceramic

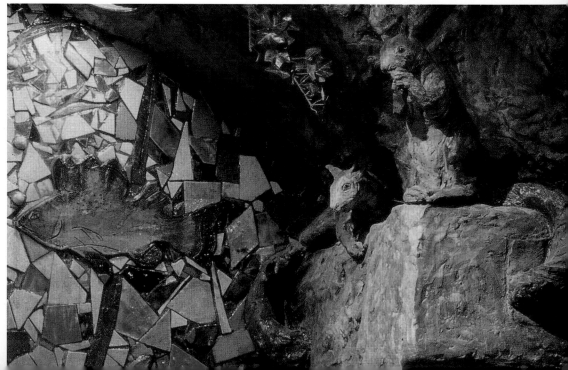

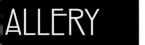

Ceramic Mural
School of Art, University of Akron, Ohio
ceramic
12' x 12' (3.7 m x 3.7 m)

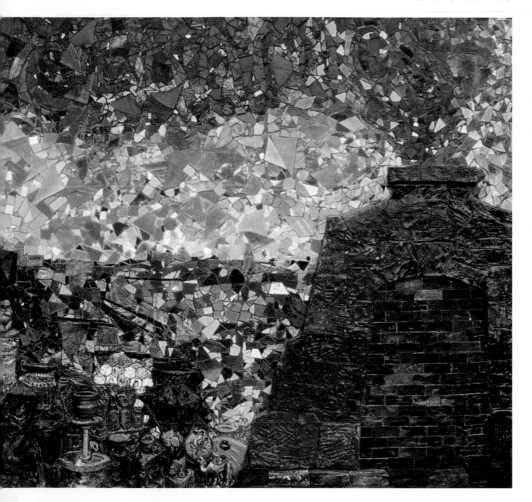

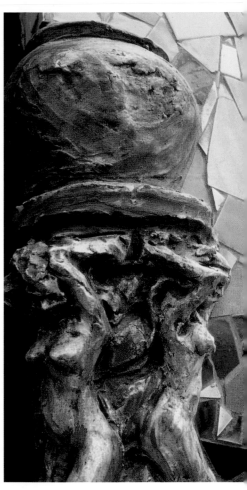

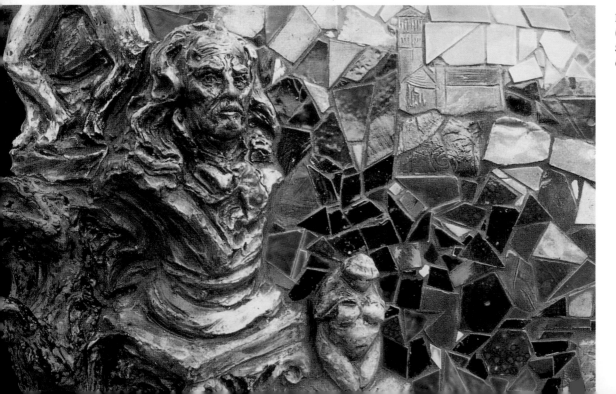

Details from **Ceramic Mural**
(above and left)
School of Art, University of Akron, Ohio
ceramic

185

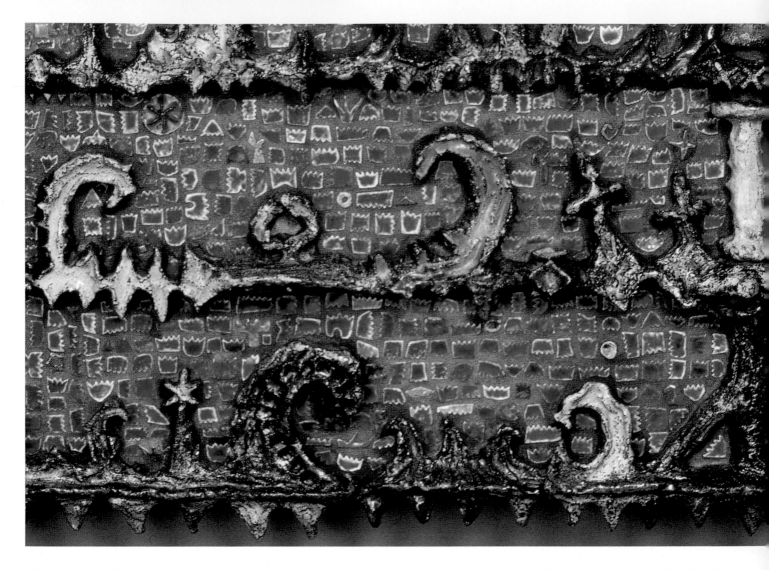

Gloria Kosco holds degrees in ceramics from the Rhode Island School of Design and the School for American Crafts at the Rochester Institute of Technology. For nine years, she worked with Mimi Strang under the umbrella of Decoratta Ornamental Terra Cotta, a collaborative artists' studio where the two investigated the relationships between ornament and architecture, often within the rigorous confines of municipal Percent-for-Art competitions and commissions. Now on her own, Kosco explores the nature of time, a favorite theme of her public works.

Although most of the visual vocabulary that appears in her public installations is re-examined in her fine arts pieces, the latter group tells a more personal story. Densely tiled with diminutive images of stars, flames, water, and wheels—sometimes cast as compasses or other forms that function as allegories for time—Kosco creates art with primitive overtones and universal appeal.

Detail from **Undercurren**

In constructing her site-specific sundials, Gloria Kosco first surveys the location, observing the interaction of light and landscape elements. Then she sets the

TECHNIQUE

center point of the circle and determines the true north heading. Generally, the artist excavates a dozen shallow forms or cavities around the circle's perimeter, making an adobe mixture from the earth.

With this mud, she builds the sundial's central gnomon and its four cardinal points. Placing the adobe mixture back into the shallow cavities, Kosco then inlays colorful bits of glazed terra cotta into the surface to complete the project. The result is twelve plaques—the adobe mixture with inlaid pieces of terra cotta—that punctuate the circle. In each of these works, the earth serves triple duty—form, molded material, and fired material—infusing symbolic and structural strength into her sundials.

"My imagery parallels my interests," says Kosco. "I am influenced by things I like, things I read about, recollections of my past, questionable occurrences, perplexing events, things that impress me, and things I know."

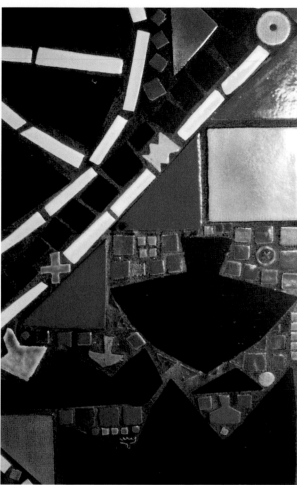

Detail from **Private Bathroom Installation**

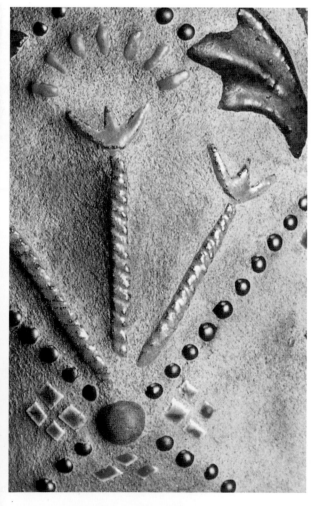

Detail from **Relative Degree of Plentifulness**

187

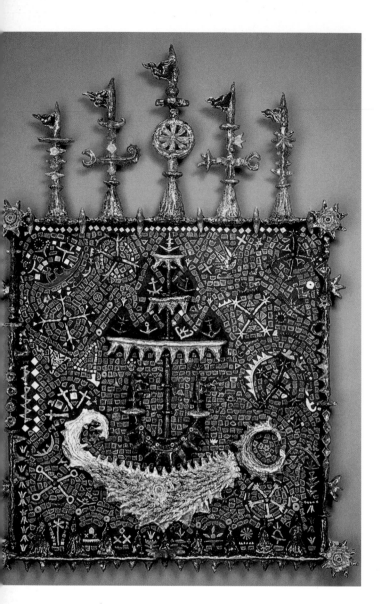

Voyage from the Temporal, III
ceramic and masonry
5.3' x 35" x 3" (1.6 m x 89 cm x 8 cm)

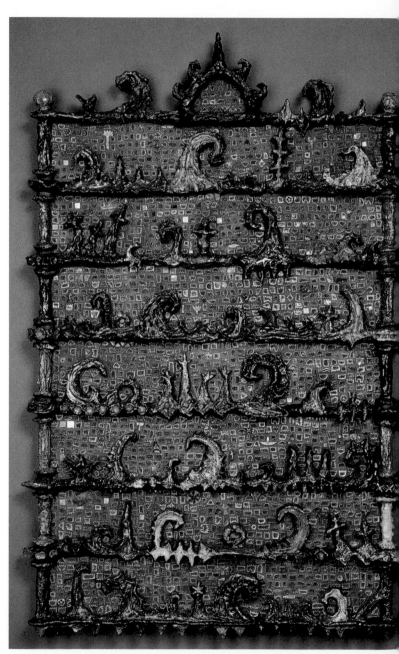

Undercur
ceramic and ma
5.3' x 33
(1.6 m x 84 cm x

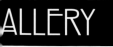

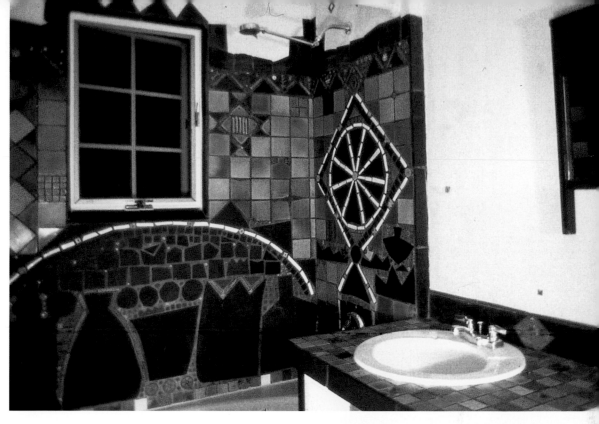

Private Bathroom Installation, a
collaboration with Mimi Strang
ceramic, slate, and masonry

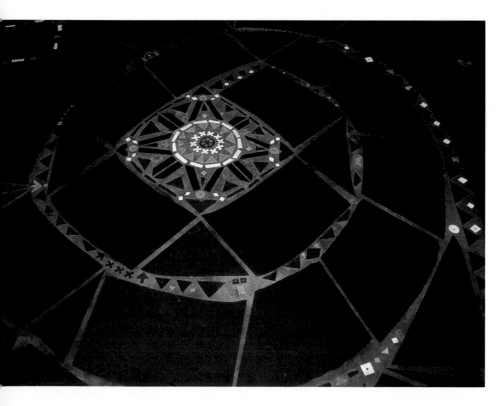

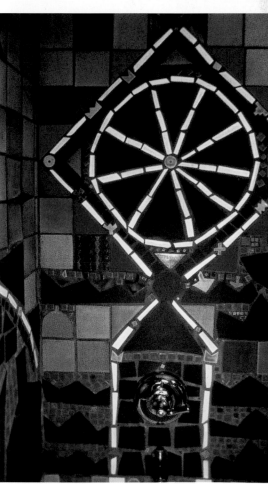

Private Kitchen Floor Installation,
a collaboration with Mimi Strang
ceramic, slate, and masonry

189

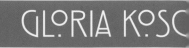

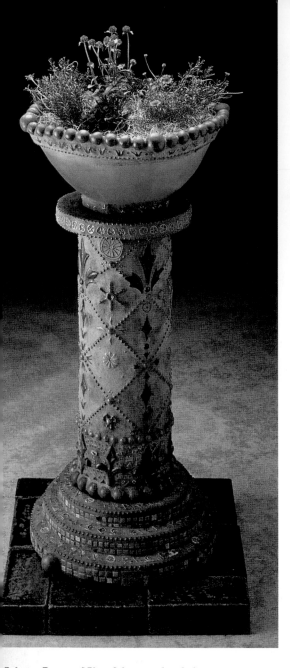

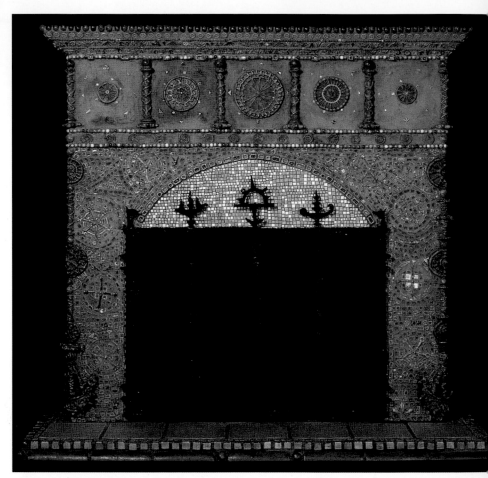

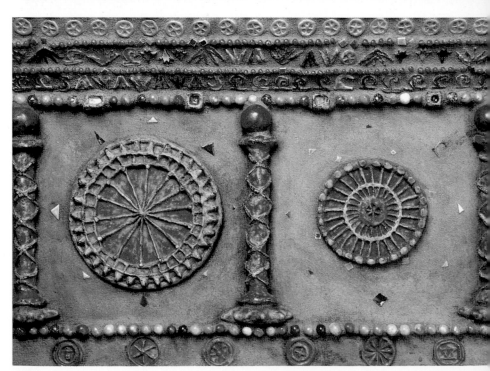

Relative Degree of Plentifulness, pedestal planter,
a collaboration with Mimi Strang
ceramic and masonry, thrown and hand-built
3.5' x 16" x 16" (1.1 m x 41 cm x 41 cm)

Time IV, Fireplace 2
(above right, detail at right)
ceramic and masonry
4.8' x 5.3' x 16" (1.4 m x 1.6 m x 41 cm)
fireplace doors, cast iron and tempered glass
28" x 36" x 1" (71 cm x 91 cm x 3 cm)

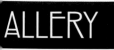

Sundial '92, a collaboration with Mimi Strang
(below, details at right)
Cedar Beach Park, Allentown, Pennsylvania
ceramic and masonry, 35' diameter (10.7 m diameter)
central gnomon, 6' high (1.8 m high), surrounded by
an inner ring of spherical time markers
and an outer ring of twelve 36" (91 cm) plaques

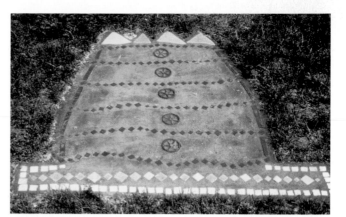

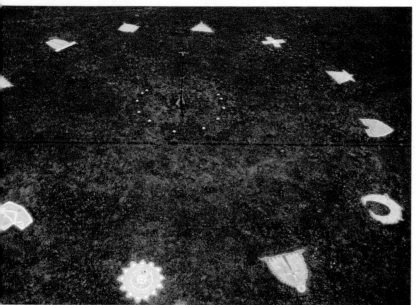

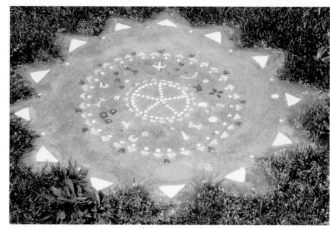

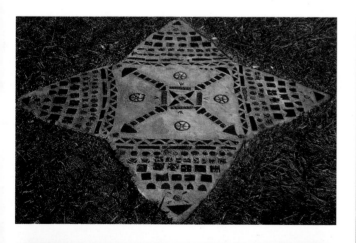

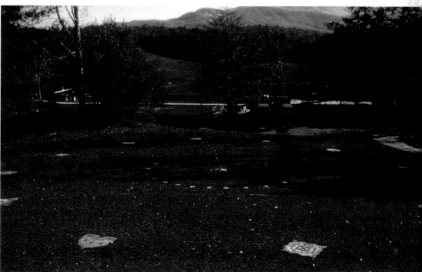

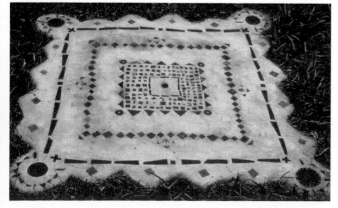

Penland Sundial, a collaboration with Mimi Strang and 20 students
(above, details at left)
Penland School of Crafts, Penland, North Carolina
terra cotta clay and modified concrete
40" diameter (12.2 m diameter)
arch-shaped time markers, 12" x 5" (30 cm x 13 cm) each

BERYL SOLLA

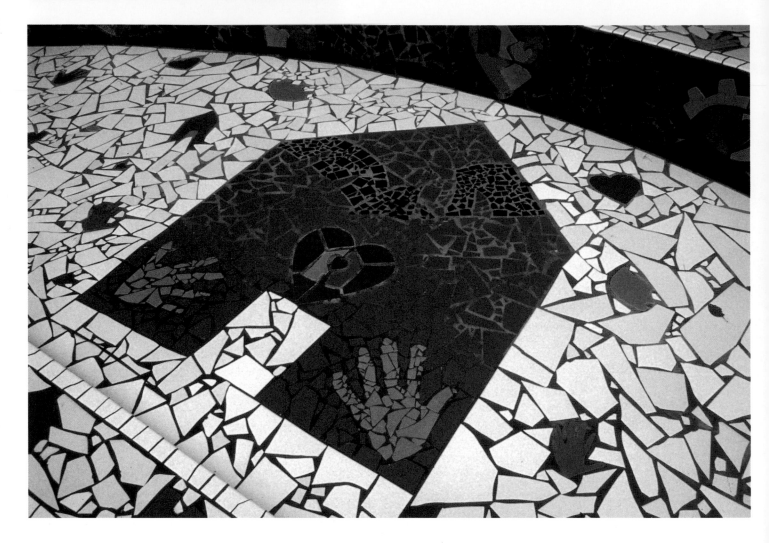

The idea that art should reflect the culture in which it is made and the people who view it aptly describes the aesthetic principle of mosaic artist Beryl Solla, more so than the prevailing view that art is a personal expression of the individual. Filled with metaphors and inspiration meant for those who will be regularly exposed to it, her site-specific works offer promise and hope.

Yet, in a medium that is difficult to imbue with personality, Solla has achieved an artistic identity that is instantly recognizable. Embedded in her two-dimensional murals are figures–tile silhouettes with charmingly clumsy and child-like edges–in solid planes of color, unencumbered by detail or texture. A Pop Art palette of striking shades, anchored by muted tones of turquoise,

primary red and yellow, lavender, and mossy green, withstands the relentless Florida sunshine and gives a nod to the varied hues of the area's Art Deco architecture. For Solla, mosaic is metaphor: broken tile that unites communities and mends shattered lives.

Detail from **Home of the Brave II**

"I believe that public art paid for by the government should reflect the needs and interests of the community using the space. If possible, I try to involve the

TECHNIQUE

local group in the piece by incorporating their history in some conceptual way or by inviting them to make tiles with me," says Beryl Solla.

For a Florida alcohol and drug recovery center, Solla designed, fabricated, and installed a work in keeping with her philosophy. Executed in two parts, *Home of the Brave* is indeed inspirational.

Embracing the entrance of an otherwise stark white stucco building is a ground-level mural of symbolism—healing hearts, hands, and houses shaded by palm trees

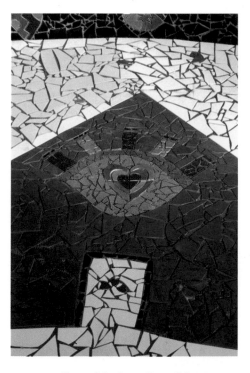

Detail from **Home of the Brave II, small fountain**

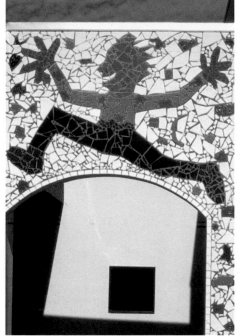

Detail from **Jump!**

are set against white and black backgrounds. These same motifs are repeated on a tiled patio and fountain in back.

At the Children's Creative Center, a daycare center and school in Miami, Solla's mosaics convey growth. Two panels featuring jumping children flank its entry, while the confetti-like pattern of the ceramics overflows onto the surrounding sidewalk.

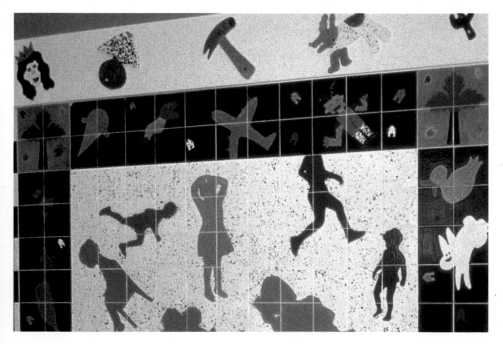

Detail from **Me and My Tropical-Fruit-Flavored Shadow**

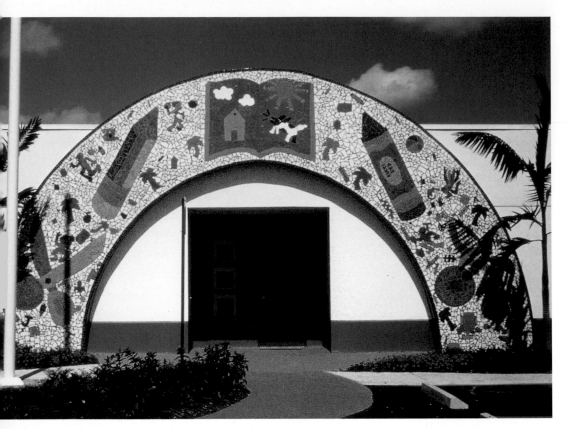

Top Ten Things
St. Agnes Rainbow Village Day Care Center,
Miami, Florida
ceramic tile
250 square feet (75 square meters)

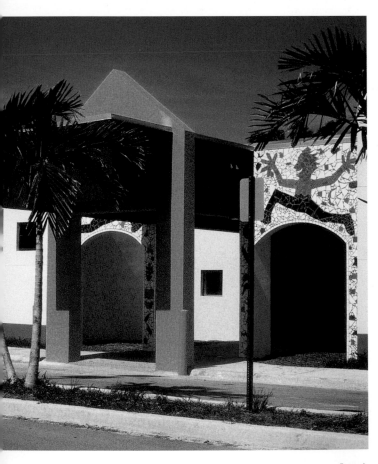

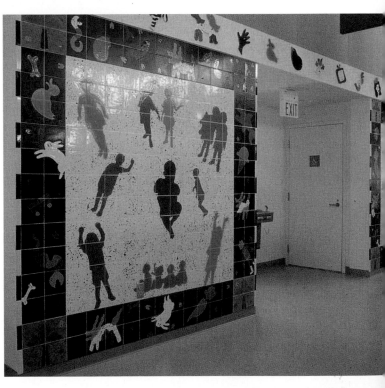

Me and My Tropical-Fruit-Flavored Shadow, 2 p
Carol Donaldson Day Care Center, Miami, F
ceram
8' x 8' (2.4 m x 2.4 m

Jump!
Florida International University
ceramic tile
180 square feet (54 square meters)

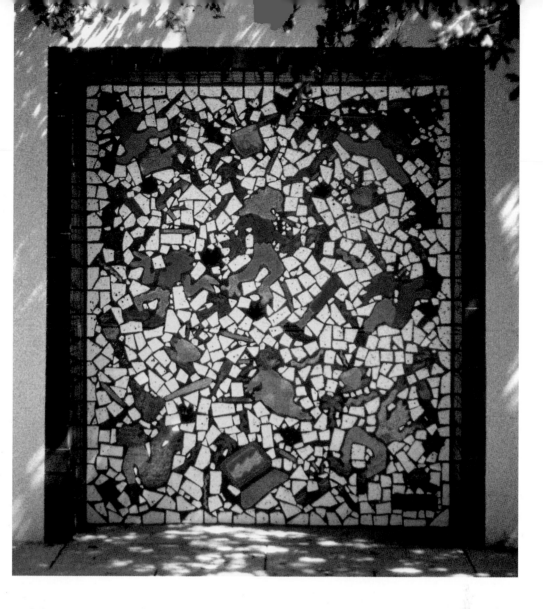

Working
Metro-Dade Building, Miami, Florida
ceramic tile
8' x 6' (2.4 m x 1.8 m)

of the Brave II, small fountain
Addiction and Recovery Center,
Springs, Florida, ceramic tile
uare feet (45 square meters)

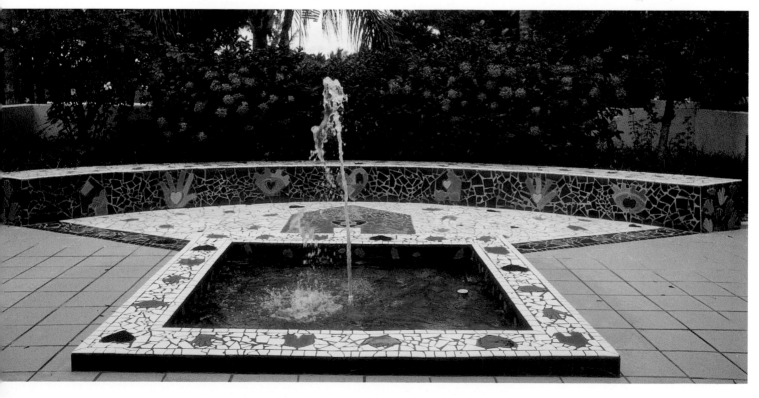

GARY STEPHENS

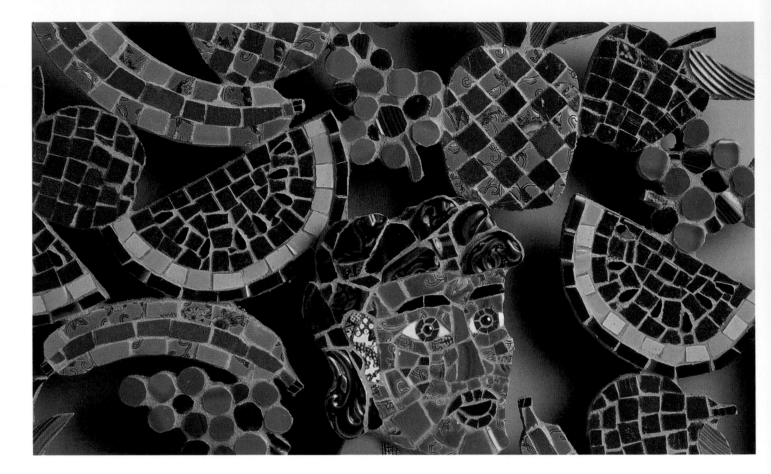

Northern California artist Gary Stephens creates life-affirming and truly unique mosaic sculptures. Using vividly colored shards of pottery and tile, he celebrates the pleasures of nature and its abundance through the colorful tropical fruit, fish, and birds that he renders within the context of stylized self-portraits. Central to much of Stephens's work are musical instruments and birds in song—highlighting an affinity for music, particularly in happy moments.

Stephens first trained as a painter, then turned to pottery and jewelry because he was fascinated with the concept of "making things." But it was mosaic sculpture that finally let him capture in three dimensions and vibrant colors the joy that he sees in everyday occurrences. His mosaics depict mermen, angels, and other mythological figures, all busy paying homage to nature's cycles and enjoying the vitality around them. Combining patterned dishware, figurines, and brilliant glazes, Stephens pieces together playful and inspiring works.

Detail from **Song of Summer (Self-Portrait II)**

"Bright colors are joyful and uplifting. I use them to counter the dark side of art often fostered by the art school culture—to be serious, analytical, critical, and

TECHNIQUE

portray unhappy emotions. Instead, my idea is to offer a happy and whimsical presentation of life," says Gary Stephens. Raised in an Arizona border town, he was exposed frequently to the direct simplicity of Mexican folk art, which Stephens says has helped shape his style.

Rather than strictly embracing traditional mosaic working methods,

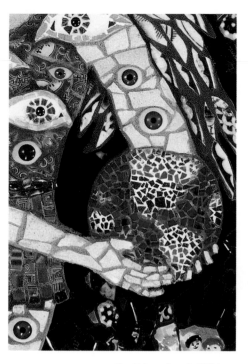

Detail from **Angel of Vision**

Stephens developed his own technique of incising *faux tesserae* into the ceramic to complete a composition. His work is greatly influenced by the shiny, busy

quality of Thai mosaic artists that he studied on his travels, as well as by the works of Rousseau, Chagall, and Matisse. Whether he is combing through boxes of dishes at yard sales or buying tea bowls by the dozen in

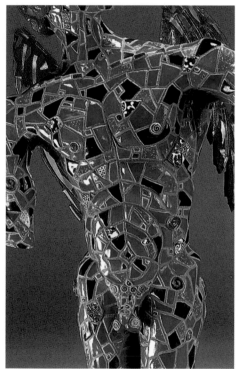

Detail from **Bobbing for Apples**

San Francisco's Chinatown, Stephens looks constantly for the perfect pattern—flowers to dot a merman's cheekbones, or scrolls and swirls for an angel's hair.

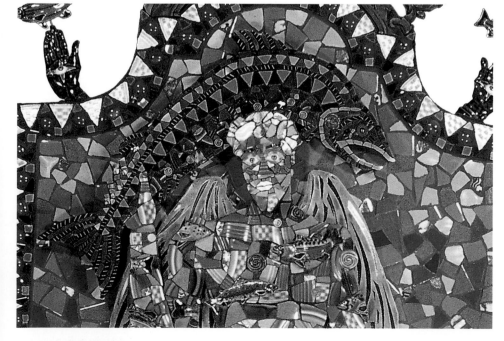

Detail from **Fish Worship**

Song of Summer (Self-Portra
mosaic on v
40" x 31" x 3" (102 cm x 79 cm x 8

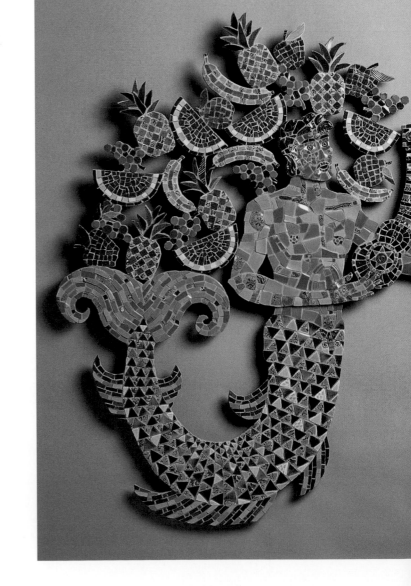

Bobbing for Apples
mosaic and low-fire ceramic
30" x 18" x 10"
(76 cm x 46 cm x 25 cm)

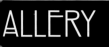

Angel of Vision
mosaic and found objects on wood
24" x 17" x 4" (60 cm x 43 cm x 10 cm)

Fish Worship
mosaic and low-fire ceramic on wood
48" x 30" x 5" (122 cm x 76 cm x 13 cm)

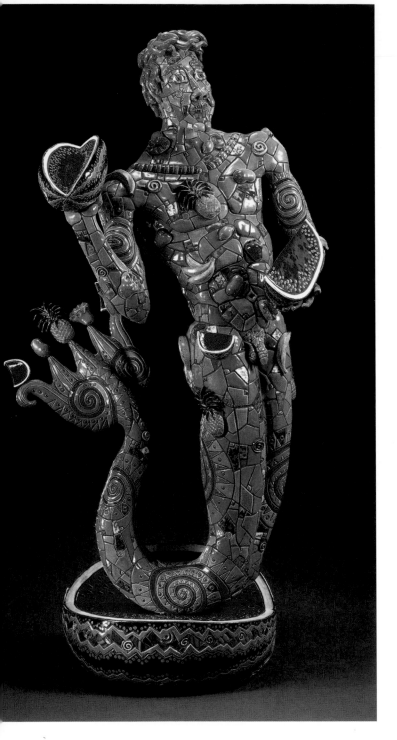

Watermelon Merman
mosaic, high-fire ceramic, low-fire glaze
36" x 19" x 12" (91 cm x 48 cm x 30 cm)

Frog Fountain with Halo of B
mosaic and high-fire cera
8' x 4' x 4' (2.4 m x 1.2 m x 1.2

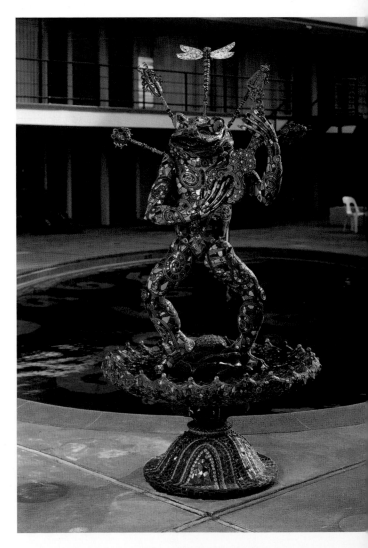

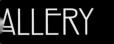

Earth Angel Sings the Wildlife Blues
mosaic on wood
40" x 34" x 5" (102 cm x 86 cm x 13 cm)

Song of Summer (Self-Portrait I)
mosaic and low-fire ceramic
28" x 20" x 5" (71 cm x 51 cm x 13 cm)

ROBERT STOUT AND STEPHANIE JURS

In their collaboration as Twin Dolphin Mosaics, Robert Stout and Stephanie Jurs expand the historic traditions of Roman and Byzantine mosaics through modern science and mathematics. Their work draws its inspiration from scientific imagery and patterns.

Their design for a walkway at the Albuquerque Museum's sculpture garden comprises two parts. First there are two sets of logarithmic spirals, appearing somewhat like the bottom of an open pine cone. The second element is a spouting, spring-like image based on a computer-generated illustration of one of the principles of fluid mechanics.

Stout has a background in drawing and painting; Jurs has a background in graphic design and crafts. Together they have completed arts projects in Alaska, California, and New Mexico.

These two dedicated artists recently relocated to Ravenna, Italy, to study Classical and Byzantine mosaic techniques, a historical and powerful mosaic tradition

that will enable them to pursue their goal of creating mosaics with twentieth-century themes.

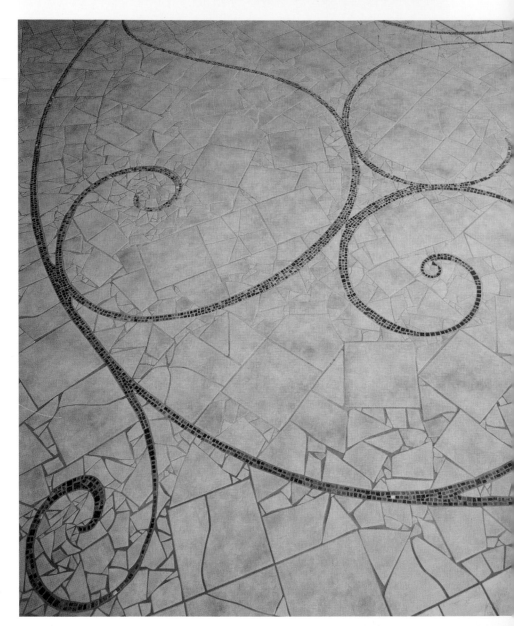

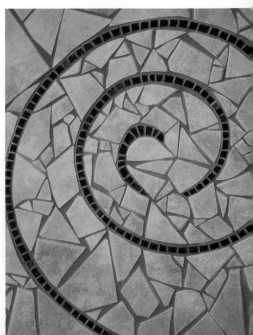

Details from
Curved Surface, mosaic entryway

Robert Stout finds that mosaics have "potential residing primarily in contemporary investigations of nature." The bounds of scientific observation have

TECHNIQUE

been pushed to extremes, and he feels "a responsibility as an artist to use this imagery, along with color, intuition, and emotion, to create pieces that describe the world in a different context."

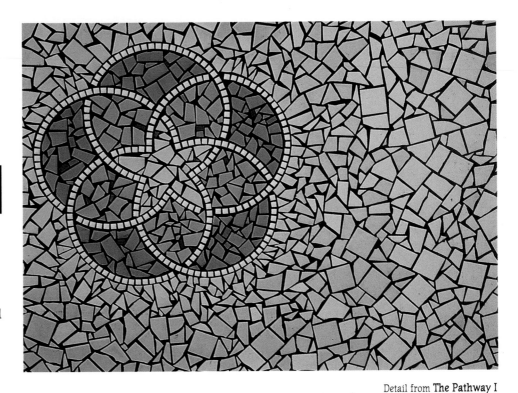

Detail from **The Pathway I**

Speaking of the scientific patterns underlying the formation of the spirals in the Albuquerque Museum walkway, Stout observes, "I value the idea that out of an original chaotic state there emerge beautiful, orderly patterns." The lace-like quality of the project owes its delicacy to the thinness of its grout lines and small *tesserae*.

In future works, Twin Dolphin Mosaics will expand on the theme of nature seen through the lenses of scientific discipline. "We find these images compelling and beautiful," they say, for they believe these concepts are perfectly suited for the complicated medium of mosaics.

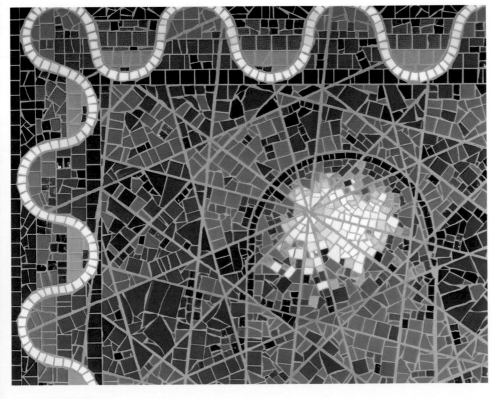

Detail from **Vita Nuova**

Curved Surface, mosaic entryway
Donelly Library, Highlands University,
Las Vegas, New Mexico
Italian- and Byzantine-style glass smalti
and Italian ceramic tile
930 square feet (279 square meters)

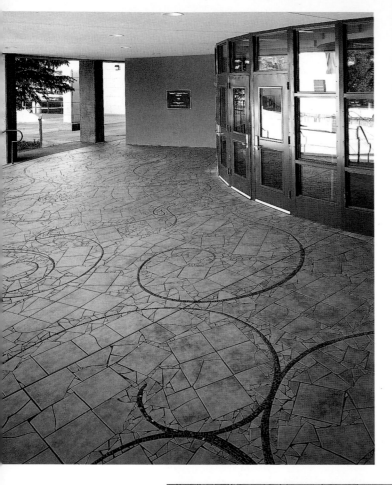

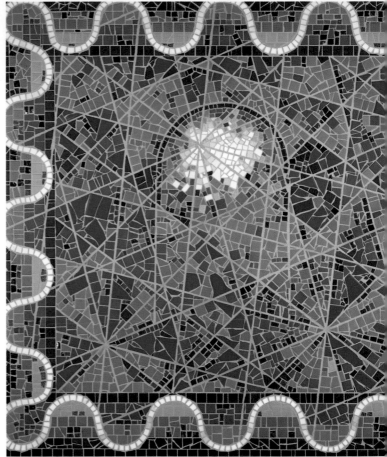

Vita N
solid body porcelain and glass sm
3.7' x 3.7' (1.1 m x 1

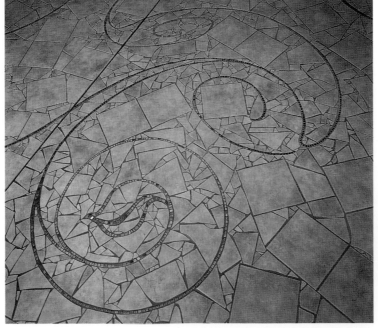

Detail from
Curved Surface, mosaic entryway

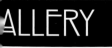

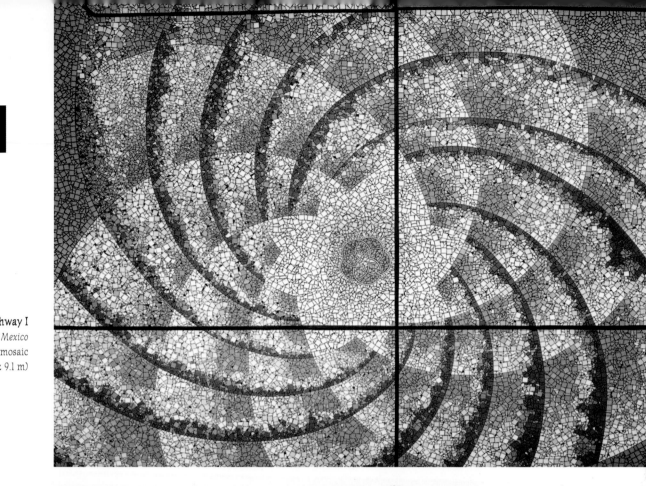

The Pathway I
Albuquerque Museum, New Mexico
tile mosaic
35' x 30' (10.7 m x 9.1 m)

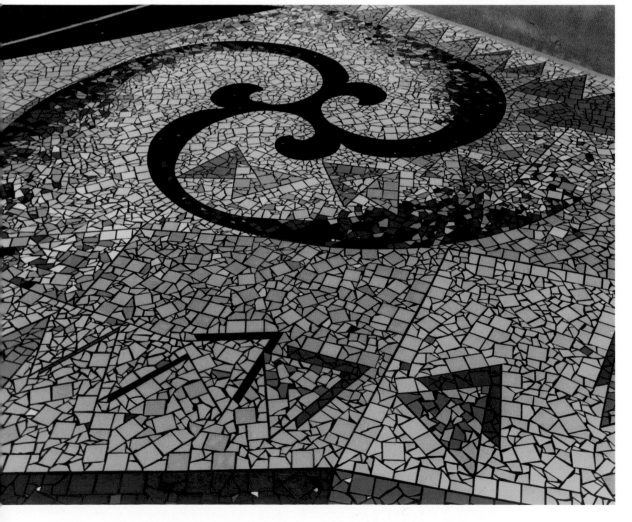

The Pathway II
Albuquerque Museum, New Mexico
tile mosaic
35' x 35' (10.7 m x 10.7 m)

STONE MOSAICS

The very nature of stone mosaics connects them to the natural world and man's ancient past. Yet, rather than being primitive, contemporary stone mosaic design is a highly evolved and sophisticated art form. Stone, rock, and rubble carefully arranged into compositions can create a look that appears to be random.

With the development of more precise cutting tools between the fifth and fifteenth centuries, stones were more easily cut into small, lightweight, uniform pieces known as *tesserae*. From that point, mosaics entered the realm of the decorative and began to appear as applications on walls and ceilings. Today they are seen in these forms and many others, from large-scale architectural ornaments to free-form sculptures to coverings for household objects.

While their individual styles diverge dramatically, stone mosaic artists Linda Beaumont, Laura Bradley, and Verdiano Marzi share some common ground. All take the viewer on a journey, although the destinations are not similar.

Beaumont's works carry the individual on a spiritual pilgrimage beyond themselves; Bradley's murals are likely to create more personal introspection; and Marzi's jagged silhouettes and rough-hewn stone take you to the natural world. The intentional rustication of Bradley's stone works and Marzi's smaller works contrast with the polished softness of Beaumont's, yet all have pieces that feature stone in a raw state suggestive of an unseen creative hand.

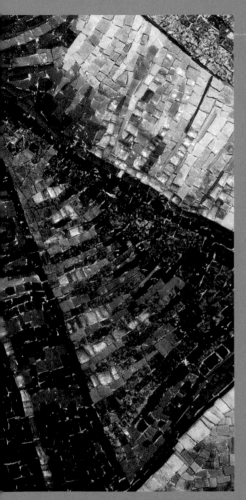

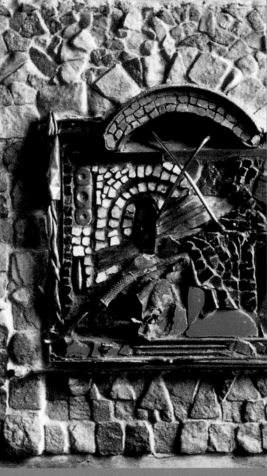

DIANO MARZI
l from
ior Wall Mosaic

LAURA BRADLEY
Detail from
Apocalypse

LINDA BEAUMONT
Detail from
Full Circle

LINDA BEAUMONT

For more than seventeen years, Seattle artist Linda Beaumont has been working in mosaics, piecing together her creations stone by stone. Considering herself a "public artist," Beaumont has a large body of work that includes paintings, traditional ceramic mosaics, and her present endeavors in stone and *terrazzo*.

Beaumont is best known for her compositions of found objects and earthy materials that at first seem simple but upon closer inspection prove to be quite complex. The surfaces of her mosaics have a generous spirit to them that invites the mind to slow down and the hand to touch. From fountains to pavements, floors, and columns, Beaumont's stone mosaics are site-specific, and her works grace both public and private facilities throughout the city of Seattle. George Chacona, a Seattle artist, developed a method for etching marble with imagery and shared his time and artistic energy with Linda during the fabrication of the Bailey Boushay Entryway and of "Full Circle."

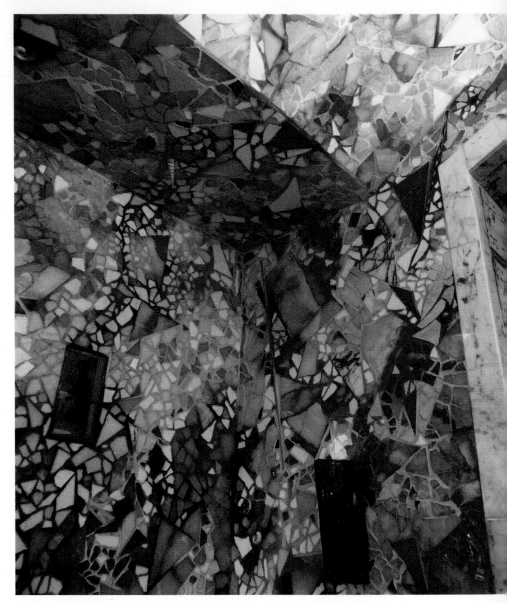

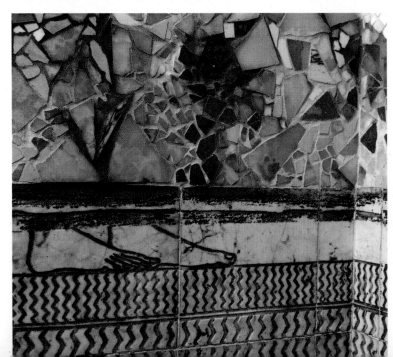

Details from **Water for Bailey Boushay, entry vestibule** (above and l

Ornate, tiled temples and cobblestone paths encountered on journeys abroad have all etched their imprint on Linda Beaumont. The work of Gaudi, the temples

TECHNIQUE

of Thailand, and the pathways of Portugal are the underlying sources of her inspiration, but Beaumont's interpretations of the projects she undertakes are purely her own.

At one of Seattle's residential care facilities for persons with AIDS, Beaumont designed and installed two stone mosaics

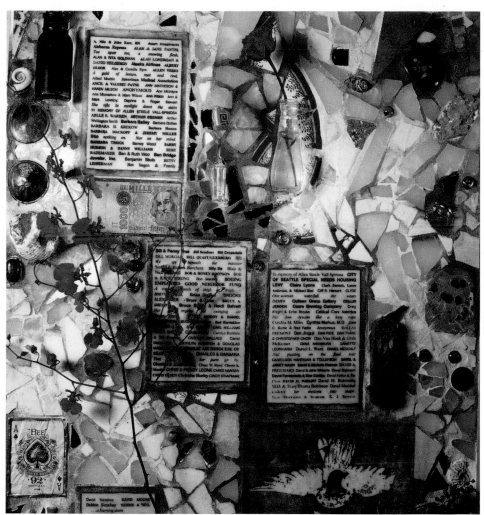

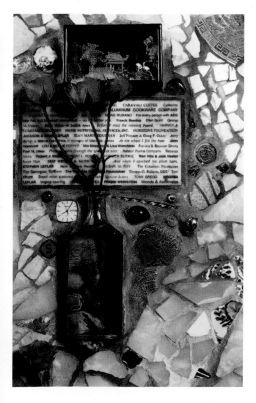

Details from **Bailey Boushay, donor recognition pillar** (above and left)

intended more for the residents than for visitors. The building is the last environment many of them will witness, she says. "The responsibility to make an entry that could touch people was too great. I needed clues, and touch was my first." She used shards of onyx and marble in sandy, earthy tones to create a gentle yet logical transitional space.

Then she embellished the stone with added imagery by etching the marble with ancient symbols such as feet walking on water and in fire, which she relates to the lives of people living with AIDS.

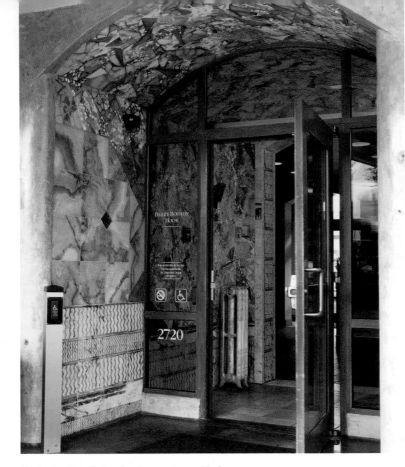

Water for Fire, Bailey Boushay, entry vestibule
AIDS Hospice
onyx and stone mosaic, embedded with mementos and etched marble
10' x 10' x 15' (3 m x 3 m x 4.6 m)

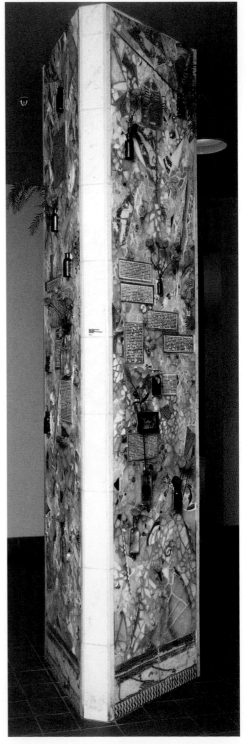

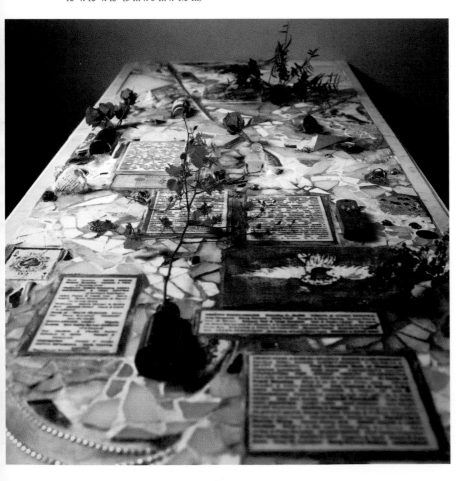

Bailey Boushay, donor recognition pillar
(above, detail at left) *AIDS Hospice*
etched marble, found objects, and mementos
3' x 3' x 3' x 10' (.9 m x .9 m x .9 m x 3 m)

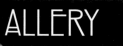

ALLERY

Step On No Pets
Animal Control Center
ceramic mosaic
10' x 15' x 8" (3 m x 4.6 m x 20 cm)

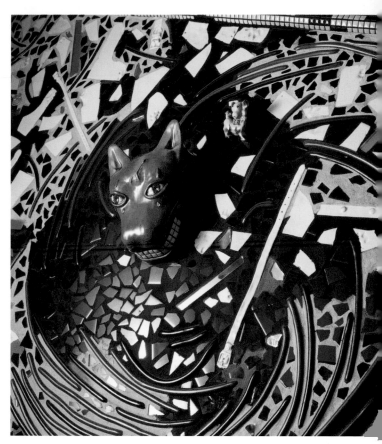

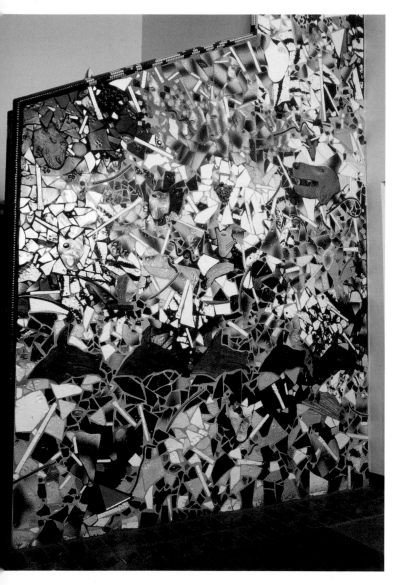

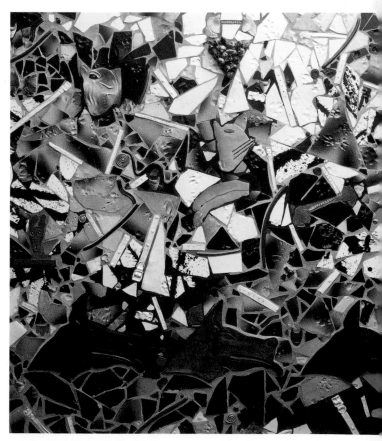

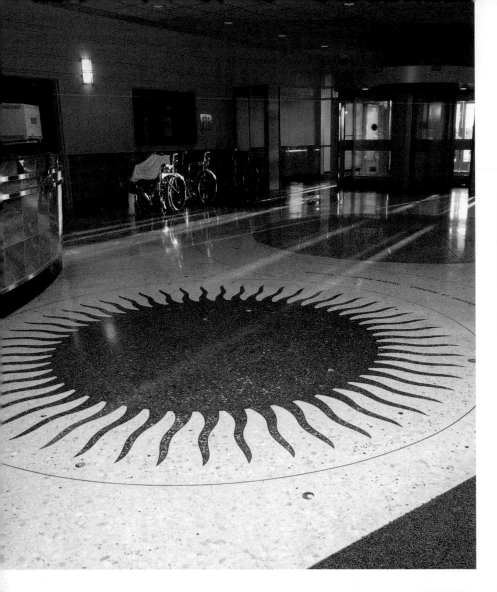

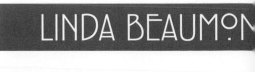

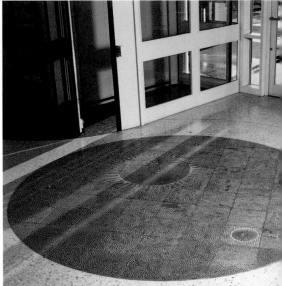

Full Circle
Harbor View Hospital
terrazzo and photo images of ancient Roman
mosaics etched into travertine and brass
1,800 square feet (540 square meters)

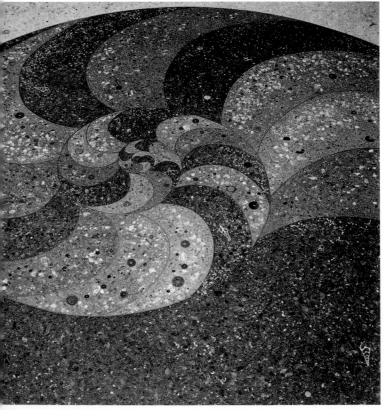

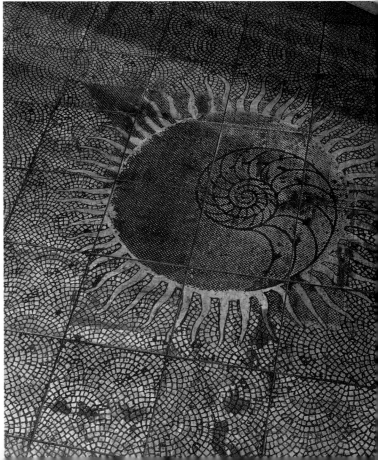

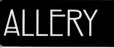

Details from **Sturgis Church, private altar**
stone and ceramic mosaic and found objects

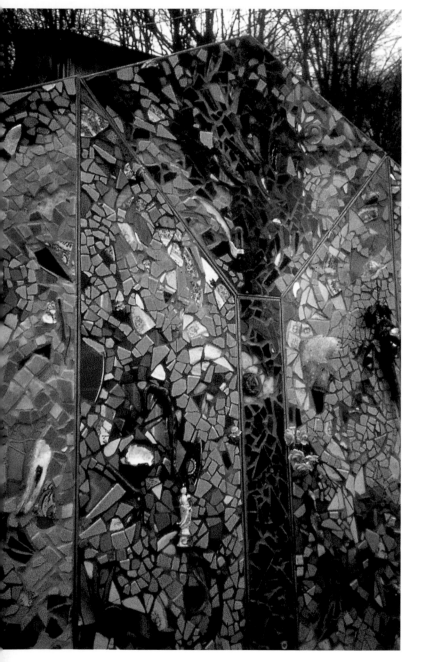

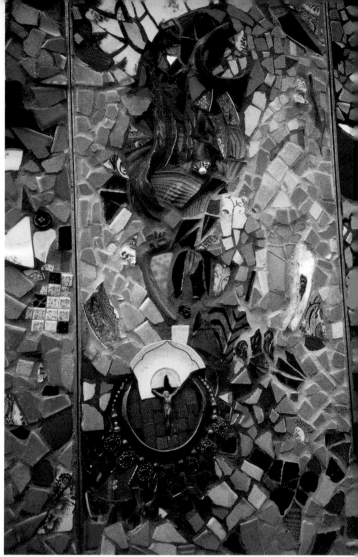

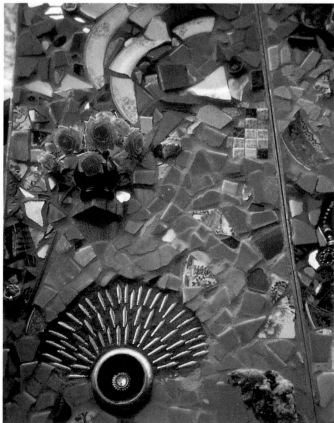

LAURA BRADLEY

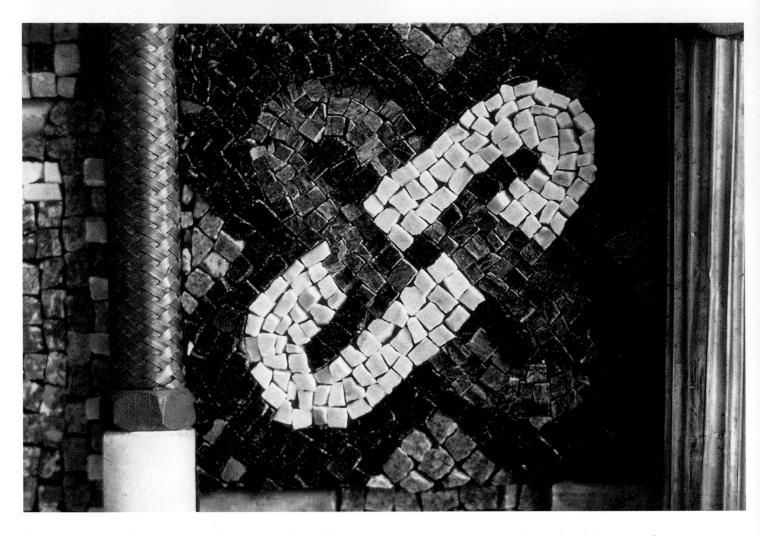

Having worked in almost every art form, Laura Bradley is also trained in some construction trades, including masonry. Her vibrant artistic stone expressions are the result of applying her training in one medium to another medium. Bradley develops ideas in collage and watercolor alongside her mosaics, and enjoys the particular constraints of working on an intimate scale: "I find the most freedom in ideas of limited space—the push and pull of a collage or the illusion of a window in watercolor may appear again as a copper door with small mosaic columns on either side."

Portals are a recurring theme throughout her work, representing communication that begins with an entry and continues with the journey through each piece. She uses portals to blend classical architecture and ornaments within her assemblages, regardless of the materials. This artistic emphasis can be seen in her commissions for the New York City Transit Authority where she has not only designed a series of subway station mosaics, but has also created a complete program of railings, gates, and grillwork.

Details from **Harmony's House**
(above and opposite)

The commitment to creating mosaics that Laura Bradley demonstrates extends far beyond her studio. Personally collecting stones to cut by hand into tesserae helps

TECHNIQUE

to immerse Bradley in her art. "I may be in the woods all day where I know there are traces of an old riverbed layered beneath the topsoil. Often, a single small stone, uncut in my hand, helps an image to rise spontaneously," she says.

She turns such images into the mosaic portals for which she is famous. Her inventive palette of materials

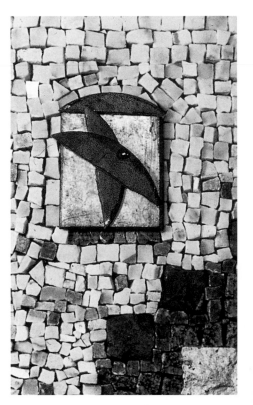

Detail from **Going Home**

includes marble and stone, and she often incorporates copper, silver, bronze, steel, mica, aluminum, and brass into her

pieces. Looking through the pictorial doorways she frames inspires a certain reverie. "Stones seem to have the quality of speaking about time—forever remembering and constantly hoping,"

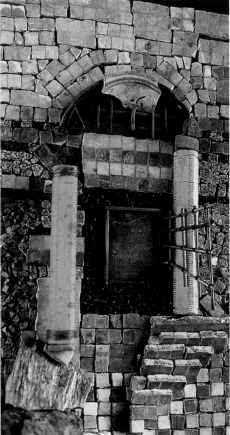

Detail from **The Open Gate**

reflects Bradley. Some of her panels cluster around openings, while others exhibit a single glimpse of another time and place.

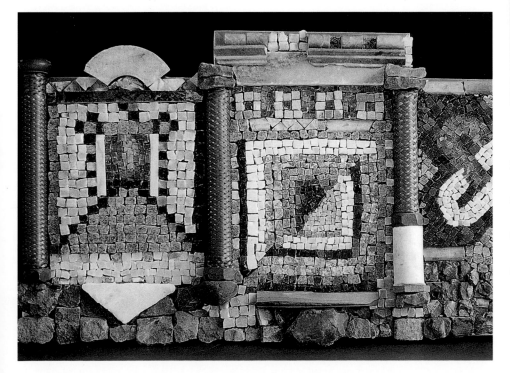

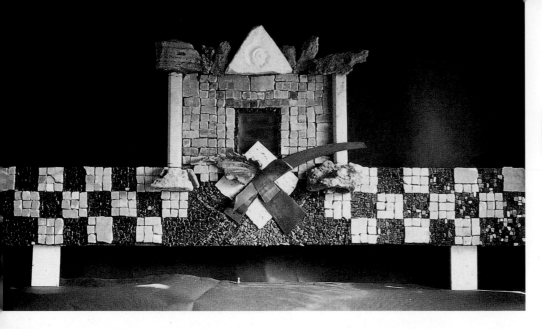

Silver Doorway
hand-cut marble mosaic, bronze,
fossil, stone, brass, silver, and ceramic
4.7' x 25" x 3" (1.4 m x 64 cm x 8 cm)

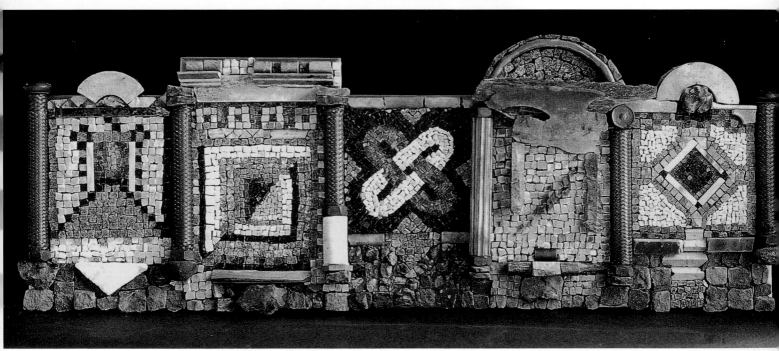

Harmony's House
hand-cut marble mosaic, stone, copper,
ceramic, and bronze
4.3' x 20" x 4" (1.3 m x 51 cm x 10 cm)

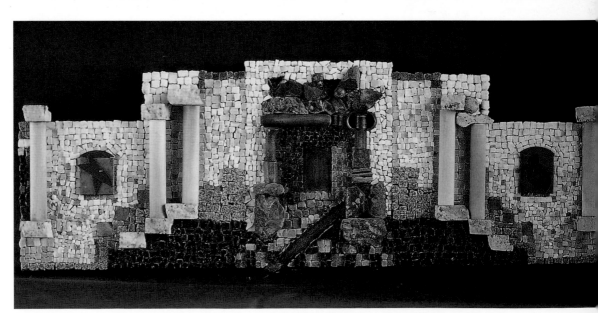

Going Home
hand-cut marble mosaic, stone,
bronze, brass, and ceramic
4' x 22" x 3" (1.2 m x 56 cm x 8 cm)

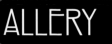

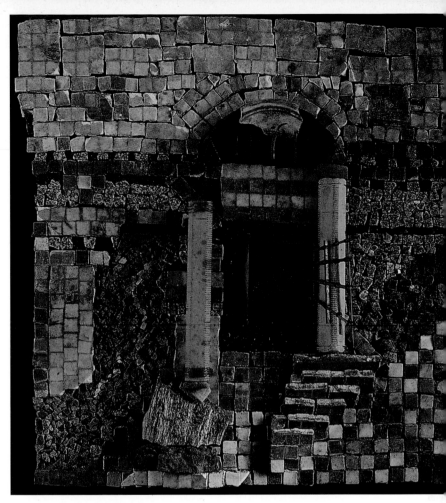

The Open Gate
hand-cut marble mosaic,
brass, and ceramic
27" x 26" x 2" (68 cm x 66 cm x 5 cm)

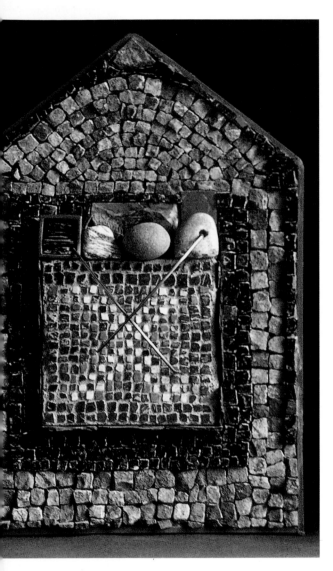

unziation I
-cut marble mosaic wall
, stone, and copper
15" x 2" (64 cm x 38 cm x 5 cm)

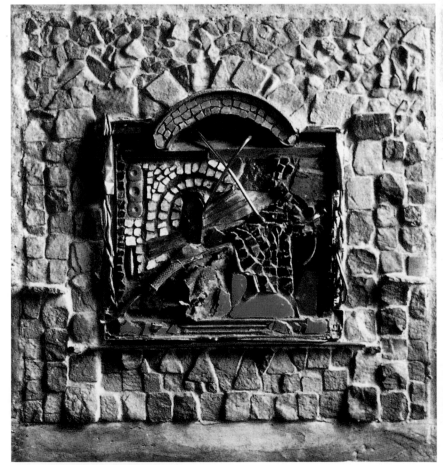

Apocalypse
hand-cut marble mosaic, stone, copper, and steel
24" x 26" (61 cm x 66 cm)

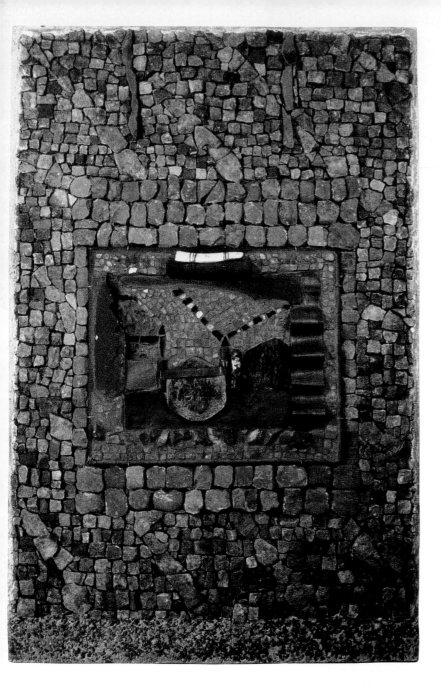

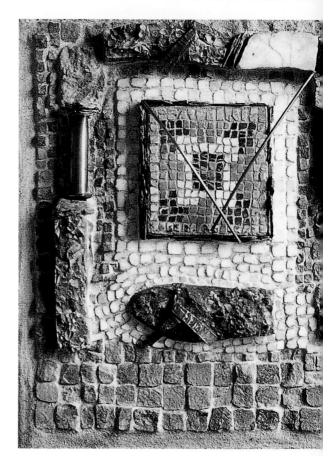

Annunziat
hand-cut marble mosaic, stone, copper, and ce
36" x 30" x 2" (91 cm x 76 cm x

When You Travel East
hand-cut marble mosaic, stone, steel, and copper
25" x 3.4' (64 cm x 1 m)

Metaphysical Clock
hand-cut marble mosaic, bronze,
lead, copper, and stone
28" x 24" x 2" (71 cm x 61 cm x 5 cm)

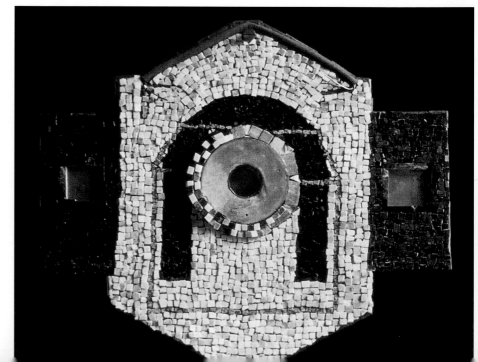

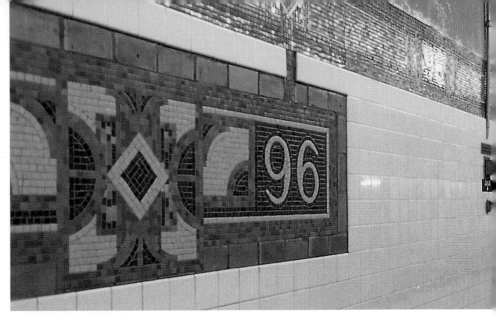

Ceramic Mosaic Panel
Commissioned by the New York City
Metropolitan Transportation Authority/Arts for Transit
96th Street Station, Lexington Avenue Subway, New York, New York
hand-cut marble mosaic
6' x 20" (1.8 m x 51 cm)

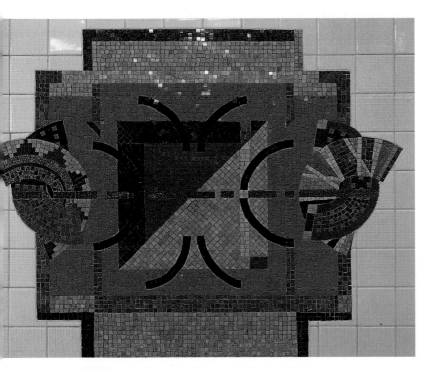

City Suite
Commissioned by the New York City
Metropolitan Transportation Authority/Arts for Transit
96th Street Station, Lexington Avenue Subway, New York, New York
hand-cut marble mosaic
4' x 4.5' (1.2 m x 1.4 m)

The Eastern Gate
hand-cut marble mosaic, stone, bronze, and ceramic
4' x 22" x 3" (1.2 m x 56 cm x 8 cm)

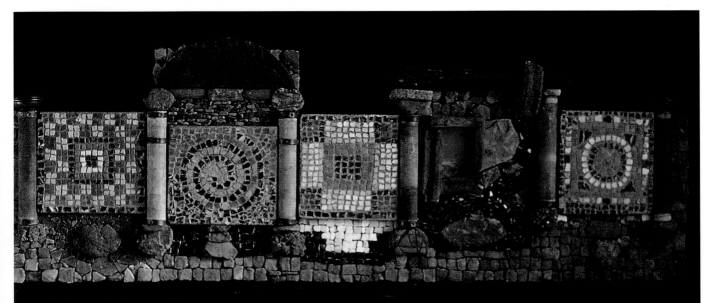

VERDIANO MARZI

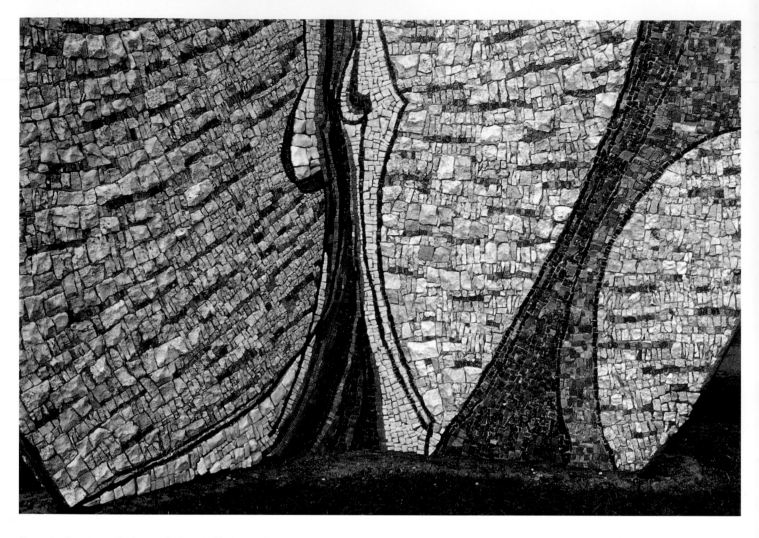

Born in Ravenna, Italy, and classically trained at such venerable institutions as the Ecole des Beaux-Arts and the Istituto d'Arte per il Mosaico, Verdiano Marzi's mosaics may be a surprise in their abstract style, but his approach to the art form remains true to tradition. "Since I was an eleven-year-old boy, I have been educated by the mosaicists of the Scuola di Ravenna. I was born there, in the city that was once the capital of the Byzantine Empire in the early Christian period," he attests.

Now a citizen of the Republic of San Marino, Marzi is dedicated to passing his skills on to the next generation.

In 1994, he developed and directed a workshop at the Louvre in Paris, France, introducing young people to mosaics. More recently, he traveled to Dahramsala, India, to teach Tibetan children the basics of the art.

Detail from **Nascita, face 1**

Creations by Verdiano Marzi can be divided into two categories: monumental works and private commissions. In the case of the former, the artist executes

TECHNIQUE

these installations personally but typically credits different painters with the designs of the mosaics. However, his private commissions are completely original. The jagged silhouettes often found in his freestanding pieces, as in the *Nascita*, and the rough-hewn stone central to many of his smaller works—*Le Repos*

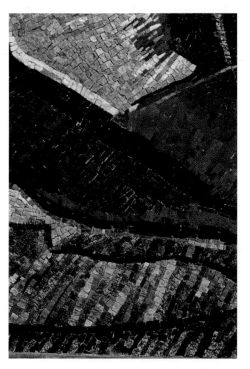

Detail from **Interior Wall Mosaic**

des Météorites is one example—are his signature. They function as an arresting contrast in form and texture to the

more regular *tesserae* that make up the remainder of the compositions.

With his pieces in collections in Germany, Japan, and throughout France, the artist maintains a well-rounded

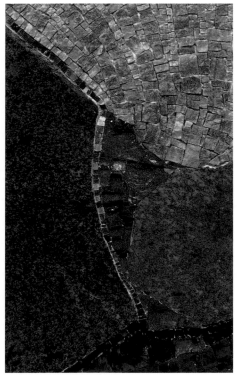

Detail from **Virginia**

approach to his craft. Marzi has steeped himself in the very foundations of mosaics by participating in the restoration of paleo-Christian pavements in southern Italy, and nineteenth and twentieth-century floors in Paris.

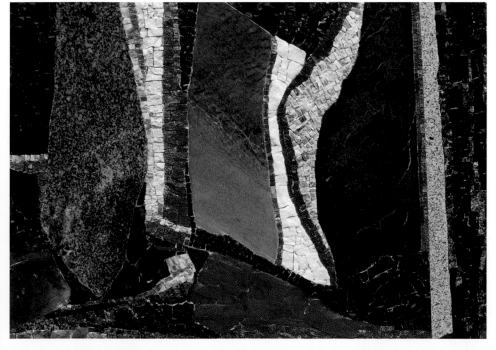

Detail from **Le Repos des Meteorites**, marble, granite, and Venetian smalti

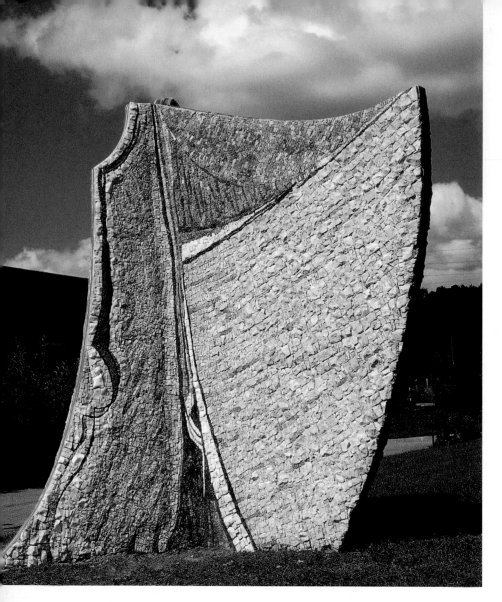

Nascita, face 2
park at Bourgouin Jallieu High School, France
marble, granite, and Venetian smalti
8.8' (2.7 m)

Sculptures
stone, marble, and concrete with
mosaic made of marble, granite,
and Venetian smalti
7.5' x 9.3' (2.3 m x 2.8 m)

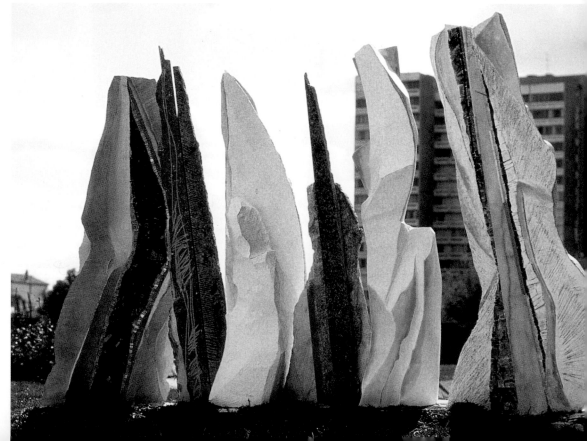

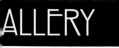

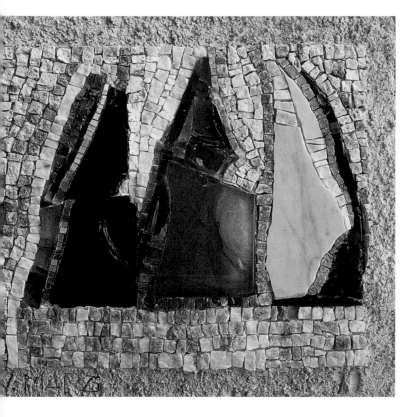

Dorata
e, granite, and Venetian smalti
1.8' (.4 m x .5 m)

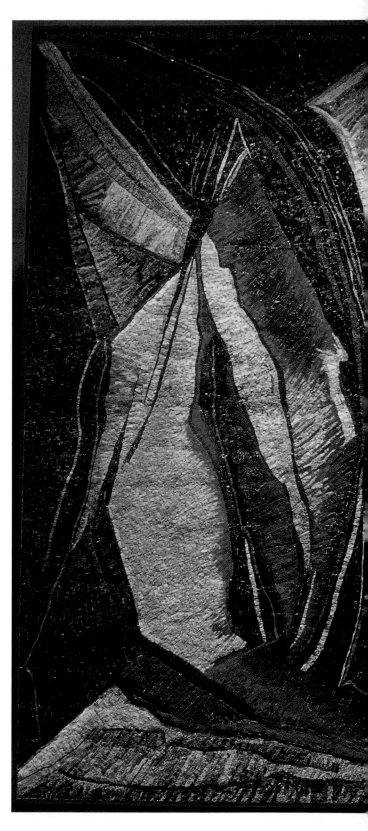

Interior Wall Mosaic
Mons Sarts Metro Station, Lille, France
marble, granite, and Venetian smalti
11.8' x 5.3' (3.6 m x 1.7 m)

St. George with Blue and Red Angels, triptych
(details below)
marble, granite, and Venetian smalti
9.3' x 3.5' (2.8 m x 1.1 m)

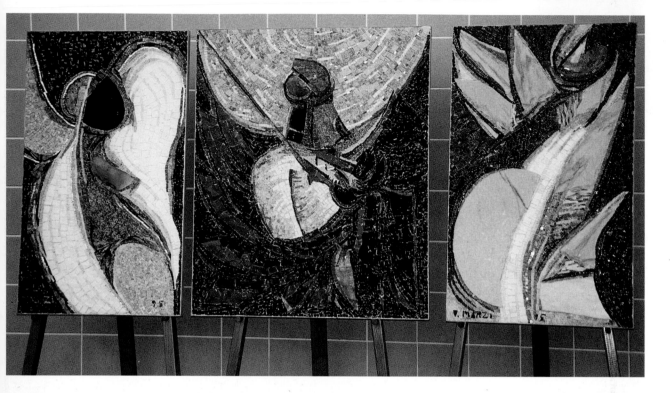

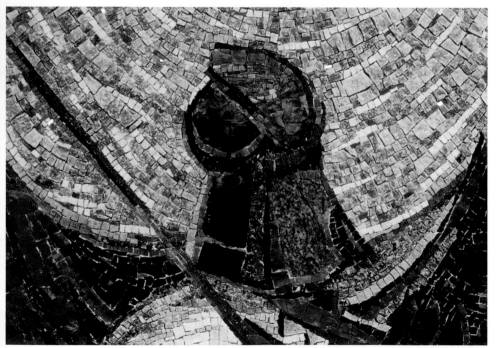

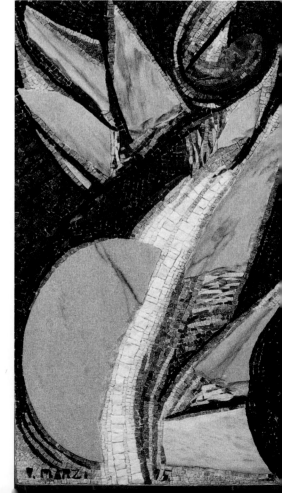

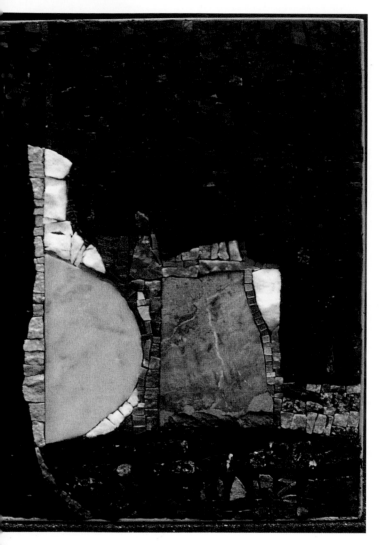

...ife

...le, granite, and Venetian smalti
...20" (60 cm x 50 cm)

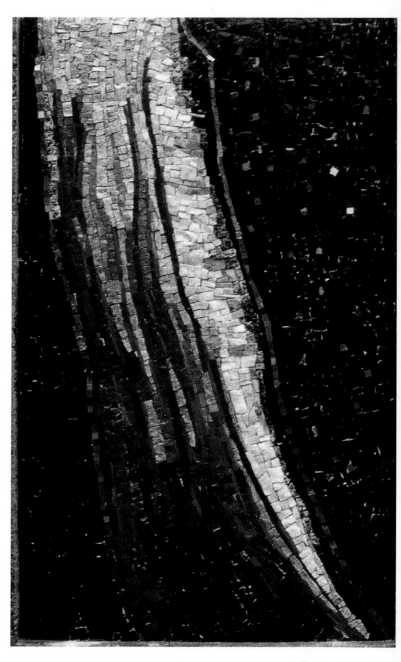

Exterior Wall Mosaic
Mons Sarts Metro Station, Lille, France
marble, granite, and Venetian smalti
24" x 3.3' (60 cm x 1 m)

MIXED-MEDIA MOSAICS

Mixed media works differ from traditional *tesserae*-based compositions in their emphasis on the parts of the mosaic rather than the whole. While incorporating an amalgam of found objects may be straining the boundaries of the art for some purists, others would argue that the mixed-media artists profiled here satisfy a set of requisites far more fundamental: the urge to collect, compose, and create.

The bridge between ceramic mosaics and mixed-media mosaics is firmly anchored by a technique called *pique assiette* ("stolen from plates"). This name was first given to the ambitious folk art endeavor of Raymond Isidore, a Frenchman who spent nearly twenty-five years blanketing his entire home with shards of cast-off crockery and dishware. Completed in the 1960s, it heralded the new, freethinking age in the development of mosaic art.

Executors of this new age, the artists whose works follow all speak from different perspectives, yet they have a common voice. Ilana Shafir's mosaic window combinations, Jane Muir's landscape compositions, the Rosenbergs' carved concrete mosaic murals, Lynn Mattson's folk art, Twyla Arthur's architectural assemblages, Val Carroll's regional murals, Carlos Alves's ocean- and culture-derived pathways and murals, Candace Bahouth's mosaic transformation of mundane objects, and Isaiah Zagar's neighborhood monuments all use fragments that come together in one fashion or another, paying homage to nature.

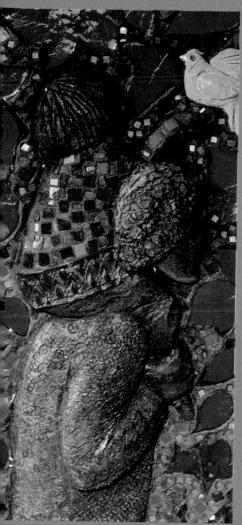

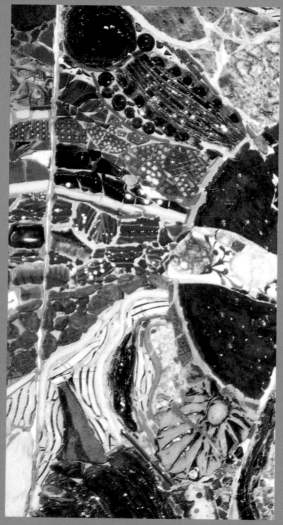

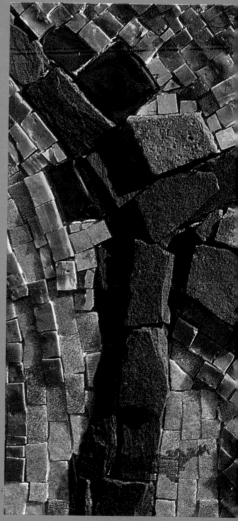

ANN KILLEN ROSENBERG
from
ren's Center Mural

ILANA SHAFIR
Detail from
Blessings

JANE MUIR
Detail from
Fruiting

227

CARLOS ALVES

Miami artist Carlos Alves creates wildly imaginative floors, ceilings, and walls. While Miami is host to most of his works, his signature creations are permanent installations in such far-off places as London, Hong Kong, and, closer to home, New York City.

With more than a decade of successful projects ranging from interior works to ceramic portraits to transit stations and swimming pools to his credit, the question of commercial production arises. Alves offers a sure response: "I could be mass-producing furniture, but I disregard that idea because I don't want my pieces to lose their integrity. I want them to be special and have their dignity." Not surprisingly, the artist also has a decidedly upfront attitude about the goals of his mosaics. "I want people to have to interact with my work, to consider it, and to consider what it makes them think about. If I succeed, then I feel like I've really accomplished something."

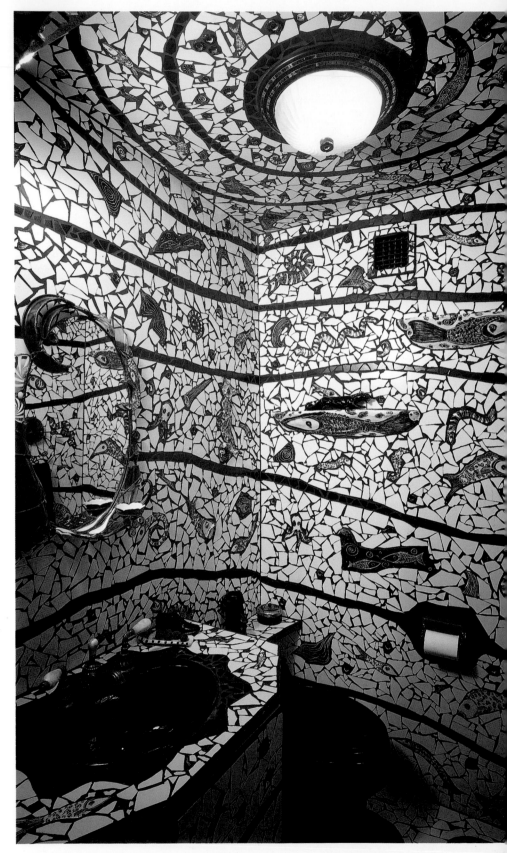

Private Bath
handmade ceramic, stained glass, and r

Carlos Alves spends a lot of time breaking and reconfiguring old ceramics, which he then uses as individual pieces in larger designs. Greatly attracted by

TECHNIQUE

the concept of recycling, Alves takes pleasure in reusing old bits and likes the idea of breaking down the pristine and fragile wholeness of an individual ceramic piece.

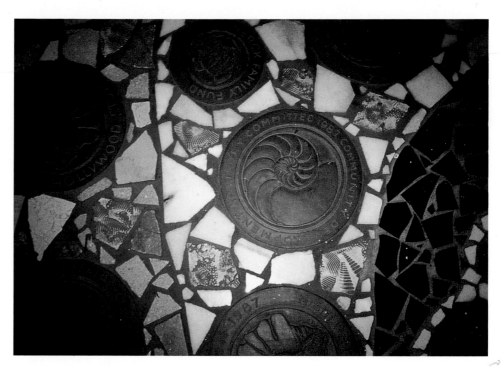

Detail from **Atlantis**, *South Florida Art Center*, assorted tile

Alves's works are closely connected to his childhood in the Miami Beach area. His Cuban roots, abundant, flowing gardens, and the years he spent in the ocean collecting shells and diving all merge together as inspiration for the spiral sea creatures and Latin symbolism that appear in his mosaics. His latest venture is exploring portraiture. Working with recycled china pieces, Alves is starting to create huge images of individuals.

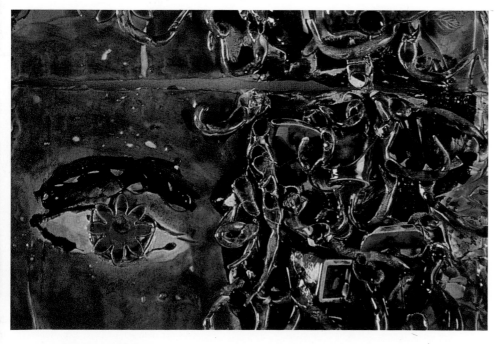

Detail from **Señorita Margarita**

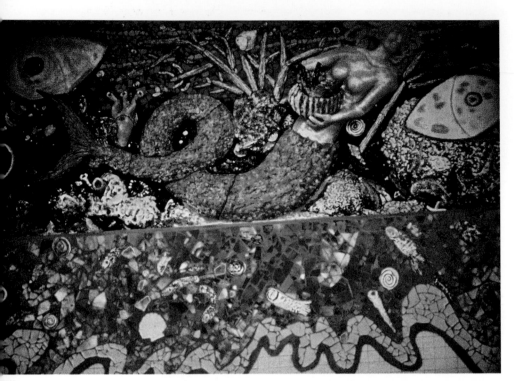

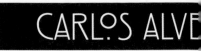

Sirena
handmade ceramic tile
26' x 6' x 14" (7.9 m x 1.8 m x 36 cm)

Save the Waters
marble, tile, and metal
1,200 square feet (360 square meters)

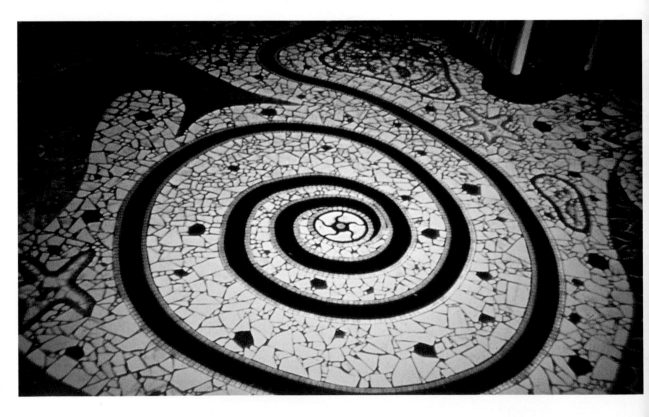

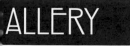

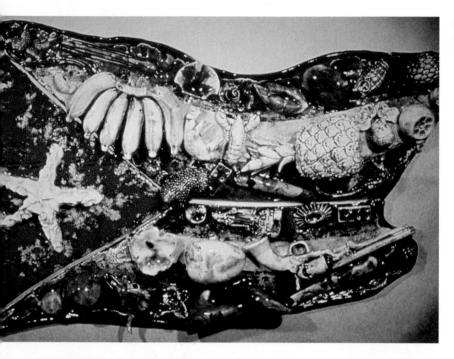

Cuban Flag
recycled ceramic tile
3.3' x 32" x 6" (1 meter x 81 cm x 15 cm)

Map of South Florida (detail)
Everglades National Park
marble, hand-glazed ceramic tile, and brass
630 square feet (189 square meters)

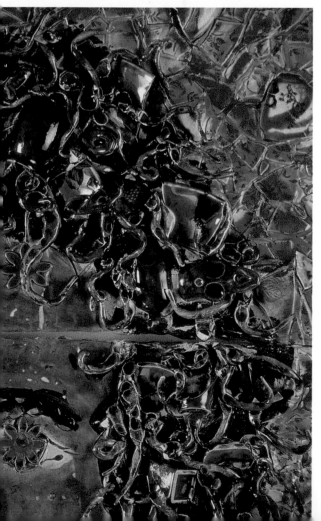

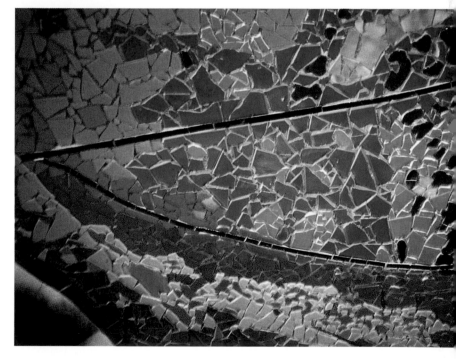

Señorita Margarita
recycled ceramic tile and fused glass
24" x 24" (60 cm x 60 cm)

TWYLA ARTHUR

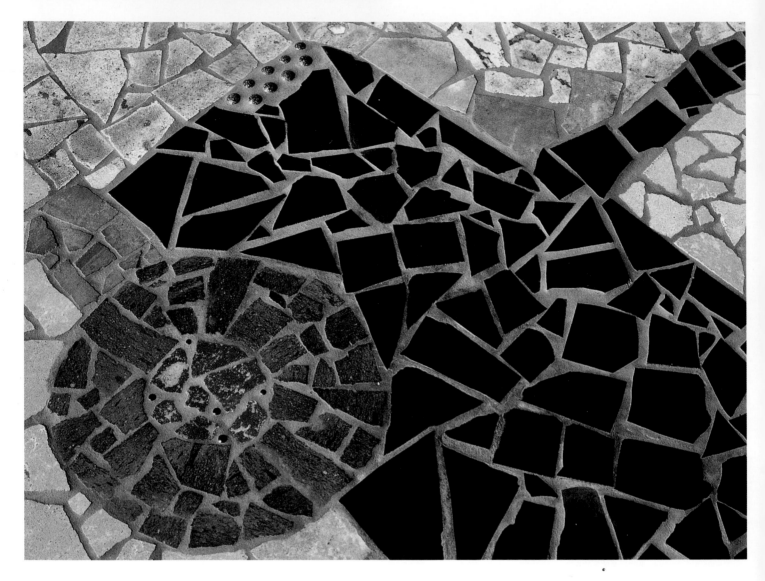

Most of Twyla Arthur's mosaics are site-specific, permanent installations, as much a part of the architecture of a building or landscape as an embellishment. This type of relationship stems from the fluidity of her work and her ability to create art that is often functional and always respectful of the space it occupies.

Trained in fine arts at Mills College, Arthur initially concentrated on sculpture and painting, but for the last ten years, assemblage has been her medium. Her mosaics include man-made ceramics and glass—however, more often than not, rock and natural stone predominate. In gardens, patios, and outdoor environments, this choice emphasizes the rustic ambience of the settings; in more refined contexts, it introduces an element of contrast. In either situation, texture takes the lead—hefty chunks, water-smoothed slabs, and pebbly surfaces invite people to touch as well as view.

Detail from **Mosaic Sidewalk**

Twyla Arthur is influenced and moved to create by primitive architecture and vernacular art. "I love the mud houses of West Africa because as an art form they

TECHNIQUE

are part of the culture, not contrived like much of western art. Traditionally women's art, the houses are sculptural in shape and painted with rich designs and colors. Their tools are primitive—most of the work is done with their hands," Arthur says.

Her work for both the terrace and interior of architect David Baker's house in Berkeley, California, reinforces her philosophy. Stones on the multilevel terrace are laid out in a flowing, organic pattern supportive of the material. Inlaid nuts, bolts, and other construction materials are a lighthearted reference to the building process, conjuring up images of an unearthed foundation. Inside the house, broken marble, concrete, and ceramic

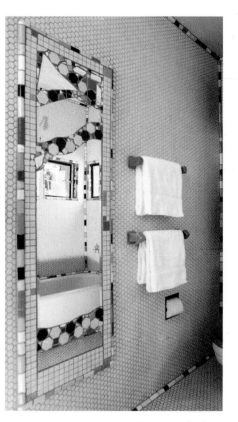

Detail from **Bathroom**

shards are laid by hand to create their own primitive sensibility in the kitchen and the bath.

Detail from **Mosaic Spoons**

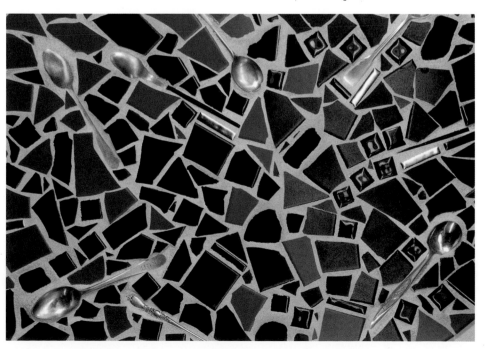

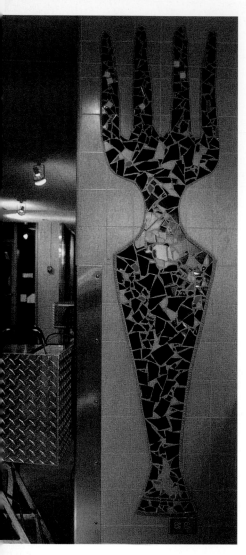

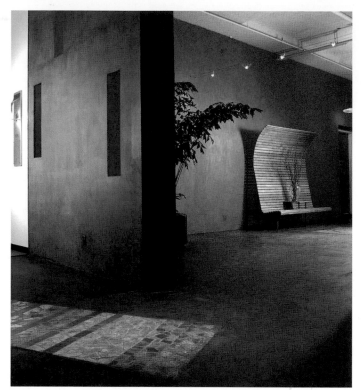

Concrete Mosaic Rug
Lobby Interior
concrete tile handmade by Buddy Rho
36" x 12' (90 cm x 3.7 m)

Mosaic Fork
UC Berkeley, Unit I Dining Hall
ceramic tile
6' x 18" (1.8 m x 46 cm)

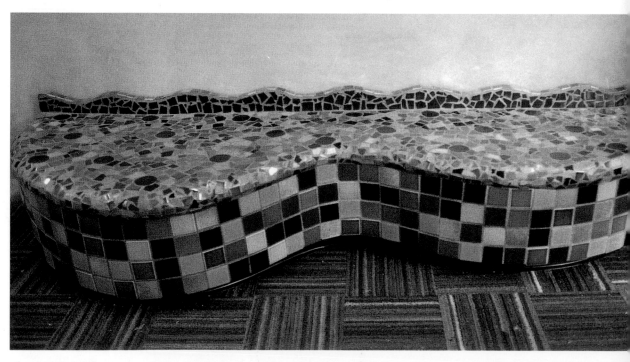

Ceramic Tile Bench
UC Berkeley, residence hall
8' x 28" (2.4 m x 71 cm)

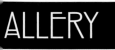

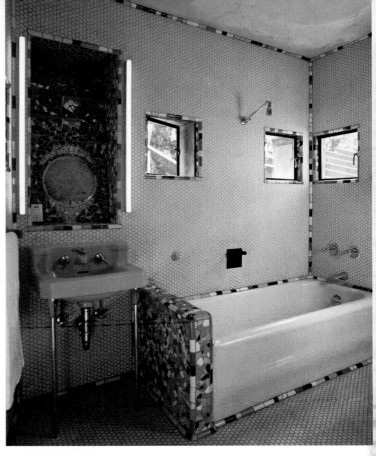

Bathroom
David Baker residence
ceramic tile and mirrors

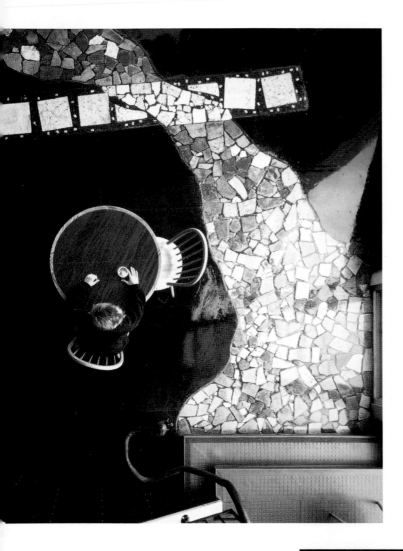

Mosaic Floor
Bison Brewing Company
concrete tile handmade by Buddy Rhodes
100 square feet (30 square meters)

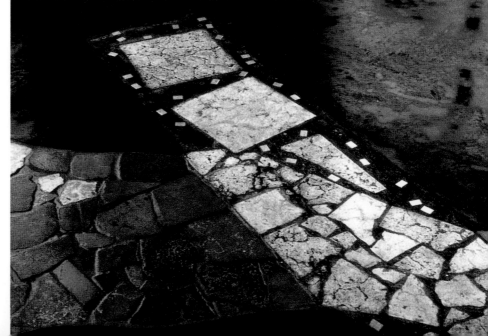

Detail from **Mosaic Floor**

CANDACE BAHOUTH

An accomplished textile artist, Candace Bahouth originally earned her reputation by weaving tapestry portraits with a three-dimensional presence to them. This attracted the curators at the Victoria and Albert Museum in London, who acquired several of these innovative pieces for their collection. The next phase of her work was devoted to intricate needlepoint designs based on medieval motifs and symbols. Eventually, these designs were turned into a successful line of commercial craft kits. Then, for a brief moment, the artist turned her attention to mosaics, but she became so enamored that she has kept her eyes (and her hands) firmly fixed on this art form ever since.

Contrary to what one might expect, the transition between needle artistry and mosaics is not a great leap for Bahouth. Both media are pattern-oriented, both are essentially additive processes involving very small components, and in this artist's case, both rely on a dynamic use of color for maximum effect.

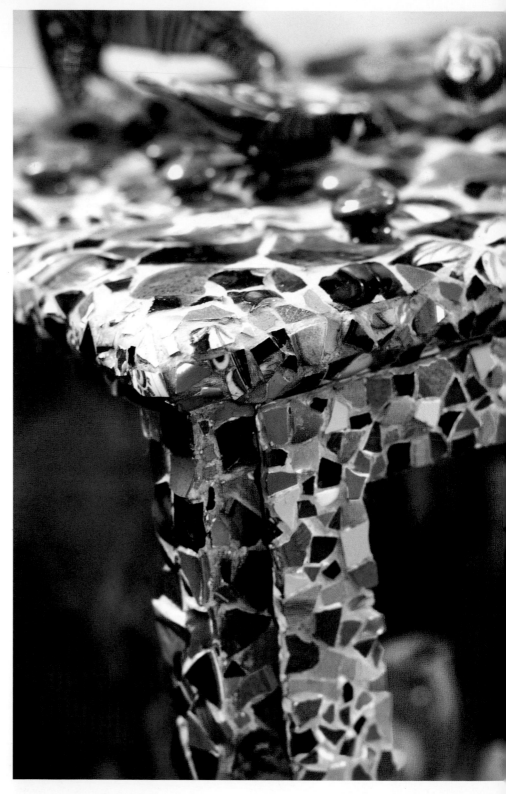

Details from **Cabinet** (above and opp

Fiber and mosaic artist Candace Bahouth could be speaking of silk threads or ceramic *tesserae* when she says, "I have a fascination with fragments and the

TECHNIQUE

redemptive metamorphosis of a thing quite ordinary into something wonderful, extraordinary, even nonsensical, amusing— an object of delight."

Transformation of the mundane into a fanciful mosaic monument is her hallmark. One brilliant example is a simple pedestal birdbath that she covered with a thick impasto of color-coordinated

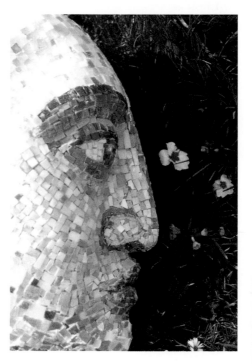

Detail from **Porcelain Head**

grout embedded with brilliant shards of mirror, glass, and ceramic. This common garden element has re-emerged as an extravagant ornament. A slight spin on

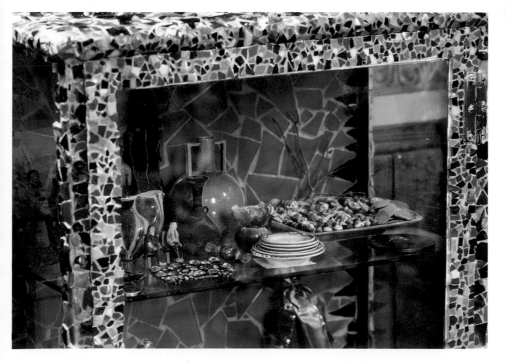

this eclectic aesthetic is the treatment she gives to a stone fence in the English countryside. The pattern of rough grey rubble is broken without warning by a vertical vein of fractured cobalt tile, an impetuous contrast to the otherwise tranquil setting that underscores

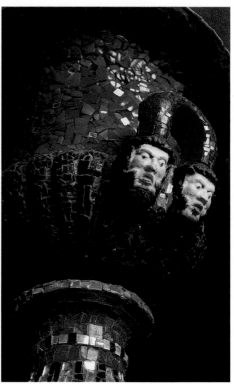

Detail from **Large Urn**

Bahouth's outlook regarding the environment. "Nature is one of life's most intense, emotional experiences, the most perfect of worlds, my main inspiration and dwelling place."

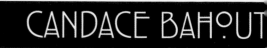

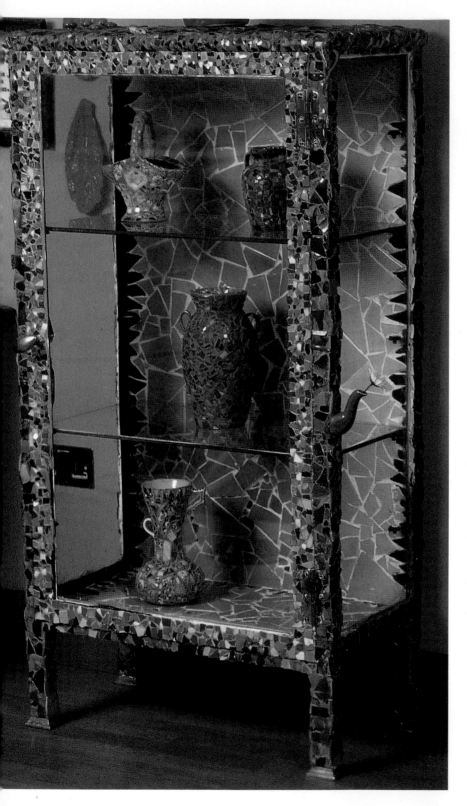

Cabinet
broken china and tile
28" x 4.4' x 15"
(71 cm x 1.3 m x 38 cm)

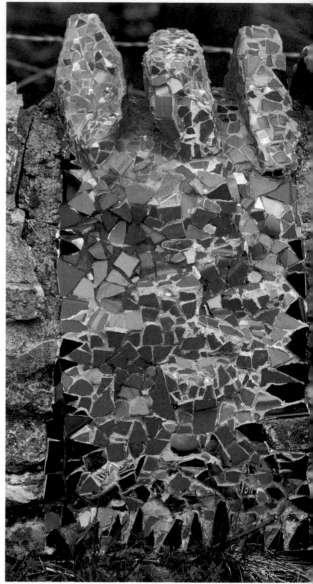

Stone
broken c
14" x 30" (36 cm x 76

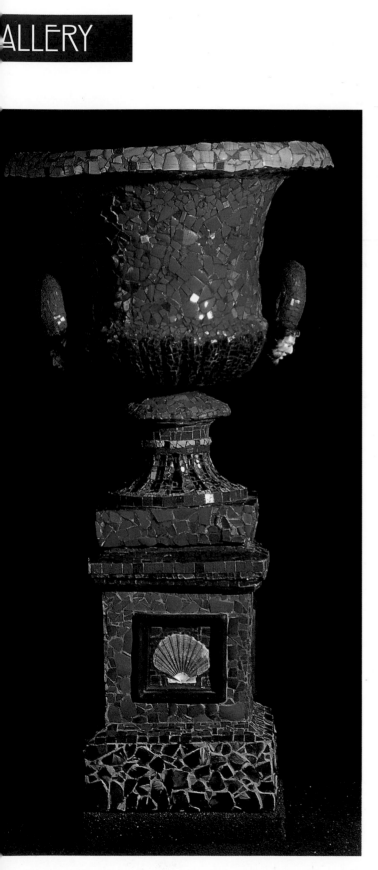

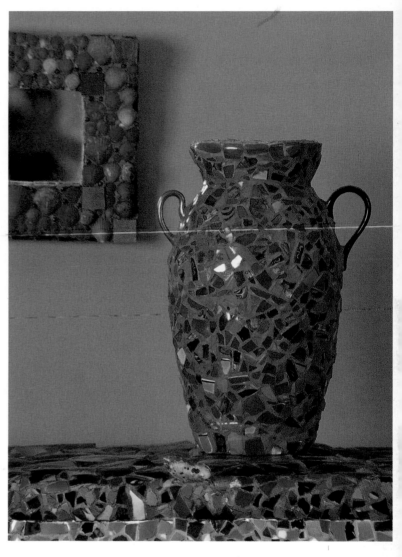

Confetti Vase
broken china and tile
12" x 8" diameter
(30 cm x 20 cm diameter)

Small Picture Frame
shells, turquoise stones, and gold leaf
10" square (25 cm square)

Large Urn
broken china, *tesserae*, and mirror
4.4' x 27" diameter (1.3 m x 69 cm diameter)

Porcelain Head
tesserae bits
22" x 18" x 10" (56 cm x 46 cm x 25 cm)

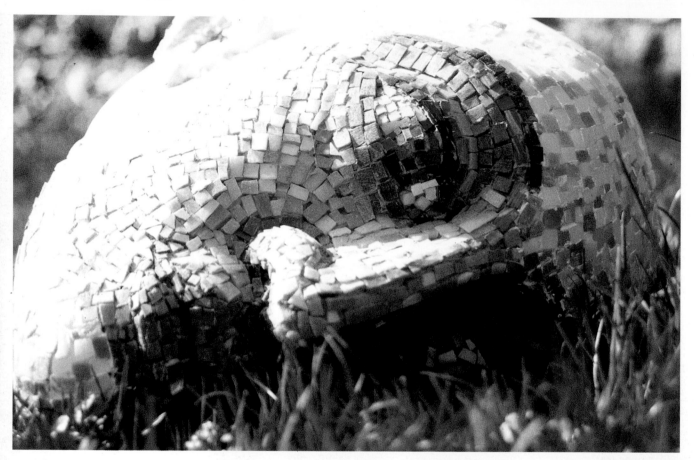

Porch with Medieval Mullion Window
cement and shells
5.6' x 9.6' (1.7 m x 2.9 m)

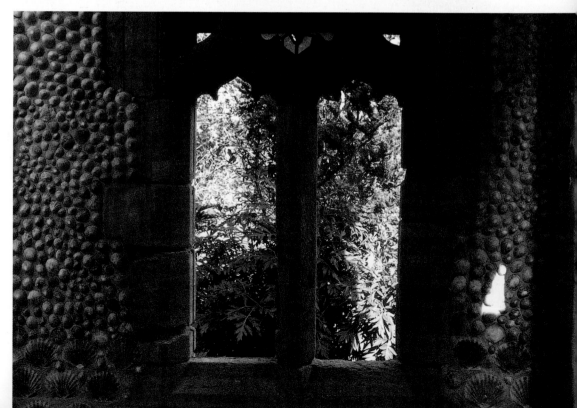

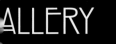

Egyptian Table
iron, cement, tesserae, and gold leaf
25" x 13" x 19"
(64 cm x 33 cm x 48 cm)

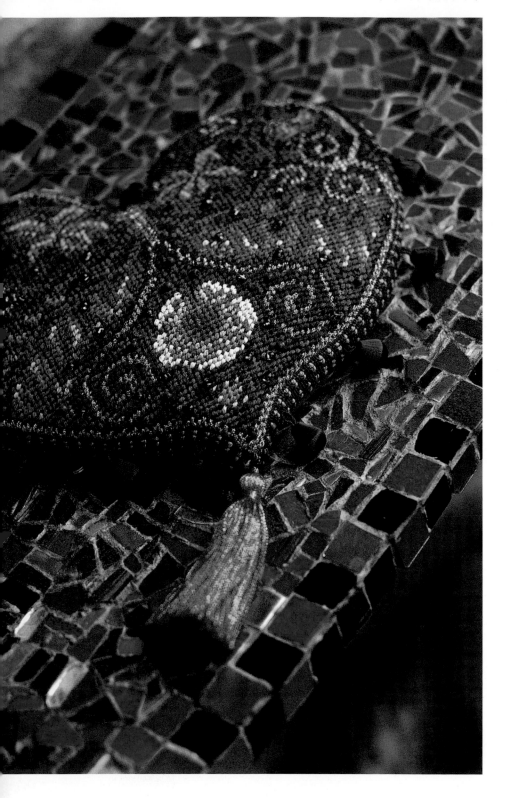

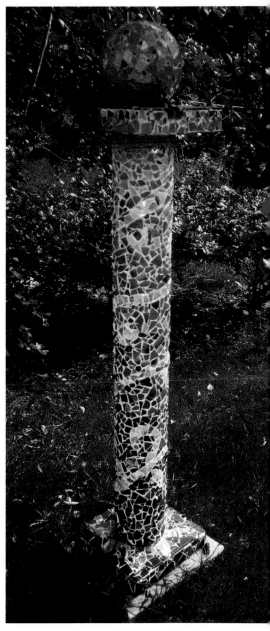

Pillar and Ball
broken china, mirror, and tile
5.8' x 14" square (1.8 m x 36 cm square)

VAL CARROLL

For nearly ten years, Val Carroll and her mosaics have been a growing presence in the Caribbean, where a number of vacation resorts have commissioned her to design, fabricate, and install large-scale projects that evoke images of nature, often as part of swimming pool or spa facilities. Just as dramatic, but less frequently on public display, are the artist's unique mosaic sculptures. Although stationary and inanimate, these abstract renditions of flora and fauna always appear to be in motion. Both *Afternoon Delight* and *Unlikely Menage x 3* depict the tidewater life that Carroll favors for her site installations.

Carroll has worked almost strictly in mosaics for the last eighteen years, but her earlier experience in painting, weaving, and sculpture is constantly being reconfigured, resulting in new directions for the evolution of her mosaics.

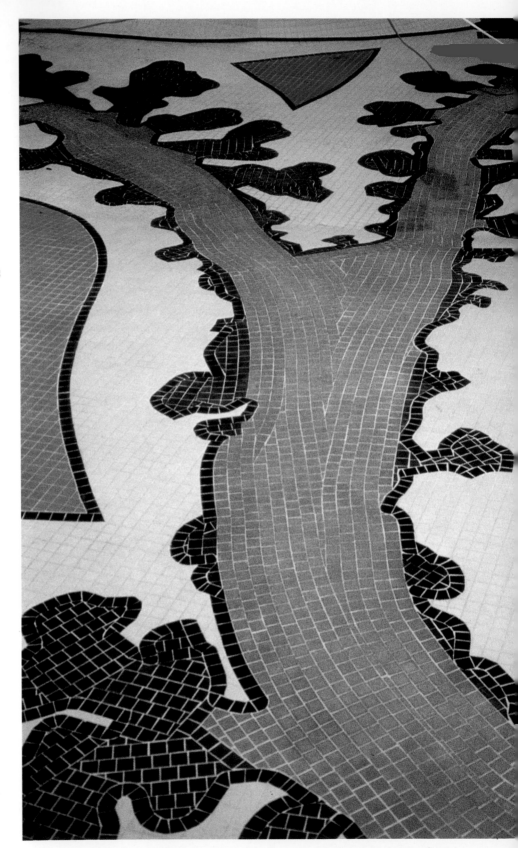

Detail from **Tidal Treasures, Fire Coral**

"Since childhood, I have had a fascination with biology and the natural world," says Carroll. That innate attraction, coupled with the 1970s attitudes about regionalism

TECHNIQUE

and the importance of preserving the unique aspects of local cultures, have greatly influenced Carroll's work through the years. "Nature remains my favorite source of inspiration," she states, and often she finds herself outside, dealing with both the joys and the discomfort nature has to offer.

One of her most important works, *Tidal Treasures*, an 18,000-square-foot

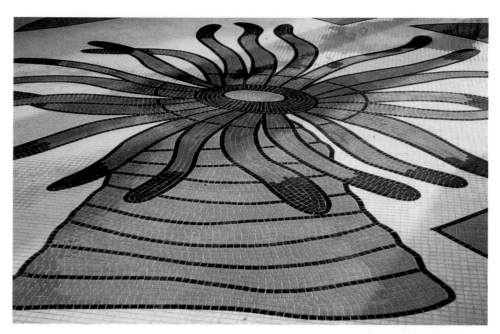

Detail from **Tidal Treasures, Anemone**

(5,400-square-meter) underwater mural, was months in the making. Humidity and island heat, along with dust and construction debris from the concurrent renovation of the adjacent hotel, made this her most challenging project, which

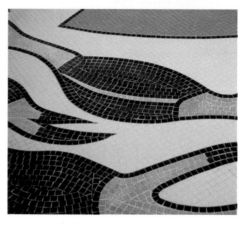

Detail from **Tidal Treasures, Seaweed**

the artist likens to "installing tile on a barbecue." But the tropical setting of Santa Lucia provided the artist with ideal inspiration—her mural depicts the region's colossal tide pool creatures like starfish and anemones, as well as fire coral, seaweed, and reef plants.

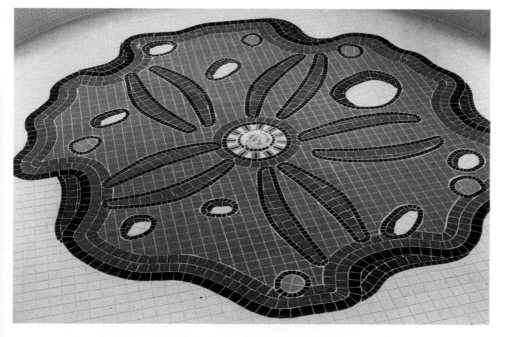

Detail from **Tidal Treasures, Sand Dollar**

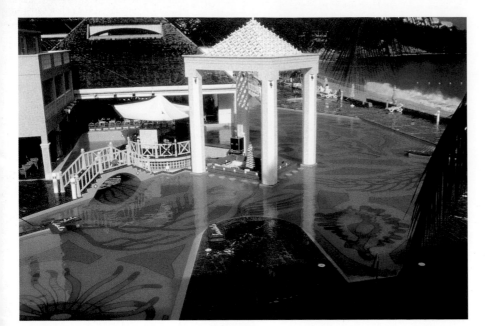

Tidal Treasures
porcelain mosaic
18,000 square feet (5,400 square meters)

Detail from **Tidal Treasures**

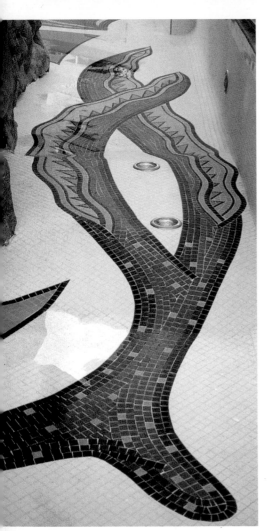

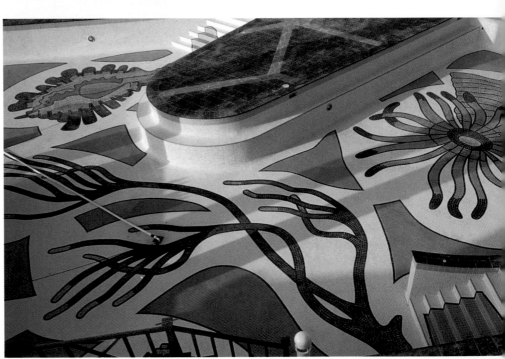

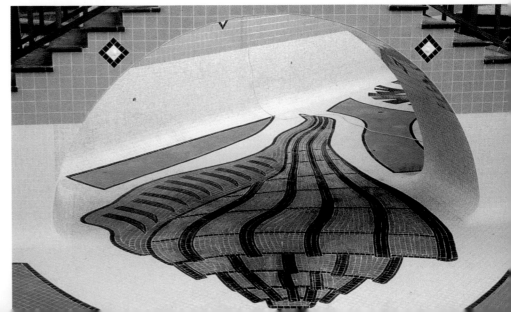

Tidal Treasures, Sea Sponge
porcelain mosaic
28' x 7' (8.5 m x 2.1 m)

Tidal Treasures, Shell (*under bridge*)
porcelain mosaic
25' x 12' (7.6 m x 3.7 m)

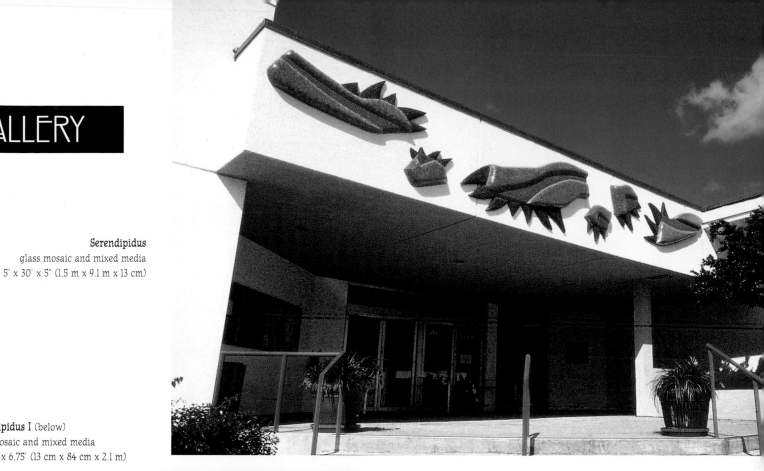

Serendipidus
glass mosaic and mixed media
5' x 30' x 5" (1.5 m x 9.1 m x 13 cm)

...ndipidus I (below)
...mosaic and mixed media
...3" x 6.75' (13 cm x 84 cm x 2.1 m)

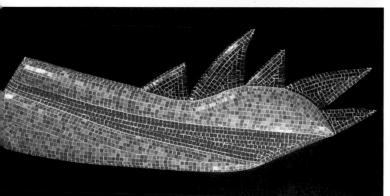

Serendipidus II
glass mosaic and mixed media
5" x 21" x 32" (13 cm x 53 cm x 81 cm)

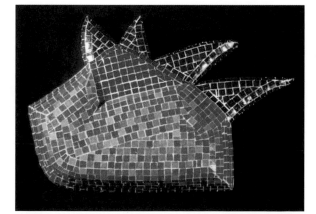

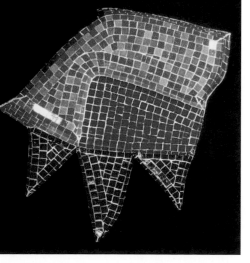

Serendipidus IV
...ss mosaic and mixed media
5" x 27" x 23"
(13 cm x 68 cm x 58 cm)

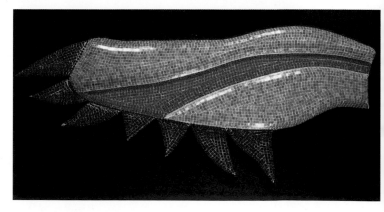

Serendipidus III
glass mosaic and mixed media
5" x 4.75' x 9' (13 cm x 1.5 m x 2.7 m)

245

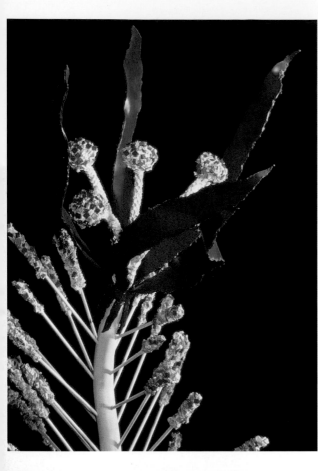

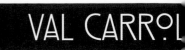

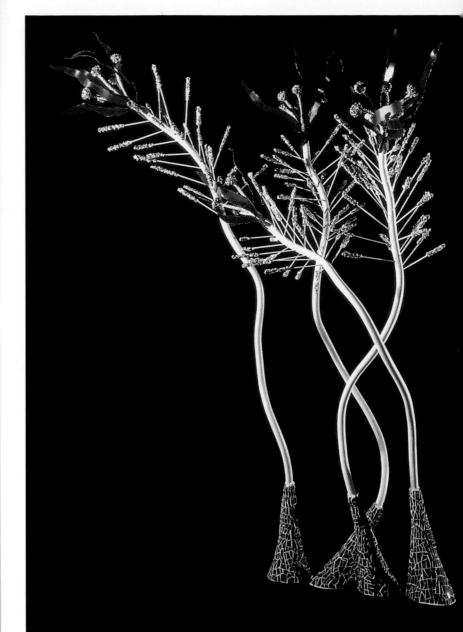

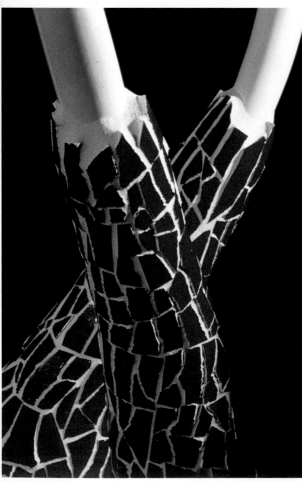

Afternoon D
ceramic mosaic, steel, and co
12' x 10' (3.7 m ×

Details from **Afternoon Delight**
(above left and left)

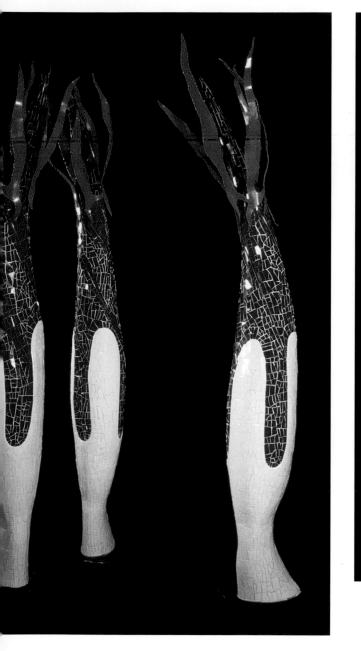

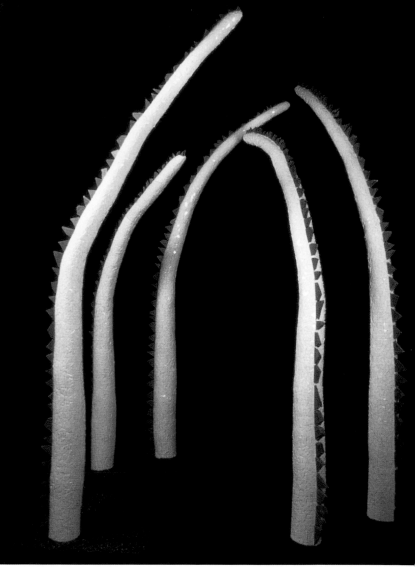

Awakenings, 5 pieces, exterior installation
ceramic mosaic, terra cotta, concrete, and steel
9' x 8" (2.7 m x 20 cm) each

Unlikely Menage x 3
ceramic mosaic, steel, and concrete
11' x 4' x 2.5' (3.4 m x 1.2 m x .8 m)

LYNN MATTSON

Lynn Mattson assembles chipped and cracked fragments of antique china, pottery, and figurines into constructions that tell a story. The secrets and compelling history of each time-worn bit are given new meaning with the artist's take on "memoryware," a popular form of American folk art from the early 1900s in which women affixed their keepsakes to containers. With her functional teapots, cookie jars, vases, and other sculptural pieces, Mattson continues this fanciful tradition of artistic narrative.

Born in San Francisco in 1958, Mattson has an extensive background in textiles and sculpted wall pieces. Her training as an artist began in seventh grade when she was sent to live in a convent for three years. One of the nuns had a giant ceramics studio, and Mattson spent most of her time there. A gift of a kiln a short time later cast her future in clay.

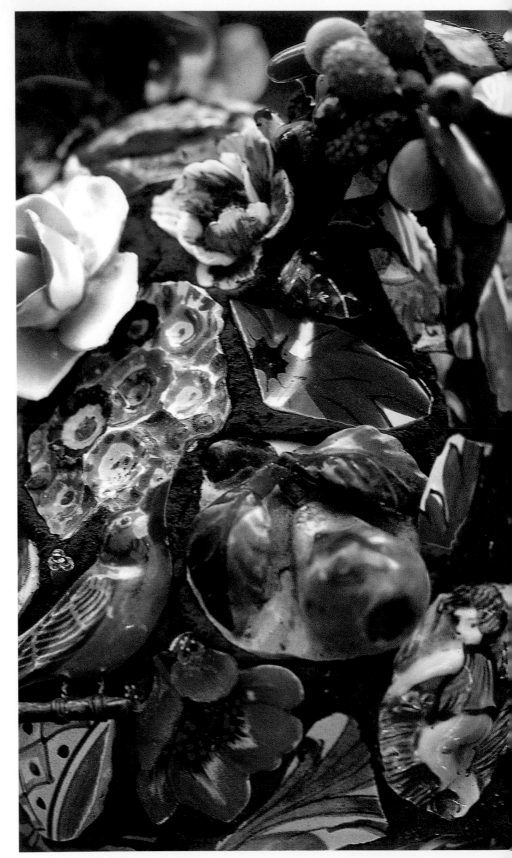

Detail from

The most important influence on Lynn Mattson's artwork is the subject she happens to be teaching at the time in her hands-on children's art history class.

TECHNIQUE

"It could be Baroque, Asian, Old World Italian, or the art of the circus," explains Mattson, "but whatever the topic, that is where I focus all of my creative energies in order to capture the true essence of the art theme."

With these shifting influences, she changes her materials. Grainy, dull green mortar binds together pieces with

Detail from **Childhood Memories, cookie jar**

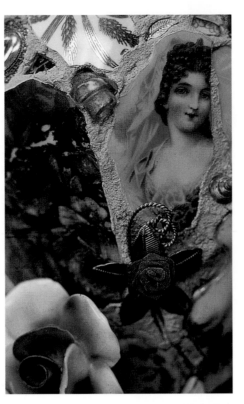

Detail from **Alexandria**

personal significance—the subdued tones, says Mattson, are contemplative and allow the importance of the individual

tesserae to be fully appreciated. When evoking an entire culture or era, the overall impact of the piece is heightened with bright hues such as electric blue or magenta. Like the memoryware of old, the worn and broken pieces that Mattson uses in her work tell her story. But in a

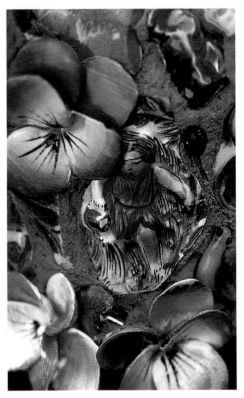

Detail from **Hallelujah**

departure from the manner of thinking of the Victorian housewives who started this craft, Mattson's vibrant constructions offer a perspective that looks toward the future.

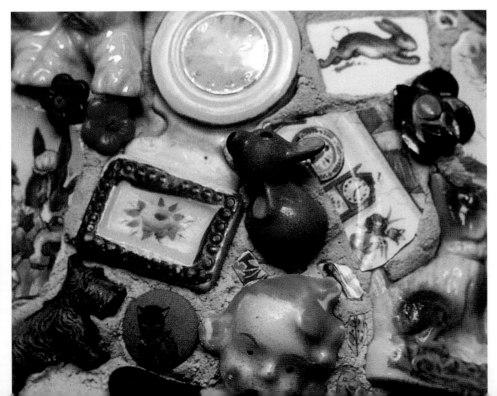

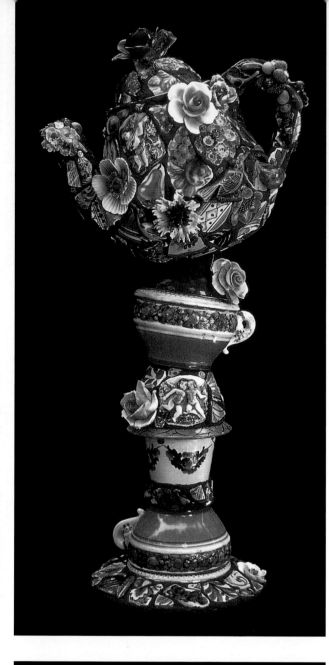

Pisa
ceramic and mixed media
19" x 9" (48 cm x 23 cm)

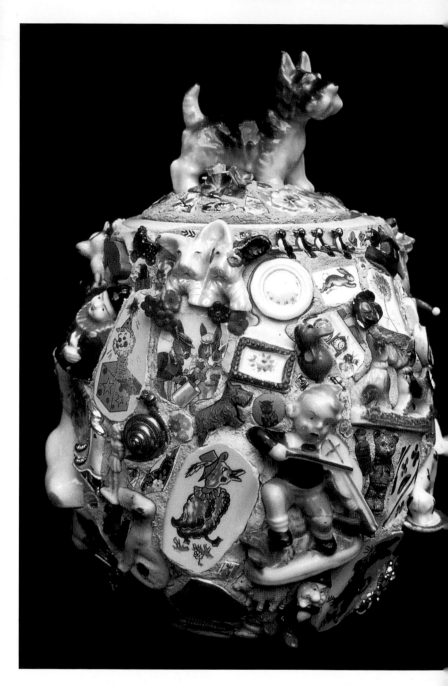

Childhood Memories, cooki
ceramic and mixed m
12" x 8" (30 cm x 20

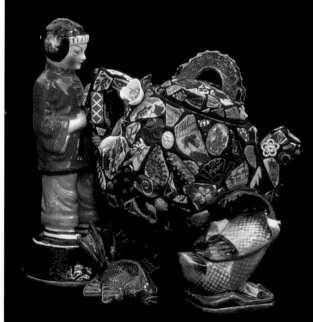

Misha
ceramic and mixed media
6" x 9" (15 cm x 23 cm)

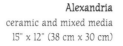

Alexandria
ceramic and mixed media
15" x 12" (38 cm x 30 cm)

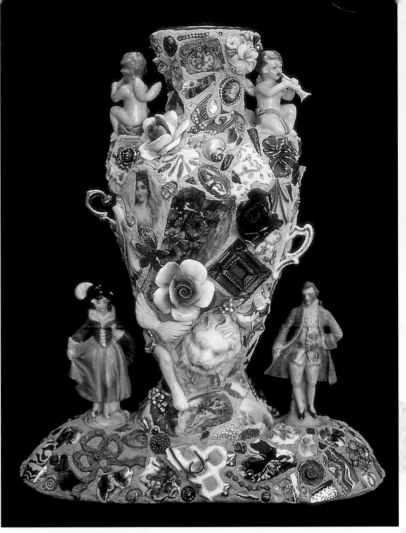

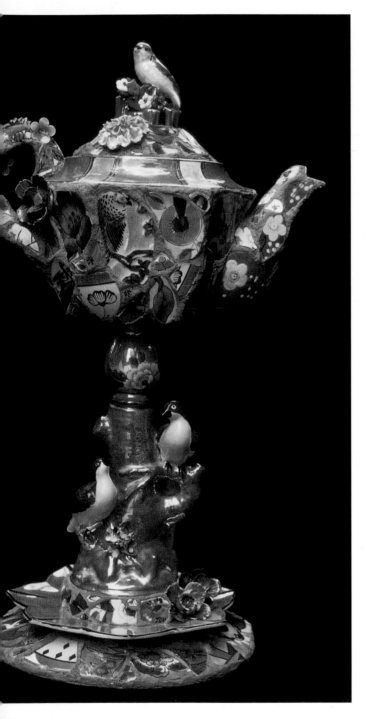

r Tree
ic and mixed media
10" (51 cm x 25 cm)

Pagoda
ceramic and mixed media
13" x 9" (33 cm x 23 cm)

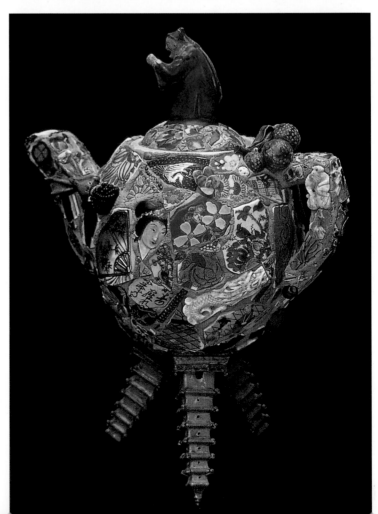

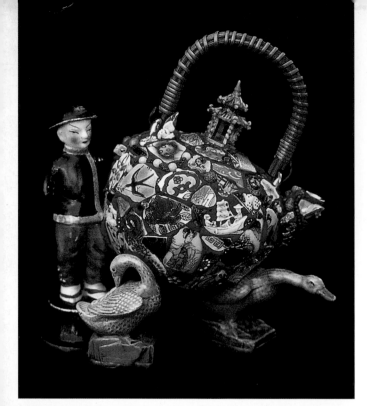

Ping
ceramic and mixed media
6" x 9" (15 cm x 23 cm)

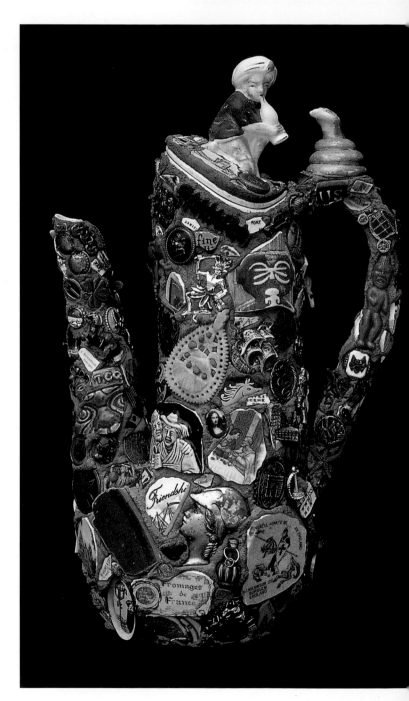

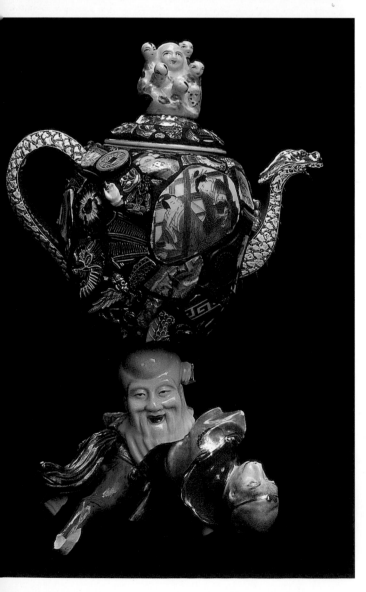

Aladdin's Tr
ceramic and mixed r
16" x 12" (41 cm x 3(

Floating Island
ceramic and mixed media
14" x 9" (36 cm x 23 cm)

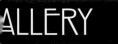

Travel Log USA
ceramic and mixed media
12" x 9" (30 cm x 23 cm)

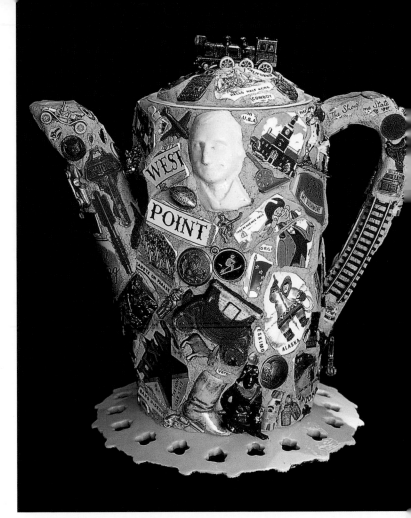

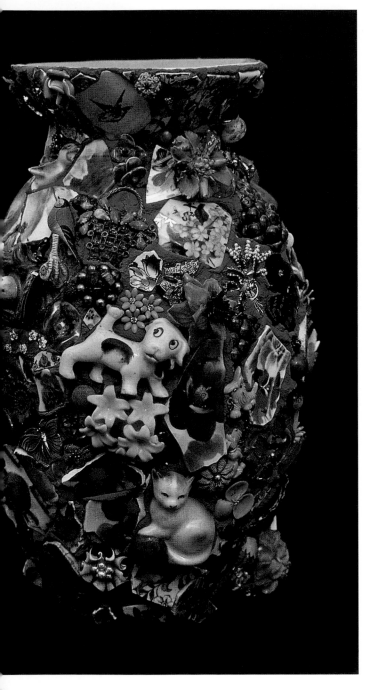

lma's Garden, San Anselmo, California
ic and mixed media
" (41 cm x 20 cm)

Mexican Bean Pot
ceramic and mixed media
11" x 12" (28 cm x 30 cm)

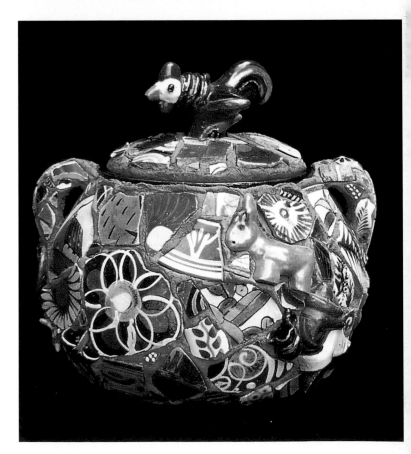

JANE MUIR

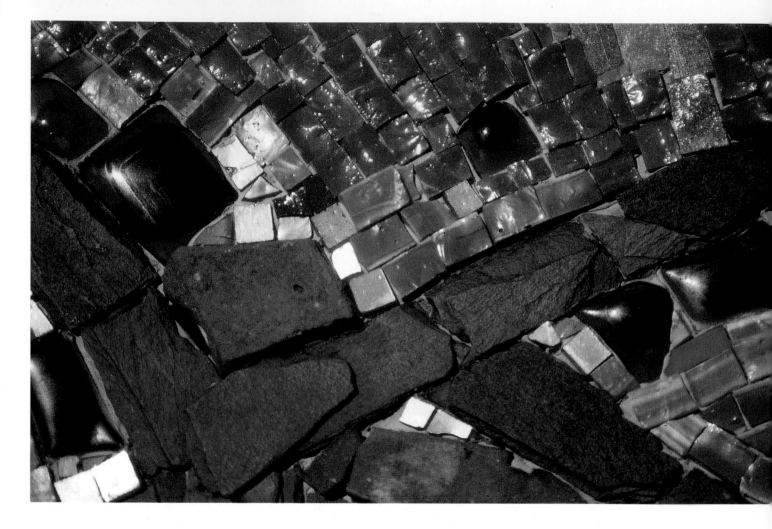

While studying medieval history at Oxford University, Jane Muir took a trip to Italy and encountered the mosaics at Ravenna, which she much admired. Her work as a mosaic artist, however, did not begin until she could no longer stand the sight of an ugly coal house door that was in clear view whenever she stood at her sink to wash dishes or clean up after two small children. With no experience, but a lot of panache, that door was boldly transformed with an Indian Tree of Life motif.

She was in her late thirties before she formally studied art—painting, sculpture, murals, and mosaics. Despite her fascination with mosaics, Muir discovered few people who shared her enthusiasm, and most even purposefully avoided it. When she set up a studio in 1968, she realized that mosaics were typically associated with "nasty coffee-tabletop kits of vitreous materials in garish colors." At that point, Muir decided to devote her career to changing such opinions and educating the public about mosaic design as an art form.

Detail from **Fruiting**

Jane Muir creates dramatically textured mosaic landscape compositions. Nature, its symbolism, and folklore exert a strong influence on her work, and many of the

TECHNIQUE

patterns she assembles suggest topographical maps or geological formations. Muir works with diverse materials, unexpectedly juxtaposing contrasts of texture, color, and reflective elements.

Rough-hewn slate, brick, gold leaf, lead crystal, and brilliant Venetian smalti find their way into the pieces she executes in high relief. Light is the most critical element to the success of her art.

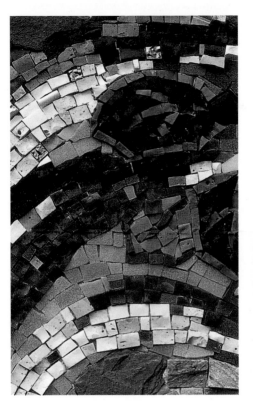

Detail from **The Leaves Be Green**

Clusters and rivers of chunky *tesserae* are deliberately sculptured into her mosaics for depth and shadow, to maneuver light where she wants it.

The influences of Botticelli, Rembrandt, Tapies, Paul Klee, and Romanesque carvings are all formative references that she says have seen her through the development of her work.

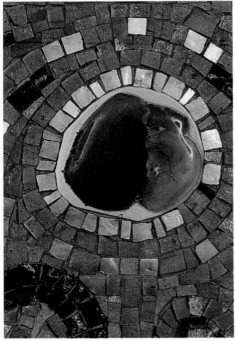

Detail from **Happy Birds**

But this artist is most influenced by the often abstract qualities of the natural environment. Weathered rocks, the sea, and mythical animals remain compelling sources of inspiration that she constantly reaches out to, for, she says, "The excitement lies in the search."

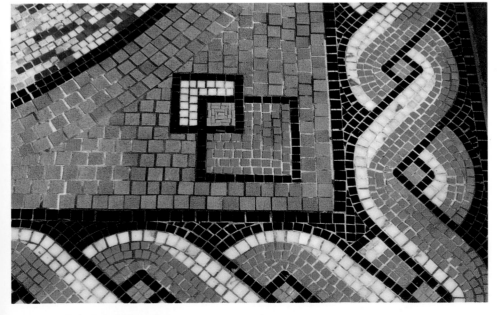

Detail from **Canterbury Longmarket**

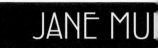

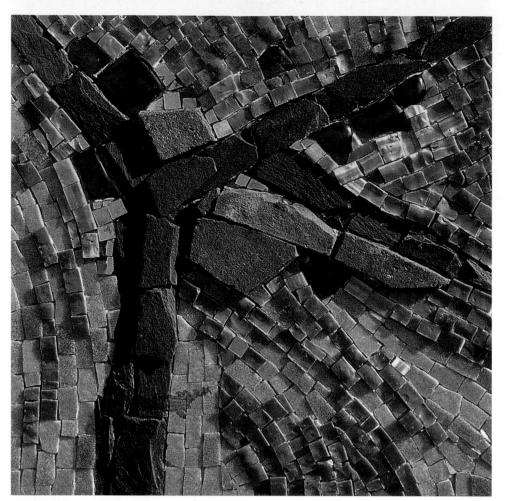

Fruiting
glass mosaic, slate, and tile
19.5" x 20" (50 cm x 51 cm)

Canterbury Longmarket
mosaic pavement, marble, high-fired stoneware,
and Venetian smalti
59 square feet (18 square meters)

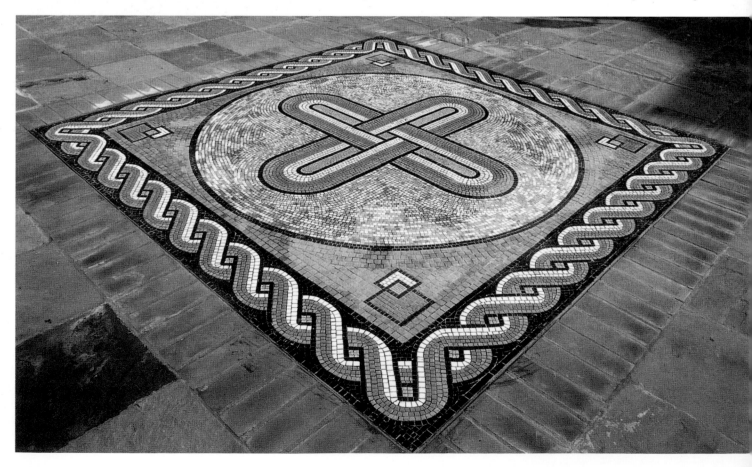

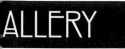

The Leaves Be Green
Venetian smalti, glass fusion, green
slate, and gold leaf
20" x 15" (51 cm x 38 cm)

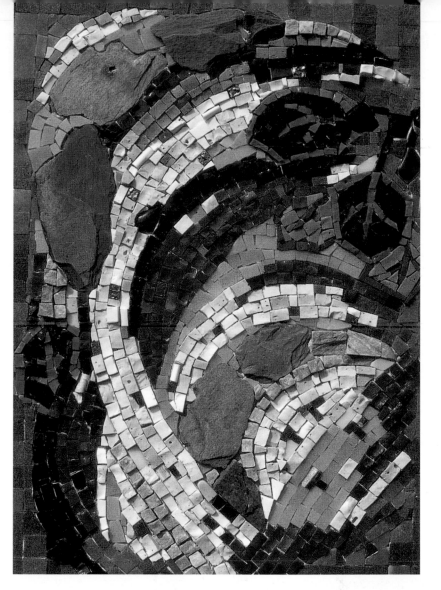

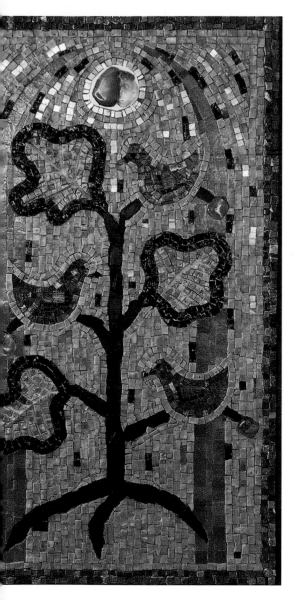

y Birds
glass fusion, and Venetian smalti
21" (92 cm x 54 cm)

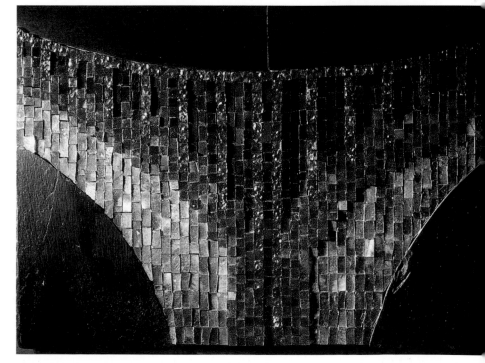

Great Cascade
slate and Venetian smalti
25" x 16" (64 cm x 40 cm)

LILLI ANN KILLEN ROSENBERG

Muralist, sculptor, and potter, Lilli Ann Killen Rosenberg is best known for her public art projects that help to enliven the cities of Boston and New York. What sets Rosenberg's work apart is the high level of community participation that she seeks for her concrete mosaic commissions. Such collaboration culminates in highly acclaimed "art in public places" that integrates the needs of a community with its architectural environment.

Frequently working with husband Marvin Rosenberg, a social worker, Lilli Ann Killen Rosenberg creates pieces layered with both personal meaning and universal significance. Much of Rosenberg's work is devoted or related to children and children's themes. Her largest commission to date is the MBTA's Park Street Station in Boston, *Celebration of the Underground*. Commemorating the opening of the first American subway in 1897, the mural is a sprawling, graphic narrative, the result of extensive interviews the artist conducted with historians, geologists, motormen, and mechanics.

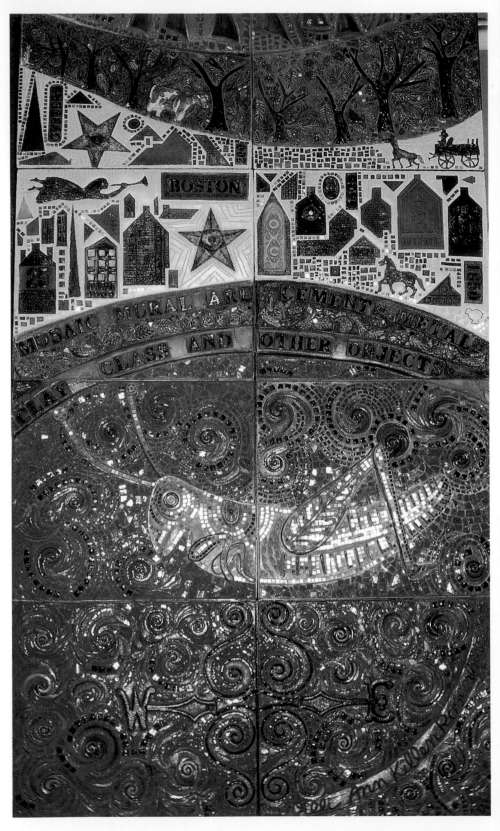

Details from **Celebration of the Underground**
(above and opposite page)

Lilli Ann Killen Rosenberg's mosaic murals are created in concrete. More than just a supporting structure, it is itself an art medium, often colored and textured.

TECHNIQUE

Sometimes carved into sculpture or cast, concrete serves as Rosenberg's invitation for community involvement. "It is the perfect medium for people of all ages to make clay pieces, collect objects, and contribute their skills for a collaborative collage, resulting in a shared sense of ownership," says Rosenberg.

She first started using concrete when working on a children's art program in New York City. She was so

inspired by their clay pieces that she embedded them into murals, sculpture gardens, and paved areas. The joyful spirit and delight in the children's imaginations helped Rosenberg brighten some very dim neighborhoods.

Like the artist's finished compositions, concrete is indestructible, and both simple and complex. Viewers are invited

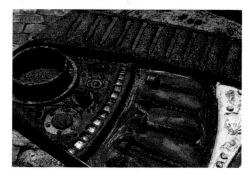

to touch the works for a tactile experience that will linger in their memories, much like the lasting impression the mosaics from the Watts Tower, a Southern California folk art dream palace, made on Rosenberg when she was a teenager.

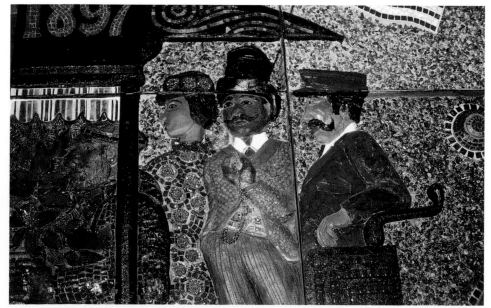

Celebration of the Underground

MBTA Park Street Station, Boston, Massachusetts
ceramic, glass, metal, and mixed media
10' x 110' (3 m x 33.5 m)

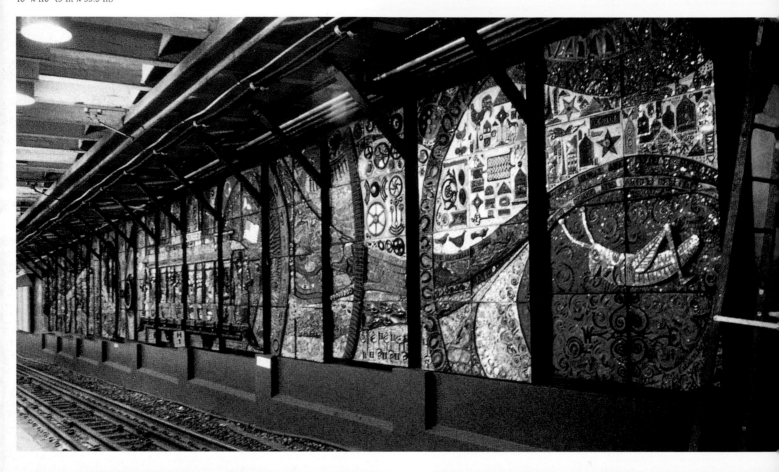

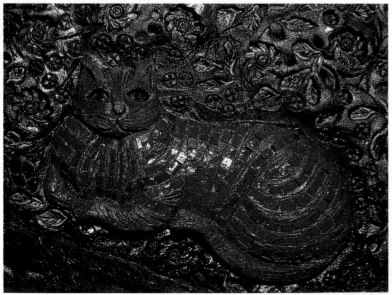

Details from **Celebration of the Underground**
(above and right)

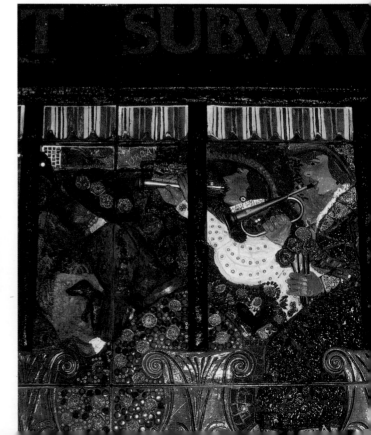

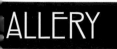

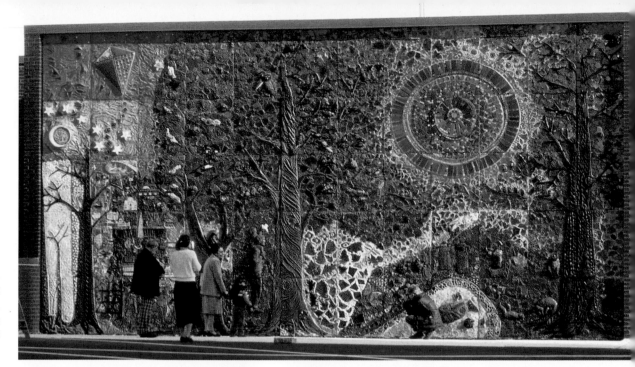

Children's Center Mural
Seasons, Philadelphia, Pennsylvania
concrete mosaic, found objects,
mixed media, and ceramic
18' x 36' (5.5 m x 11 m)

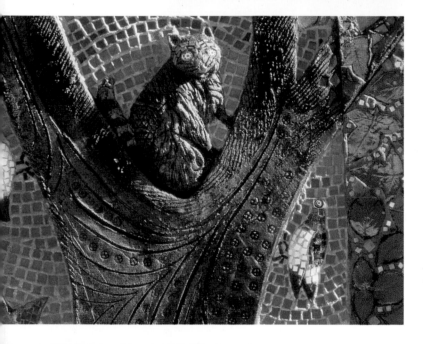

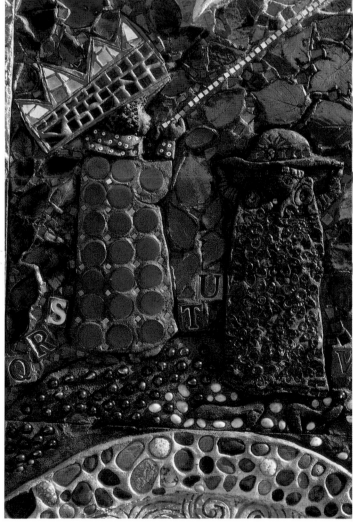

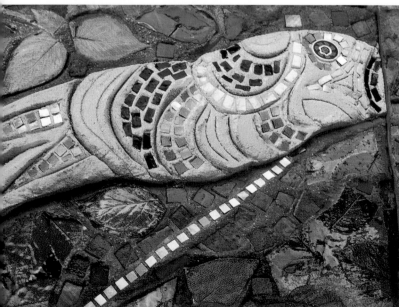

Details from **Children's Center Mural**

ILANA SHAFIR

For Ilana Shafir, the first step on the path to her life as an artist was taken among simple peasants in a tiny Yugoslavian village where her family sought refuge from the Nazis. A seventeen-year-old, she was so affected by the courage and strength of these villagers that she began to paint their portraits and the landscape. Born in Sarajevo, Shafir attended the Zagreb Academy of Arts after the war. In 1949, she immigrated to Israel and settled in Ashkelon to work as an artist and teacher, and there she began creating mosaics.

The Netzach Israel Synagogue in Ashkelon is brightened by Shafir's unique signature—a stained glass window and mosaic combination within a single frame. This dual-form mosaic is designed around the daily ebb and flow of light—bright Mediterranean daylight passes through the glass and then slowly fades into the night's shadows, giving center stage to the opaque tesserae. This aesthetic interplay and transformation of light make Shafir's mosaics easily identifiable.

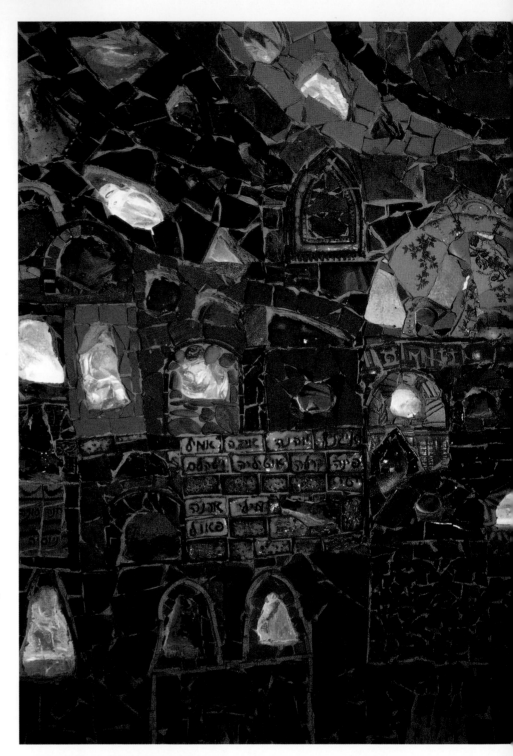

Detail from **Jerus**
(above and opp

Primarily a self-taught mosaicist, Ilana Shafir's works are fabricated from a variety of traditional and unexpected materials. These include seashells,

TECHNIQUE

ceramic pieces, broken china, natural stones, pebbles, minerals, and gold and silver tesserae. Her mosaics have a spiritual atmosphere characterized by a dynamic flow upward toward the sky. Her materials inspire her artworks: "There is always a one-of-a-kind stone, piece of ceramic, or broken handle with

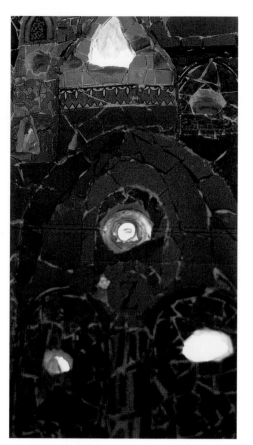

Detail from **Jerusalem**
(includes the sign "Z" that the artist and her sister wore as Jewesses during World War II)

which I begin my work. The mosaic grows with its own laws of composition and texture but is always related to that first piece."

After thirty years as an artist in her community, Shafir has ready sources

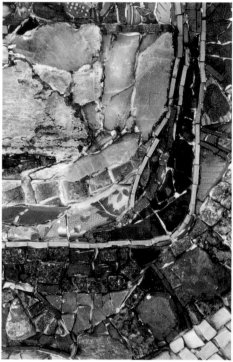

Detail from **The Big Gate**

of materials. "All the town knows that my studio is the address to deposit broken ceramics. From time to time, someone stands admiring one of my mosaics and says, 'Now I see what she has done with my broken china set!'"

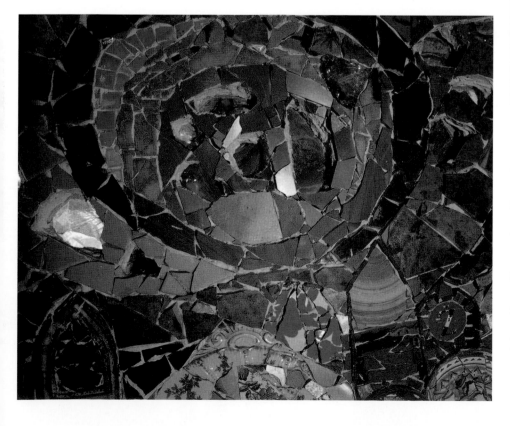

Jerusalem
colored glass from Murano, broken ceramic, and found objects
5.8' x 36" (1.8 m x 90 cm)

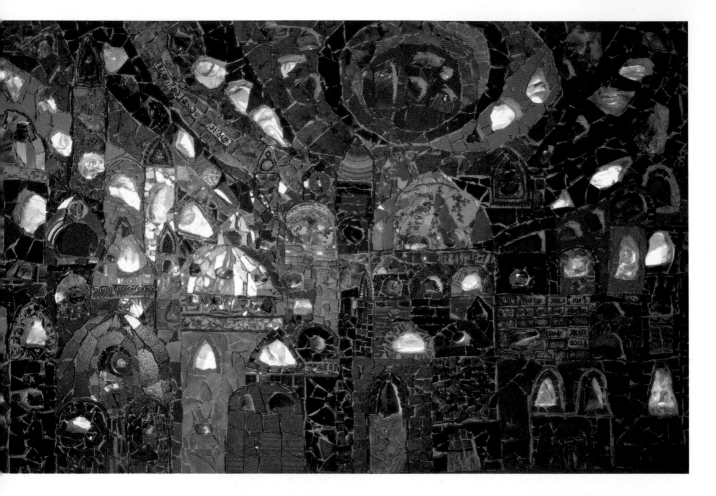

The Closed Gate
gold smalti, marble *tesserae*, shells,
corals, broken ceramic, pebbles,
found objects, and sandstone
32" x 24" (80 cm x 60 cm)

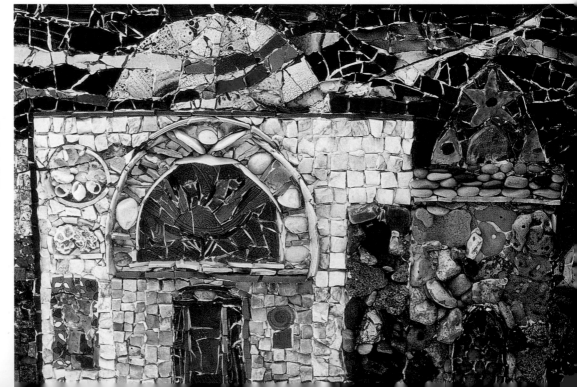

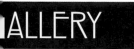

Star
ceramic, pebbles, shells, green
eilat stones, and gold and silver smalti
20" x 28" (50 cm x 70 cm)

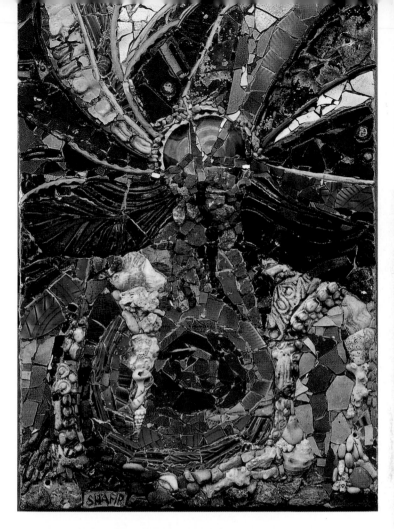

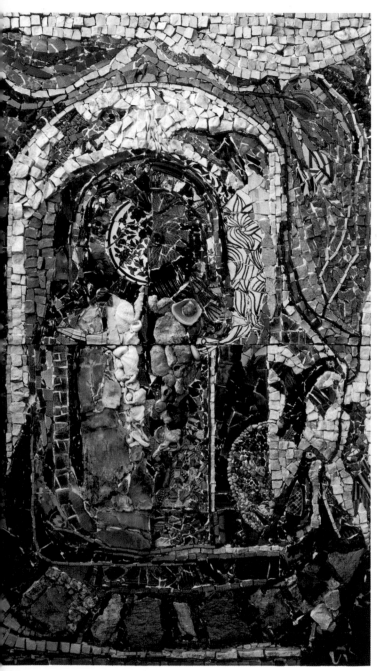

Big Gate
smalti, marble *tesserae*, basalt, granite, eilat, arad, and alabaster stones,
en ceramic, pebbles, shells, and corals
x 4' (80 cm x 1.2 m)

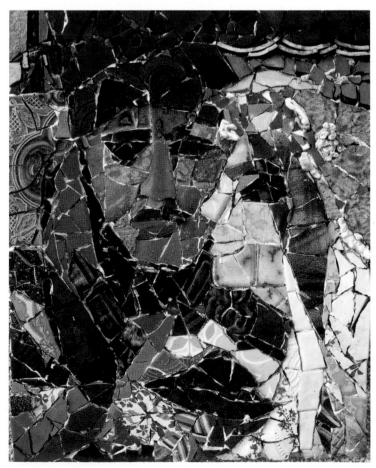

Wedding
broken and cut ceramic and corals
16" x 20" (40 cm x 50 cm)

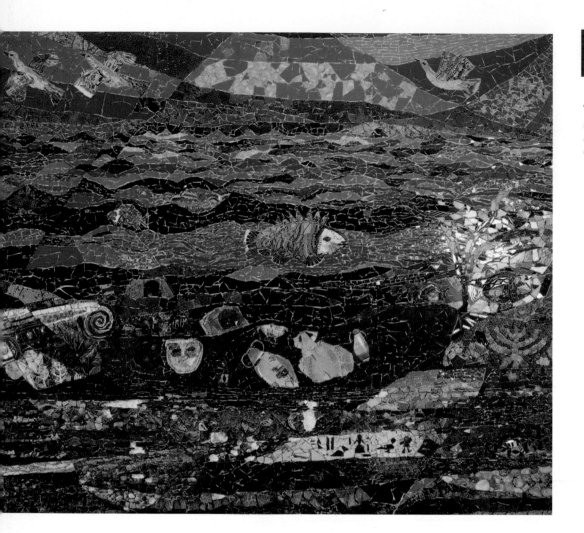

The Soil of Ashkelon
stone *tesserae*, natural stones, pebbles, broken ceramic, ceramic tiles, and handmade ceramic
9.8' x 8.3' (3 m x 2.5 m)

Mural at the Entrance Wall of the
Woldenberg Community Center, Ashkelon
stone *tesserae*, natural stones,
pebbles, broken ceramic, ceramic tiles,
and handmade ceramic parts
10' x 6.5' (3 m x 2 m)

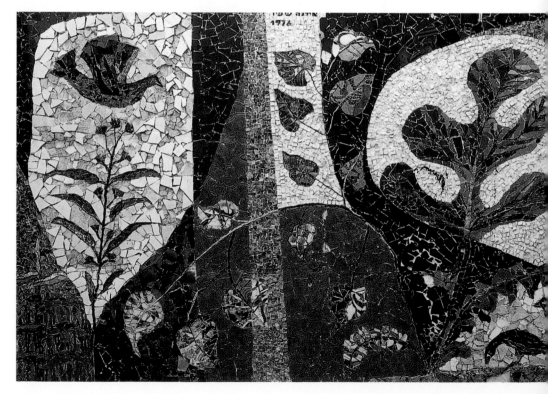

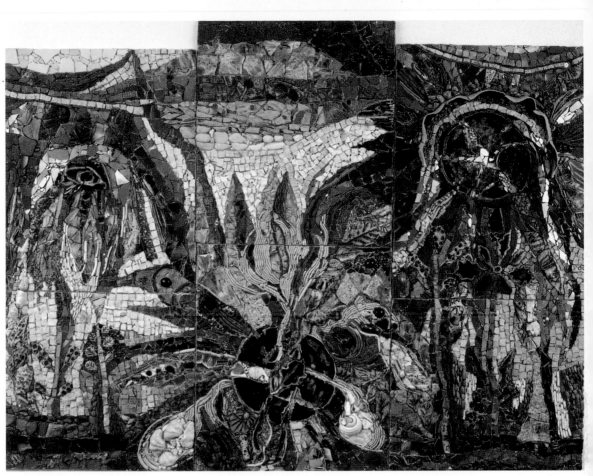

Blessings
broken ceramic, handmade ceramic parts,
pebbles, marble *tesserae*, gold and
silver smalti, glass, corals, and shells
5.8' x 4.8' (1.8 m x 1.4 m)

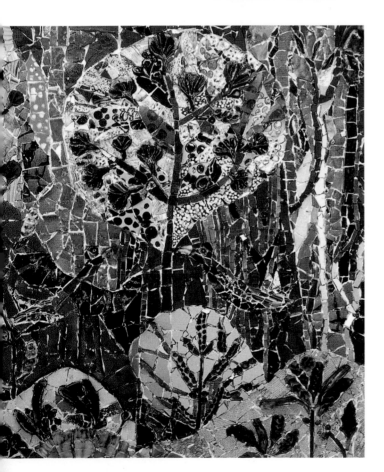

en
made ceramic parts, broken ceramic, and marble *tesserae*
24" (90 cm x 60 cm)

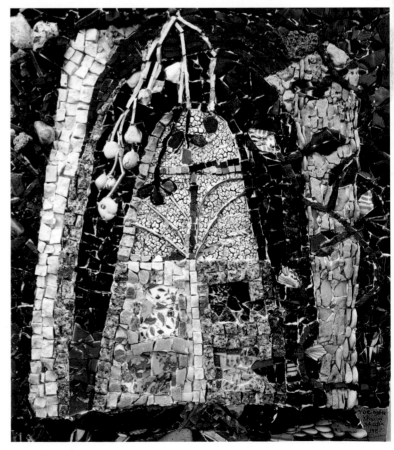

The Flower Gate
broken ceramic, stone *tesserae*, gold smalti, pebbles, and glass
27" x 31" (68 cm x 78 cm)

ISAIAH ZAGAR

For more than twenty-five years, Isaiah Zagar has been fashioning an extensive body of folk art, embellishing interior and exterior walls throughout Philadelphia with mosaics. Although at first the public looked askance at his murals, these works are now highly acclaimed and much admired for their rich contribution to the city's fabric. Zagar has transformed at least twenty bland and dispirited settings in the South Street and Old City neighborhoods into enclaves of surprise and delight. While not physically connected, these wall murals establish a distinct public art environment that Zagar calls a psychically contiguous system of parks.

Originally trained as a printmaker and painter, Zagar studied at the Pratt Institute in Brooklyn, New York, and then switched to mosaics. His executions are not purely architectural ornaments, for they embody an individual aesthetic and a strong, unified vision, one that turns nondescript architecture into colorful sculpture.

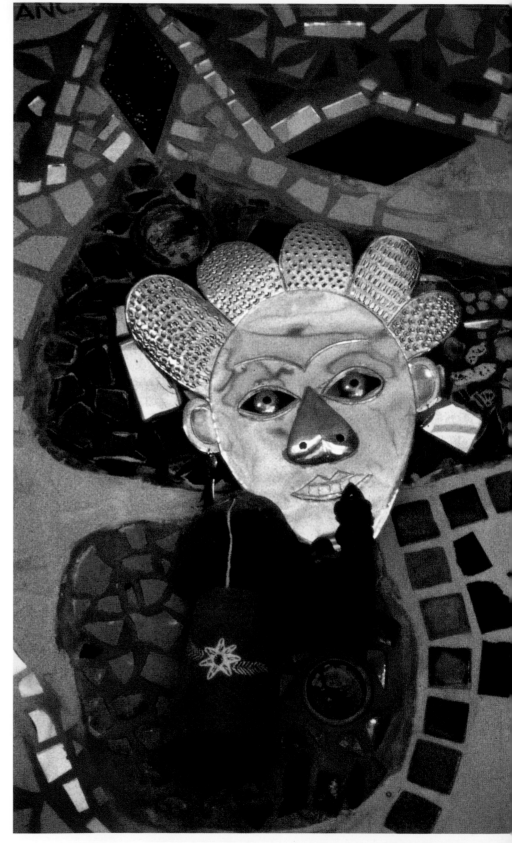

Detail from **Kater Street Stu**

Isaiah Zagar's mosaic installations transform masonry facades, walls, and stairwells that were once expressionless into dazzling abstractions of tile, mirror, and

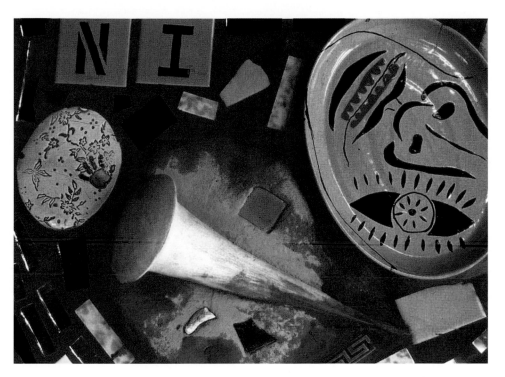

Detail from **A Day in America**

TECHNIQUE

found objects. Every surface is completely covered, painted in minute and imaginative detail. Embedded into his murals are spiraling, twisted, or upside down messages from Zagar spelled out in pieces of broken mirror or tile. Despite the large size of his projects—up to 6,000 square feet (540 square meters)—Zagar works without a plan.

Greatly influenced by the rich, distinctive colors found in the cultures of

South America, where he worked for five years as a craft developer with the Peace Corps, Zagar adopted these brilliant hues into his own work. He uses these colorful references as a cultural link, believing that art is a universal language capable of joining widely disparate peoples. The influence of Marcel Duchamp, Antonio Gaudi, and outsider artists can also be seen in his mosaics. Zagar's work has been referred to as an artistic expression of the concept that things don't need to be "either/or"—instead they can be both/and."

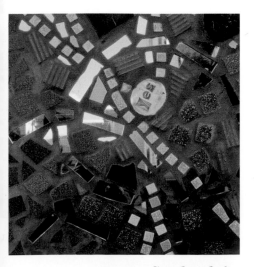

Detail from **Kater Street Studio**

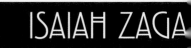

Kater Street Studio,
entranceway interior
tile mosaic
12' x 15' (3.7 m x 4.6 m)

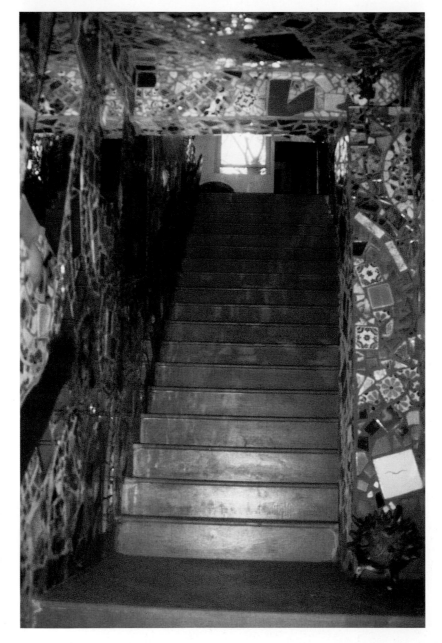

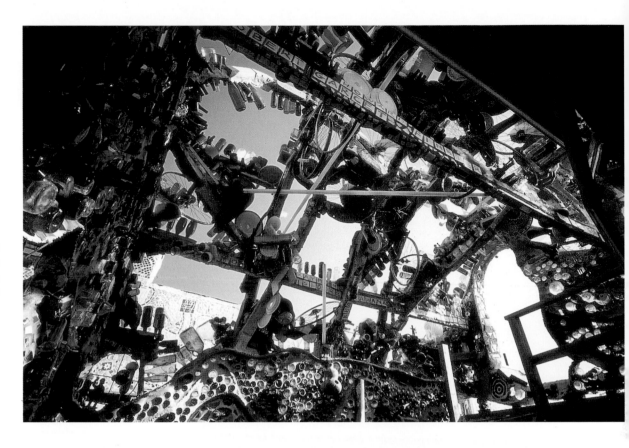

er Street Studio, Canopy on South
Street side
mixed media mosaic
30' x 40' (9.1 m x 12.2 m)

Kater Street Studio, exterior
mixed media mosaic
20' x 30' (6.1 m x 9.1 m)

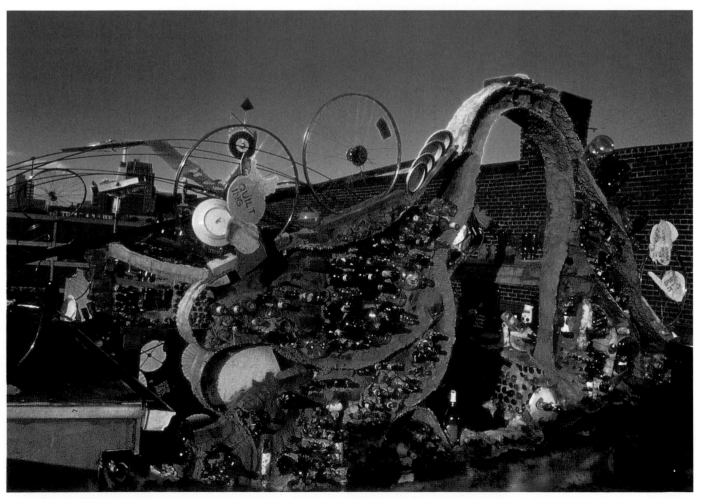

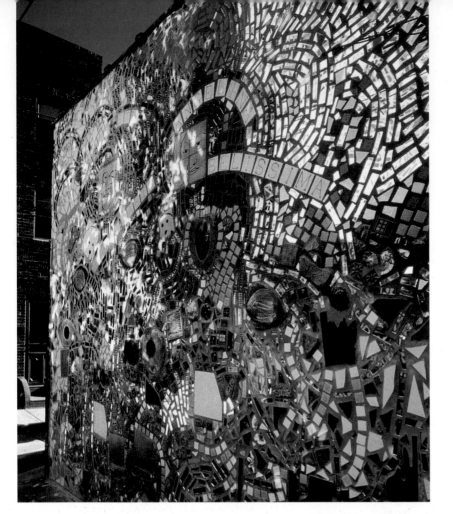

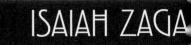

Pemberton Street Wall
mixed media mosaic
12' x 25' (3.7 m x 7.6 m)

Mildred Street Wall
mixed media mosaic
8' x 30' (2.4 m x 9.1 m)

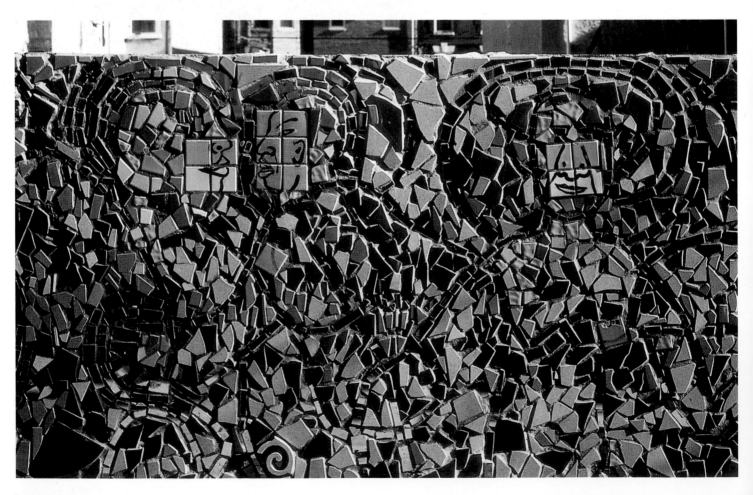

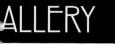

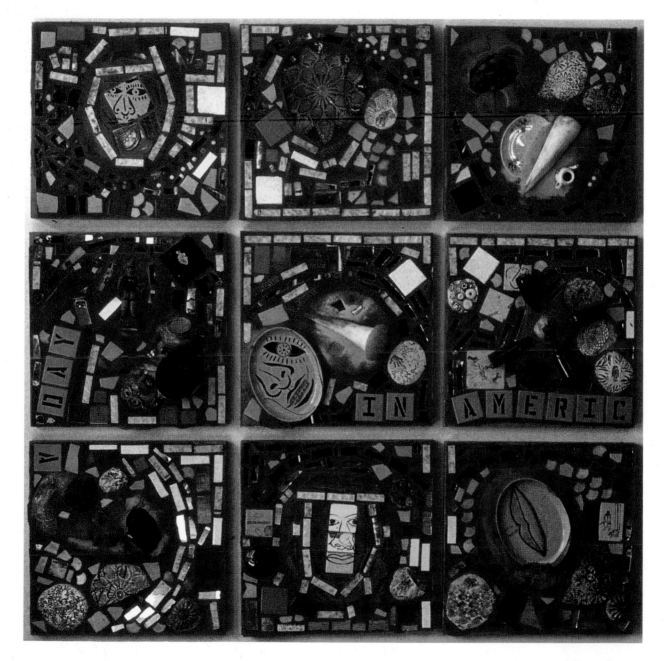

A Day in America
mixed media
88" x 88" (224 cm x 224 cm)

Waving Strings
natural stones and
colored cement
4' x 32" (1.2 m x 80 cm)

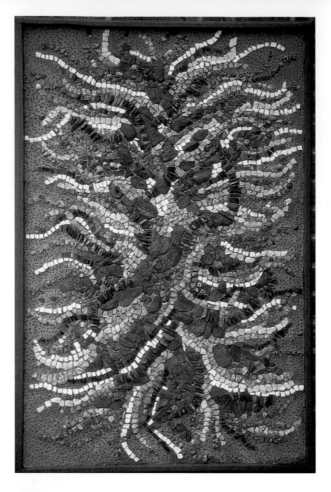

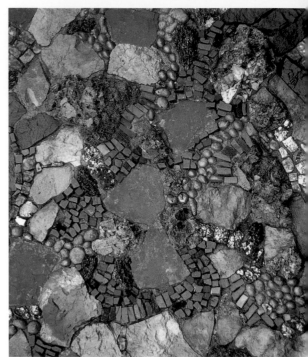

Detail from **Fire**, glass and gold

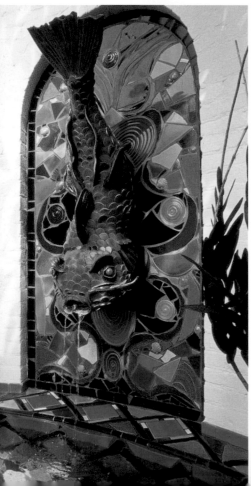

Catalan Fish Fountain
ceramic tile and ferro cement
8' x 7' x 3.5' (2.4 m x 2.1 m x 1.1 m)

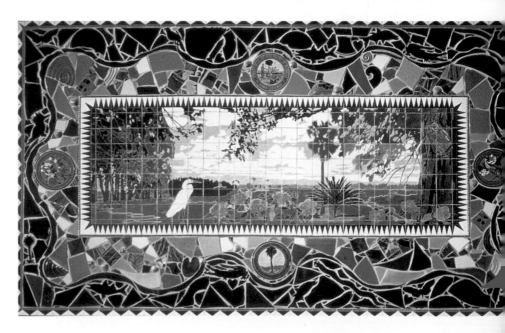

Ceramic Tile M
Home Savings of America, Pembroke Pines, F
8' x 12' (2.4 m x 3

After Van der Weyden
clay and found objects
24" x 24" (60 cm x 60 cm)

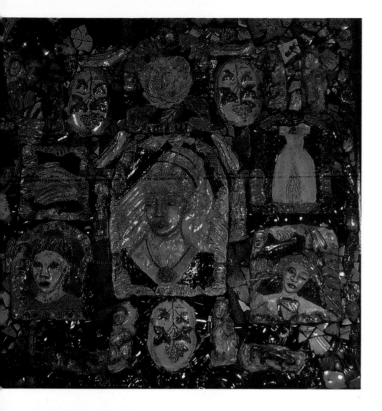

**Greenhouse
and Aviary**
mosaic collage and
handmade tiles
6' x 26" (1.8 m x 66 cm)

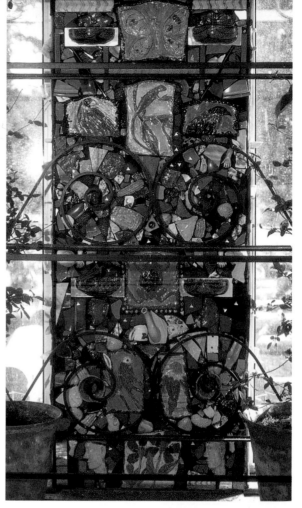

ARBARA FIELD

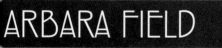

Dream's Peak (right)
mosaic tile panels
6.7' x 24" (2 m x 60 cm) each

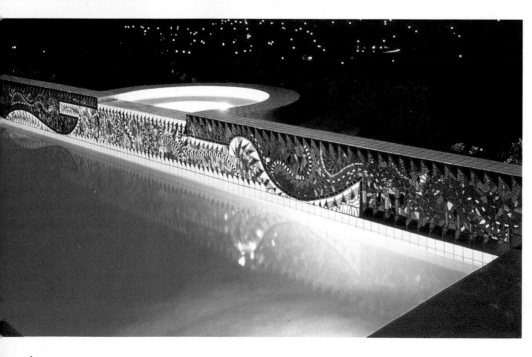

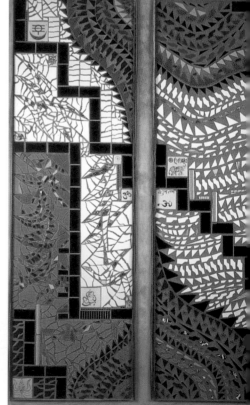

.arazad
ic tile
3.5' (12.2 m x 1.1 m)

275

MERLE FISHMAN AND DAVID CATRAMBONE
Venus
glass and marble
3' x 11' (.9 m x 3.4 m)

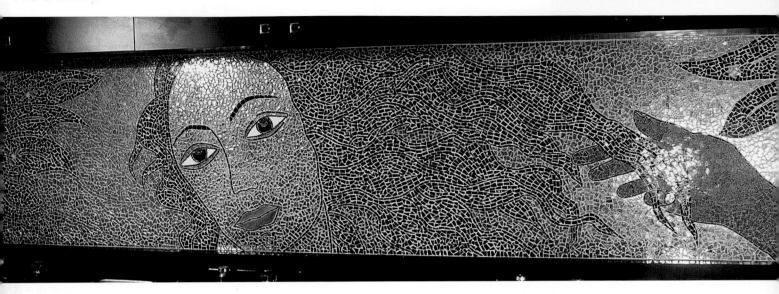

MERLE FISHMAN AND
DAVID CATRAMBONE
The Wave
ceramic tile
5' x 9' (1.5 m x 2.7 m)

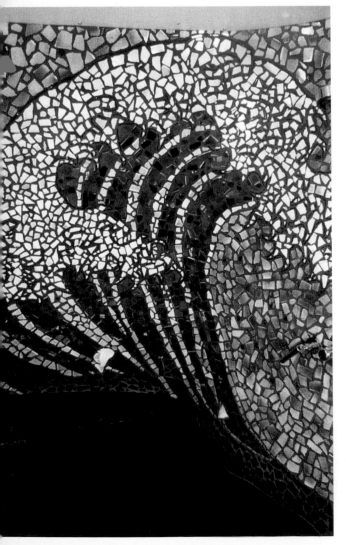

DAVID CATRAMBONE
Crucifix
linoleum mosaic
8' x 4' (2.4 m x 1.2 m)

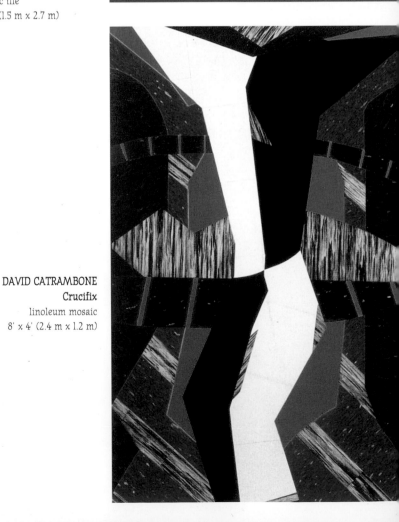

Danza del Cerchio (below, detail below left)
Port of Seattle, Washington
glass mosaic, 11' x 43' (3.4 m x 13.1 m)

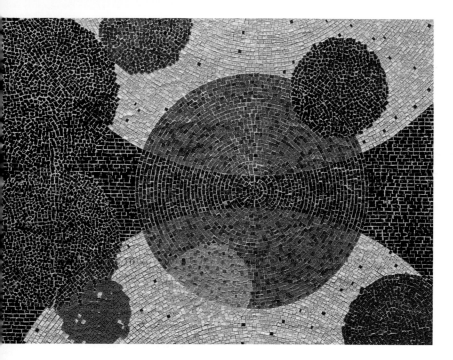

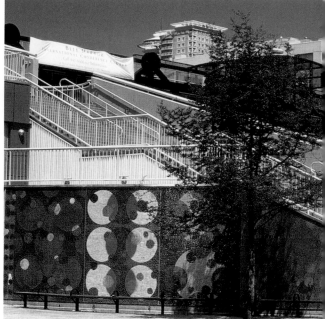

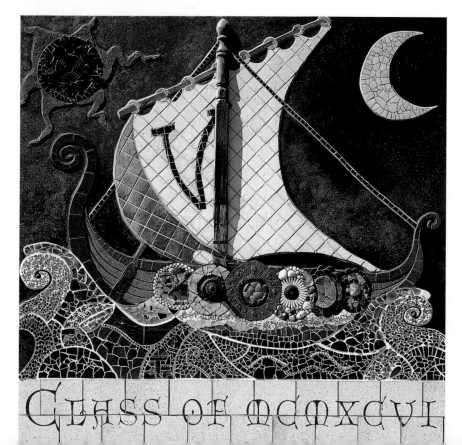

Valley Vikings
Valley High School, Albuquerque, New Mexico
ceramic and glass tiles, found objects,
gemstones, and seashells
10' x 10' (3 m x 3 m)

Union Square
14th Street Subway, New York, New York
marble, granite, onyx, slate, sandstone, brick,
old tiles, Italian glass, and tumbled glass beads
5.5' x 8.6' (1.7 m x 2.6 m)

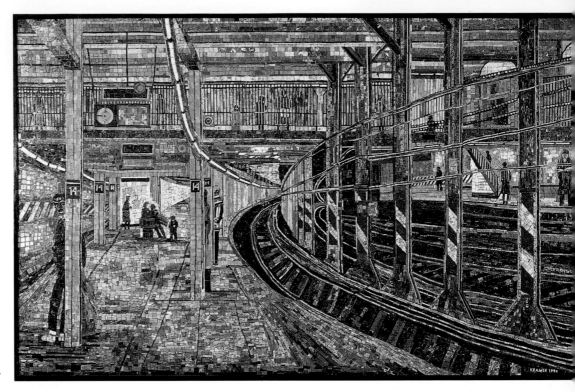

Detail from **Screen of Four Seasons, Summer**
marble, gold, silver, and smalti

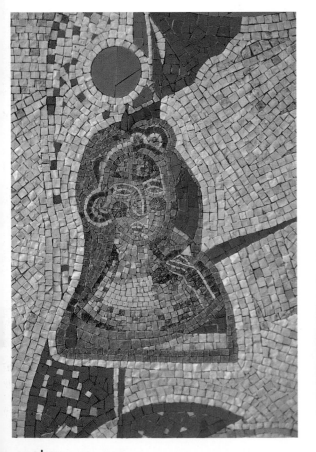

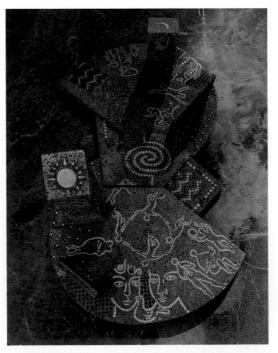

Earth of Delight and Sorrow
marble, gold, silver, and cocciopesto
3' x 24" x 24" (.9 m x 60 cm x 60 cm)

LEN MICHAELS

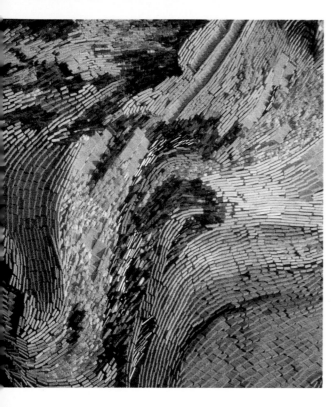

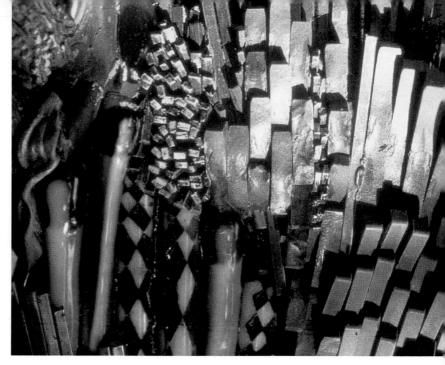

Detail from **Assemblage**
AIA Headquarters, Detroit, Michigan
tile, cameo glass, and bronze

Detail from **Assemblage** (left)
Detroit Receiving Hospital, Michigan
tile and metal

IFFORD MYERS

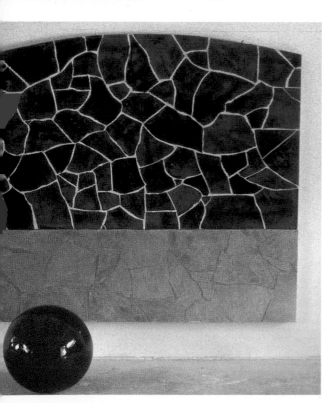

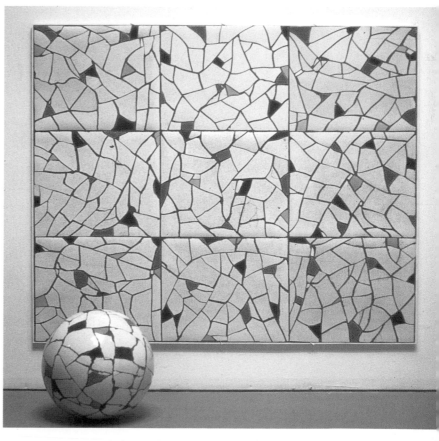

Remark (*Le Monde Rien***)**
glaze on clay
5' x 6' x 20" diameter
(1.5 m x 1.8 m x 51 cm diameter)

Poolside with Red Ball (left)
glaze on clay and flagstone
5' x 5.5' x 20" diameter
(1.5 m x 1.7 m x 51 cm diameter)

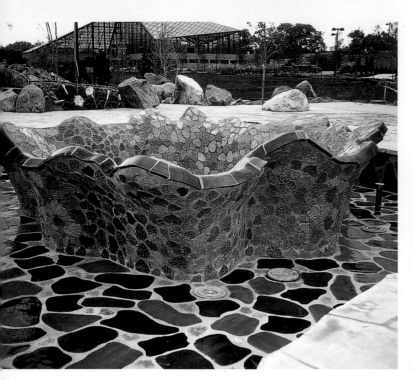

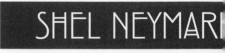
SHEL NEYMARK

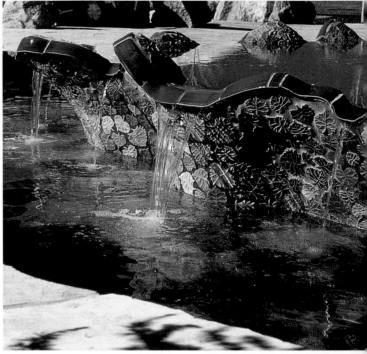

Details from **The Rosalie Doolittle Fountain**
(above and right)
Rio Grande Botanic Garden, Albuquerque, New Mexico
ceramic and tile mosaic

Angels Tend My Garden, table
ceramic
4' x 3' x 3' (1.2 m x .9 m x .9 m)

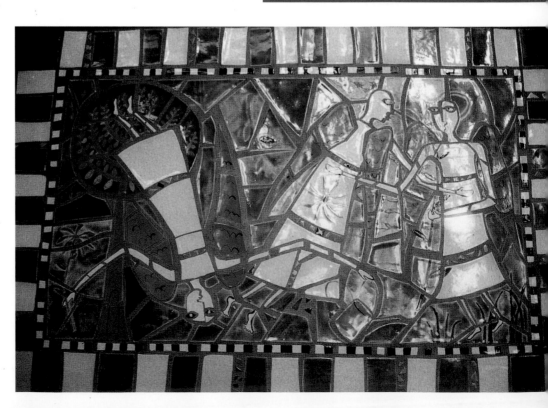

EDRO ROMERO

New Mexico Low Rider Bench
ceramic on cement
5' x 16' x 4' (1.5 m x 4.9 m x 1.2 m)

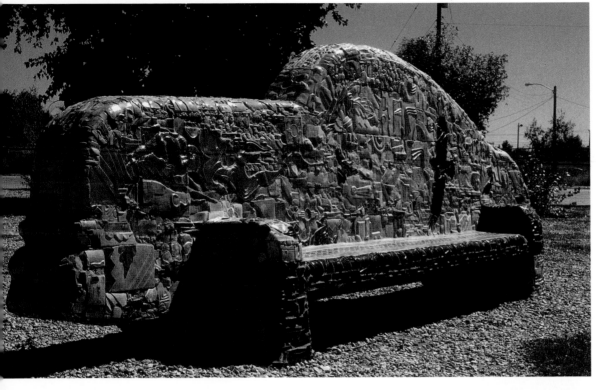

APRIL SHELDON

Patio and Outside Fireplace
(right and below)
Carmel, California
ceramic tile mosaic

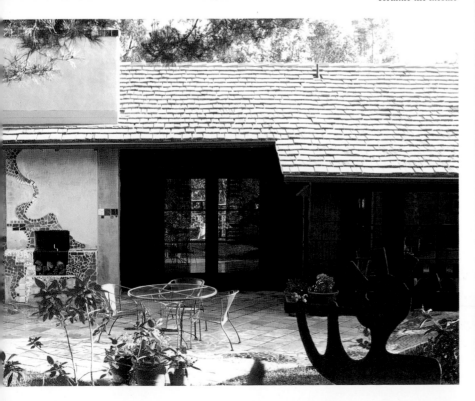

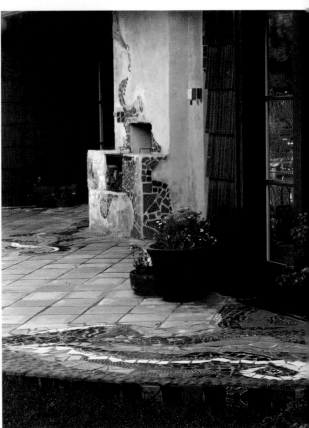

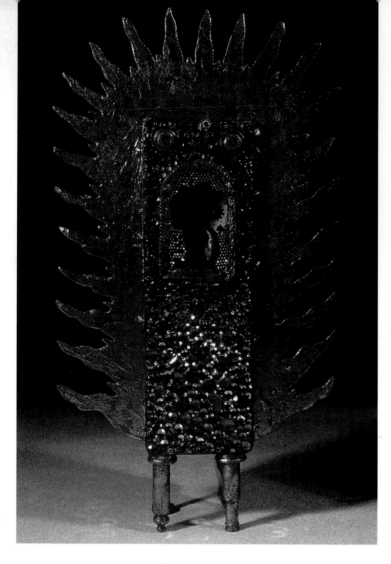

He Speaks of Possible Futures
rhinestone, mosaic, and mixed media
19" x 10" x 4" (48 cm x 25 cm x 10 cm)

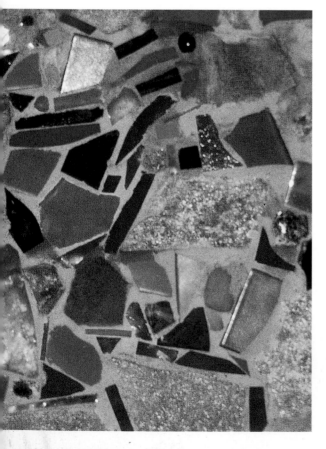

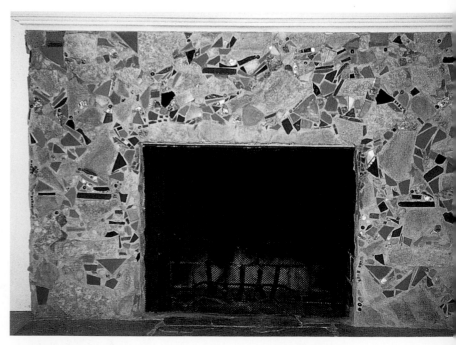

Fireplace (above, detail left)
natural stone, ceramic tile, glass, mica, and crystals
6' x 3.9' x 6" (1.8 m x 1.2 m x 15 cm)

Home Sweet Home
ceramic mosaic and found objects
5.6' x 14" x 11" (1.7 m x 36 cm x 28 cm)

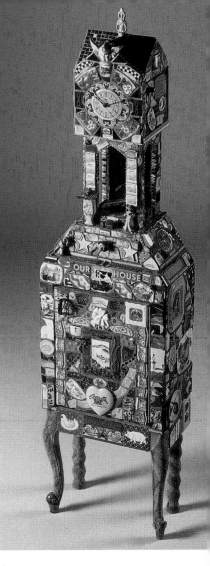

?E AND STEVE TERLIZZESE

Detail from **Clock of Ages**
ceramic mosaic and found objects

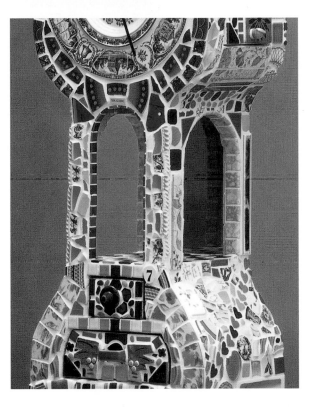

INA YANKOWITZ

Exploded: dining table
ceramic and granite
29" x 9.2' x 3.5' (74 cm x 2.8 m x 1.1 m)

Slipped Covers
chairs with granite inlay and copper edging
3.3' x 20" x 20" (1 m x 51 cm x 51 cm)

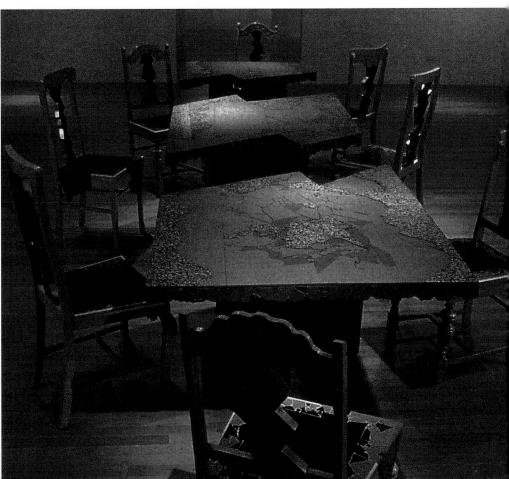

ARTIST DIRECTORY

Erin Adams
5551 Florence Terrace
Oakland, CA 94611

Carlos Alves
1043 Lincoln Road
Miami Beach, FL 33139

Twyla Arthur
2007 West Summit
San Antonio, TX 78201
twylaa@earthlink.net

Harriet Backer
Heyerdahlsrei 18
0386 Oslo, Norway

Candance Bahouth
Ebenezer Chapel
Pilton, Somerset
BA4 4BR
England

Marlo Bartels
2307 Laguna Canyon Road, #7
Laguna Beach, CA 92651

Linda Beaumont
1517 12th Avenue
Seattle, WA 98122

Linda Benswanger/Mozayiks
612 East 9th Street, #3
New York, NY 10009
212-677-7834

Ellen Blakeley
3244 Folsom Street
San Francisco, CA 94110

Joseph Blue Sky and Donna Web
943 Dopler Street
Akron, OH 44303

Laura Bradley
241 West Broadway
New York, NY 10013

Val Curtis
6040 SW 28th Street
Miami, FL 33155

Sara Curtis
St. Louis, MO
givethemroots@aol.com

Patty Detzer
2083 Fir Island Road
Mt. Vernon, WA 98273

Barbara Field
473 Medicine Bow Road
Aspen, CO 81611

George Fishman
103 NE 99 Street
Miami Shores, FL 33138
305-758-1141
mosaics@telocity.com
georgefishmanmosaics.com

Merle Fishman
David Catrambone
Projectile
4630 Saloma Avenue
Sherman Oaks, CA 91403

Ann Gardner
4136 Meridian Avenue N
Seattle, WA 98103

Melissa Glen Mosaics
73 Locust Street
Holliston, MA 01746

Peter Kaskiewicz
Apricot Salmon Productions
5110 ½ Guadalupe Trail, NW
Albuquerque, NM 87107

Sonia King
1023 Sarasota Circle
Dallas, TX 75223
214-824-5854
sonia@mosaicworks.com
www.mosaicworks.com

Gloria Kosco
P.O. Box 223
Silverdale, PA 18962

Edith Kramer
95 Vandam Street, Apt. 3F
New York, NY 10013

Haruya Kudo
7-7-9-202
Togashira, Toride
302 Japan

Deb Mandile
Plum Island, MA
debra1234@aol.com

Andrew Martin
369 B Third Street
PMB 105
San Rafael, CA 94901
andrew_martin@adidam.org

Verdiano Marzi
14, rue Louise-Michel
93170 Bagnolet
France

Doreen Mastandrea
144 Moody Street
Waltham, MA 02453
paintaplate@juno.com

Lynn Mattson
25302 Calle Beccerra
Laguna Niguel, CA 92677

Glen Michaels
4800 Beach Road
Troy, MI 48098

Robin Millman
Lexington, MA
daffodillish@aol.com

Jane Muir
Butcher's Orchard, Main Street
Weston Turville
Aylesbury, Bucks
HP22 5RL
England

Gifford Myers
1267 Boston Street
Altadena, CA 91001

Bridgette Heidi Newfell
10 Orange Street
Newburyport, MA 01950
978-465-5969

Shel Neymark
P.O. Box 25
Embudo, NM 87531

Felice Nittolo
Via A. Codronchi, 61
48100 Ravenna
Italy

Lucio Orsoni
Cannaregio, 1045
30121 Venice
Italy

Cathy Raingarden
c/o Christensen Heller Gallery
5831 College Avenue
Oakland, CA 94618

Margaret F.H. Reid
2 Stone House
Howey, Llandrindod Wells
Powys LD1 5PL
England
011-44-1597-825517
mfhreid@polyopol.kc3ltd.co.uk

Pedro Romero
P.O. Box 16422
Santa Fe, NM 87506

Lilli Ann Killen Rosenburg
Marvin Rosenberg
4001 Little Applegate Road
Jacksonville, OR 97530

Diana Maria Rossi
1747 Oregon Street
Berkeley, CA 94703

Ilana Shafir
Kapstadt Str. 2
Ashkelon 78406
Israel

April Sheldon
477 Bryant Street
San Francisco, CA 94107

Connie Sheerin
Crafts a la Cart
P.O. Box 246
Lansdowne, PA 01950
610-262-8162
concraft@aol.com

Beryl Solla
1222 NW 83rd Avenue
Coral Springs, FL 33071

Mark Soppeland
576 Fairhill Drive
Akron, OH 44313

Aimee Southworth
Lexington, MA
southctm@aol.com

Joan di Stefano Ruiz
P.O. Box 24605
Oakland, CA 94623

Gary Stephens
36 Martens Boulevard
San Rafael, CA 94901

Robert Stout and Stephanie Jurs
Twin Dolphin Mosaics
Via Bartonlini, 8
48100 Ravenna
Italy
011-39-0544-456-345
sjurs@racine.ravenna.it

Susan Strouse/Artful Gardens
Boston, MA

Kelly Taylor
Taylor Design Studio
672 Gateway Drive
Suite 610
Lessburg, VA 02175
703-443-0825

Zoe and Steve Terlizzese
511 46th Street
West Palm Beach, FL 33407

Bruce Winn
Roseberry-Winn Pottery and Tile
669 Elmwood Avenue
Providence, RI 02907
www.roseberrywinn.com

Nina Yankowitz
106 Spring Street
New York, NY 10012

Isaiah Zagar
c/o Synderman Gallery
(Rick Synderman)
303 Cherry Street
Philadelphia, PA 19106

RESOURCES

Crafts a la Cart
P.O Box 246
Lansdowne, PA 19050
USA
610-394-0992
concraft@aol.com
www.craftsalacart.com

Glass Crafters Stained Glass Inc.
398 Interstate Court
Sarasota, FL 34240
USA
800-422-4552
http://glasscrafters.com

James Hetley Stained Glass Supplies Ltd.
Glasshouse Fields
London, E1W 3JA
United Kingdom
020-7780-2344

Mosaic Matters
The online magazine for all things mosaic
www.users.dircon.co.uk/~asm/index.htm

Mosaic Mercantile
P.O. Box 78206
San Francisco, CA 94107
USA
877-966-7242
http://mosaicmercantile.com

Mountaintop Mosaics
Elm Street
P.O. Box 653
Castleton, VT 05735
USA
800-564-4980
www.mountaintopmosaics.com

Mosaic Workshop
1A Princeton Street
London, WC1R 4AX
United Kingdom
020-7831-0889
www.mosaicworkshop.com

National Artcraft Co.
7996 Darrow Road
Twinsburg, OH 44087
USA
888-937-2723

The Partner One Corporation
(wrought iron tables)
458 Satinwood Way
Chula Vista, CA 91911
USA
800-474-7168

TileMosaics.com
P.O. Box 15101
Long Beach, CA 90815
USA
562-715-6511
www.tilemosaics.com

Tower Ceramics Ltd.
9–15, Wenlock Road
London N1 7SL
United Kingdom
020-7251-6959

Wits End Mosaics
5224 West State Road 46
Box 134
Sanford, FL 32771
USA
407-323-9122

ABOUT THE AUTHORS

Formerly a development editor with HarperCollins, Leslie Plummer Clagett has been editor-in-chief of *SF magazine* and *New York Arts Journal*. The author of the *Travel & Leisure Guide to San Francisco and the Wine Country* (Macmillan), she has produced and written many articles on culture and the design arts.

Celie Fago began working with polymer clay in 1991 after years of working as a painter and sculptor. Her jewelry combines polymer with metalworking and with Precious Metal Clay. She's a highly regarded, generous, and innovative teacher who has done groundbreaking work combining these materials. She's one of six senior instructors of Precious Metal Clay worldwide and was invited by master metalsmith Tim McCreight to be Mitsubishi's PMC liaison to the polymer clay community in 199.

Mary Ann Hall is a writer and editor with an enduring interest in arts, crafts, and design. She was the founding editor and director of content of Craftopia.com and the editor-in-chief of *Handcraft Illustrated*. As a longtime artist and crafter, she has studied and worked in several areas, including jewelry- and metalworking, painting, polymer-clay sculpture, glassblowing, and furniture making. She lives in Virginia.

Anna Kasabian has 29 years of experience as a writer, editor, and communications professional. She writes about interior design, food, garden crafts, home and garden preservation projects, and architecturally significant properties. She has written 7 books and many magazine articles.

JoAnn Locktov is a former film producer and currently a decorative painter and ardent admire of mosaic art. Her search to learn more about the intriguing art form of mosaics led to her collaboration on this book. As a graduate of University of California Berkeley in Economics and Art History, JoAnn used her background, artist's eye, and love of fine crafts to assemble this meaningful and engaging study of modern mosaic work.

Ceramic artist and color maven Doreen Mastandrea works in Lexington, Massachusetts, where she runs Paint a Plate Studio. Her ceramic sculptures have been shown in various galleries. She has also created numerous mosaic installations and taught mosaic workshops at several schools in the Boston area. She is the author of *Ceramic Painting Color Workshop*.

Livia McRee is a craft author and designer who has written and contributed to many books, including *Easy Transfers for Any Surface, Quick Crafts, Ceramic Painting Color Workshop, Paper Shade Book* (all from Rockport Publishers), and *Instant Fabric: Quilted Projects from Your Home Computer* (Martingale & Company). She lives in Massachusetts.

Sandra Salamony is an art director and writer living in Cambridge, Massachusetts. She has designed crafts for many magazines and books. She is the author of *Hand Lettering for Crafts*.

Georgia Sargeant started drawing, sewing, and building things as a child and never stopped. After studying studio arts in college, she became a graphic artists, reporter, and editor. From 1997 to 2001 she was the editor of the quarterly newsletter of the National Polymer Clay Guild, where she featured and wrote about leading polymer clay artists around the world.